Retrieving Doctrine

Essays in
Reformed Theology

Oliver D. Crisp

IVP Academic

An imprint of InterVarsity Press
Downers Grove, Illinois

InterVarsity Press
P.O. Box 1400, Downers Grove, IL 60515-1426
Internet: www.ivpress.com
E-mail: email@ivpress.com

InterVarsity Press® is the book-publishing division of InterVarsity Christian Fellowship/USA®, a movement of students and faculty active on campus at hundreds of universities, colleges and schools of nursing in the United States of America, and a member movement of the International Fellowship of Evangelical Students. For information about local and regional activities, write Public Relations Dept., InterVarsity Christian Fellowship/USA, 6400 Schroeder Rd., P.O. Box 7895, Madison, WI 53707-7895, or visit the IVCF website at <www.intervarsity.org>.

ISBN 978-0-8308-3928-5

Design: Cindy Kiple
Image: AquaColor/iStockphoto

Printed in the United States of America

Library of Congress Cataloging-in-Publication Data

Crisp, Oliver.
 Retrieving doctrine / Oliver D. Crisp.
   p. cm.
 Includes bibliographical references and index.
 ISBN 978-0-8308-3928-5 (pbk.: alk. paper)
 1. Reformed Church—Doctrines—History. 2. Theology.
Doctrinal—History. I. Title.
 BX9422.3.C75 2009
 230'.42—dc22

                                                                      2010052963

P	21	20	19	18	17	16	15	14	13	12	11	10	9	8	7	6	5	4	3	2	1
Y	29	28	27	26	25	24	23	22	21	20	19	18	17	16	15	14	13	12	11		

For Jeremy and William:
multum valet coniunctio sanguinis.

Contents

Preface

It is a strange and seldom noted fact that theologians spend much of their time in the company of the dead. This is inevitable, since theology is inextricably bound up with the Christian tradition. In order to make progress in doctrine, theologians must expend a great deal of time and effort listening intently to what thinkers of the past have to say about matters touching the divine, quizzing them on the views they espouse. Only then will they be in a position to make some contribution of their own. This traffic between the shades of dead divines (or, at least, their literary remains) and their living successors is not always unproblematic. But the best theology seeks to engage those voices from the past most congenial to the task of passing on the faith, once delivered to the saints.[1]

Nicolo Machiavelli captures something of this *tête-à-tête* when he reports his own intercourse with intellectuals of the past in the following manner:

> When evening comes, I return to my house, and I go into my study; and on the threshold, I take off my everyday clothes, which are covered with mud and mire, and I put on regal and curial robes; and dressed in a more appropriate manner I enter into the ancient courts of ancient men and am welcomed by them kindly, and there I taste the food that alone is mine, and for which I was born; and there I am not ashamed to speak to them, to ask them for the reasons for their

---

[1] As Kathryn Tanner puts it, 'Knowledge of Christianity in other times and places is a way, then, of expanding the range of imaginative possibilities for theological construction in any one time and place, a way of expanding the resources with which one can work.' In *Jesus, Humanity and the Trinity: A Brief Systematic Theology* (Minneapolis: Fortress Press, 2001), p. xviii.

actions; and they, in their humanity, answer me; and for four hours I feel no boredom, I dismiss every affliction, I no longer fear poverty nor do I tremble at the thought of death: I become completely part of them.[2]

This volume attempts to follow Machiavelli's example, and engage theologians of the past in conversation in order to bring their ideas to the table of contemporary theological reflection. What is envisaged here is the retrieval of their ideas for the purposes of constructive dogmatics. Consequently, the thinkers discussed in the following chapters are not treated as advocating views that are simply a set of problems that must be stepped over or circumvented. Rather, they are approached in the spirit of collegiality, as those whose ideas might be used as resources for theology today; hence the title of this book.[3]

It is often said these days that all theology is contextual in nature. The theology contained in this volume is unabashedly Reformed, the theologians whose ideas are the subject of the chapters being representatives of that tradition. Some are well known, and there are chapters that deal with issues that have been mined before (although, of course, I think there is more to be said on each topic that is treated in this way). But others are figures whose work does not have a wide currency beyond those that take a professional interest in their ideas. So, alongside chapters dealing with the work of John Calvin, Jonathan Edwards and Karl Barth, there are chapters on aspects of the theology of the post-Reformation scholastic theologian, Francis Turretin, the nineteenth-century American German-Reformed theologian, John Williamson Nevin, and the Scottish Reformed theologian, John McLeod Campbell.

Theological retrieval is not the same as historical theology, although the two are closely related.[4] A collegial approach to theology involves

---

[2] *The Portable Machiavelli*, ed. And trans. P. Bondanella and M. Musa (Harmondsworth: Penguin, 1969), p. 59.

[3] See John Webster, 'Theologies of Retrieval' in John Webster, Kathryn Tanner and Iain Torrance, eds., *The Oxford Handbook of Systematic Theology* (Oxford: Oxford University Press, 2007), pp. 584 and 585 respectively.

[4] See, for example, Brian Gerrish's excellent book *Tradition in the Modern World: Reformed Theology in the Nineteenth Century* (Chicago: University of Chicago Press, 1978) which is a paradigm of careful historical-theological scholarship whose merits are not merely or narrowly historical in nature. In fact, Gerrish deals with two theologians also tackled here: John Williamson Nevin and John McLeod Campbell.

bringing the ideas of the past into the present. But it does not necessarily imply agreement with everything past theologians have said. There is such a thing as collegial disagreement, and this is also reflected in what follows. In each of the essays contained in this volume the emphasis is upon making sense of certain theological issues, problems and concerns that often have a philosophical as well as theological aspect. In each case, the ideas of the past are shown to have importance for the theology of the present, even where they have to be 'corrected' or where their ideas are incomplete or, perhaps, mistaken in some respect.

The essays are divided into three sections, which reflect key themes in Reformed theology. The first division concerns creation and providence. We begin with a recommendation of John Calvin's understanding of these twin doctrines. In recent discussion of creation and providence, the sort of view Calvin advocates is often thought to be hopelessly out of date. However, through a careful analysis of Calvin's doctrine it turns out that Calvin has much to say to those involved in the contemporary discussion, and that his views are far from otiose.

Then, in a second chapter, Karl Barth's reworking of the doctrine of creation is brought into dialogue with the work of the post-Reformation Reformed Orthodox. In this chapter the emphasis is upon the dialectic of theological give-and-take that one can see in Barth's work as he reflects on the Reformed tradition. In some ways he echoes what his forebears had to say. In other ways he departs from the tradition in innovative and interesting ways. Even if one is not wholly won over to Barth's account, there is much in what he says with which contemporary Reformed theologians can usefully engage. There are other Reformed theologians who have made important contributions to our understanding of creation and providence. But Calvin and Barth stand as two theological giants, whose work merits consideration in a book like this one.

The second section deals with the twin themes of sin and salvation. The first essay concerns Jonathan Edwards' understanding of the imputation of original sin. In it, I set out several ways in which Reformed theologians have understood this doctrine. Then Edwards' doctrine is discussed, with reference to the secondary literature on his work. I argue that other treatments of Edwards' doctrine, by a range of divines from the nineteenth century to the present, have misunderstood what he is attempting to say. In this way, the essay is an attempt to correct certain misreadings of this aspect of his doctrine of original sin as a contribution to Reformed theology.

There follows an essay on Francis Turretin's discussion of the necessity of the Incarnation. In his magisterial *Institutes of Elenctic Theology*, the textbook of theology which was the fruit of his years teaching at the Genevan Academy, Turretin sets forth the view that the Incarnation occurred because of the sin of human beings. It is necessary only as a consequence of God ordaining that a world where sin occurs should obtain, where God decrees that he will save some number of his human creatures that fall into sin. But given that God does ordain such a world, and deigns to save some number of fallen humanity, not only is some means by which salvation is obtained necessary. It turns out that, for reasons superficially similar to Anselm's *Cur Deus Homo* argument, God must bring about salvation via a God-man. Nothing less is required in order to save sinful human beings. Turretin's argument raises a number of serious problems. For one thing, it seems counterintuitive to think God could not have brought about salvation via some other, less costly means than the Incarnation. In which case, it looks like the Incarnation is unjustified. A second concern has to do with how Turretin's argument can be squared with a robust account of divine freedom and aseity. If the Incarnation is in some sense necessary, in what sense was God free to withhold Incarnation? Finally, in this chapter, consideration is given to an objection based on the modal implications of Turretin's account of the necessity of the Incarnation. It transpires that Turretin adopts certain assumptions about the divine nature which conflict with other things he says about the hypothetical necessity of the Incarnation. Only by adjusting this element of Turretin's reasoning does his argument appear to make complete sense.

John McLeod Campbell was a nineteenth-century Scottish Presbyterian minister ejected from his parish in Rhu by the Church of Scotland for his novel ideas about the atonement. He spent the majority of his subsequent career pastoring an independent congregation in Glasgow. There he laboured in relative obscurity after his expulsion until, towards the end of his life, his work was recognized as being a seminal contribution to Scottish theology. In recent times his account of the nature of the atonement has been championed by Thomas and James Torrance as an antidote to the (supposedly) severe high Calvinistic understanding of the need for atonement to placate divine retributive justice. Interestingly, it was reading some remarks by Jonathan Edwards that was the catalyst for McLeod Campbell's own doctrine of the atonement. In this chapter I argue – against the Torrances and, to some extent, McLeod Campbell himself – that the internal logic of his doctrine does not need the revision to the doctrine of God that he thought it did. In fact, one could take his notion of non-penal substitution, as I call it, in a rather different and much more Edwardsian direction. The result is a novel understanding of the nature of the atonement that owes it origins as much to Edwards as to Campbell. Although I do not endorse Campbell's account of the atonement, the 'Edwardsian' version of the doctrine set forth in this chapter shows that the underlying logic of Campbell's position can be taken in a rather different direction than Campbell himself was desirous of, which may well merit further consideration.[5]

Whether or not Karl Barth's views imply a doctrine of universalism has been the subject of considerable dispute in recent theology. In the last chapter in the second section, I set out the logic of Barth's position, in an attempt to make sense of his doctrine. I argue that Barth's view can be taken in one of two directions: either it is a species of necessary universalism, or it is not a coherent whole. Barth himself denied his view was a version of universalism. But if that is right, then his work contains several competing strands of thought which do not appear to add up. It may well be that there is more than one doctrine at work in Barth's account, which is what has led to the sometimes bitter disputes about his theological legacy on this important topic.[6]

The third section begins with a consideration of Calvin's doctrine of impetration, that is, petitionary prayer. Or, rather, it brings to bear the resources of Calvin's doctrine on the problem of the apparent pointlessness of petitioning God if God has ordained all that will come to pass. Having set out the requirements for a Calvinian doctrine and examined what Calvin has to say on the matter, I offer a defence of this Calvinian view of impetration. It turns out that petitioning God is not necessarily pointless even if, like Calvin, we think

---

[5] I have attempted to set out a preliminary version of my own views on the nature of the atonement as a work of penal substitution in 'Original Sin and Atonement', Thomas P. Flint and Michael C. Rea, eds. *The Oxford Handbook of Philosophical Theology* (Oxford: Oxford University Press, 2009), ch. 19.

[6] I explore this matter further in 'On the Letter and Spirit of Karl Barth's doctrine of Election: A Reply to O'Neil' in *Evangelical Quarterly* LXXIX (2007): 53–67, and 'Barth and Jonathan Edwards on Reprobation (and Hell)' in David Gibson and Daniel Strange, eds. *Engaging with Barth: Contemporary Evangelical Critiques* (New York: T&T Clark, 2008), pp. 300–322.

that all things are determined by divine fiat. This is important given the recent philosophical interest in impetration, much of which proceeds on the assumption that the determinism of a theologian like Calvin cannot make sense of petitionary prayer.

The eighth chapter considers John Williamson Nevin's doctrine of the Church. Alongside his younger (and better known) colleague Phillip Schaff, Nevin was the leading light of the so-called Mercersberg theology. This originated in the seminary of the German Reformed Church in Mercersberg, Pennsylvania, at which both Nevin and Schaff taught. Nevin went on to become President of Franklin and Marshall College and to defend what he thought of as traditional Calvinist views on the nature of the Church and the Eucharist, notions which, he feared, were being eroded by the theological pragmatism of evangelists like Charles Finney. In fact, matters were more complicated than this suggests. Nevin was accused of taking his Calvinism in the direction of high churchmanship, rather like – in England at the same period – John Henry Newman and John Keble were involved in taking Anglicanism in a much more 'high church' direction. However on inspection it appears that Nevin's account of the Church is thoroughly Reformed. What distinguishes his position is its debt to Romanticism and, in particular, to an organic and holistic understanding of the nature of the Church. This is unusual in the Reformed tradition, but not without precedent, as we shall see in the final chapter on Edwards. I argue that Nevin's doctrine of the Church has much to commend it to contemporary Reformed theologians for whom a properly catholic, evangelical ecclesiology is something to be welcomed.

The final chapter revisits the controversy over the qualifications for communion in which Jonathan Edwards became embroiled at the end of his ministry in Northampton in the 1740s. Famously, Edwards changed his mind about what qualifies a person for communion. Having begun his ministry by accepting the inclusive approach of his immediate predecessor and maternal grandfather, the formidable Solomon Stoddard, Edwards began to have qualms about Stoddard's approach. He eventually revised his grandfather's views in the direction of a much stricter set of qualifications for communion. In this chapter I argue that Edwards' change of heart was a consequence of his views on the Church. He had come to hold that the Church was an organic whole, in a way similar to the position Nevin would later take up. This, he thought, had implications for how one should administer the ordinance of Communion, which led him to revise his views. But rather than being draconian measures, Edwards' doctrine turns out to be of a piece with his eschatological vision of the nature and purpose of the Church in the plan of God. I argue that his revised position, which led directly to his dismissal from Northampton, should cause contemporary Reformed theologians to think again about whether their own ecclesiology is 'high' enough.

I close with some acknowledgements and thanks. First, the acknowledgements: a number of the essays that appear in this volume have been published previously. I am grateful to several journals and publishers for allowing the following to be reprinted here: 'John Calvin on Creation and Providence' in Sung Wook Chung, ed. *John Calvin and Evangelical Theology: Legacy and Prospect* (Milton Keynes: Paternoster, 2009), ch. 3; 'Karl Barth on Creation' in Sung Wook Chung, ed. *Karl Barth and Evangelical Theology: Convergences and Divergences* (Grand Rapids: Baker Academic and Milton Keynes: Paternoster, 2007), ch. 4; 'On the theological pedigree of Jonathan Edwards' doctrine of imputation' in *Scottish Journal of Theology* 56 (2003): 308–327; 'Non-penal substitution' in *International Journal of Systematic Theology* 9 (2007): 415–433; 'On Barth's denial of universalism' in *Themelios* 29 (2003): 18–29; and 'Jonathan Edwards and the Closing of the Table: Must the Eucharist be Open to All?' in *Ecclesiology* 5 (2008): 1–21.

Finally, some words of thanks. There are various people whose help in the preparation of this volume has been invaluable. Robin Parry has been a great encouragement and a first-rate interlocutor over the years, and was the first person to whom I turned when I first conceived of this book. Other friends and colleagues have also helped me to think through some of the thorny issues that led to the composition of each chapter. These include Paul Avis, William Evans, David Gibson, Paul Helm (who has commented on each chapter), Stephen Holmes, Bruce McCormack, Benjamin Myers, Stuart Noble, Myron B. Penner, Michael Rea, Robert Sherman, Douglas Sweeney, Eddy Van der Borght and Alan Torrance. I am particularly grateful to William Storrar as Director and Thomas Hastings as Director of Research (fondly known as 'the Dean') of the Center of Theological Inquiry, Princeton, where the final sections of this book were written while I was a resident member and Scheide Fellow in Theology in the academic year 2008–2009. It has been a privilege to spend time in this unique intellectual community.

Claire, Liberty, Elliot, and Mathilda Crisp have helped me too, often in very practical ways. Living with a scholar can be trying, especially when he seems to spend much of his time cloistered with 'dead friends'. But they have borne it cheerfully, and with gentle humour. For that I am very grateful.

This book is dedicated to Jeremy Luke Crisp and William Samuel Crisp, my brothers.

PART I

CREATION AND PROVIDENCE

CHAPTER ONE

John Calvin on Creation and Providence

> One does not read Calvin. One does not think of reading him. The prohibition is more absolute than it ever was against Marx, who always had the glamour of the subversive or the forbidden about him. Calvin seems to be neglected *on principle*.
>
> – *Marilynne Robinson*[1]

For some modern theologians, the doctrines of creation and providence found in the work of a classical theologian like John Calvin either need significant adjustment, or must be done away with altogether in favour of a very different understanding of God's relation to his creation.[2] An example of the former, more modest reassessment

---

[1] Marilynne Robinson, *The Death of Adam: Essays on Modern Thought* (New York: Picador, 1998), p. 12.

[2] Back in the 1960s Langdon B. Gilkey summed up much of the mood of the modern theology of his time when he said 'Providence, then, is a difficult doctrine for us in our day to ponder, difficult alike to us morally and rationally and apparently opposed to our fundamental beliefs in creaturely autonomy and finite causality' ('Providence in Contemporary Theology' in *The Journal of Religion* 43 (1963): 181). But this problem is still in evidence today. Charles Wood, in commenting on Gilkey's essay, observes that 'The situation has not changed markedly since Gilkey wrote. Put plainly, the doctrine [of divine providence] has simply been overwhelmed by the challenges it has faced' ('Providence' in John Webster, Kathryn Tanner and Iain Torrance eds. *The Oxford Handbook of Systematic Theology* [Oxford: Oxford University Press, 2007], p. 93). Things are not quite so bleak for the doctrine of creation, which has been the subject of considerable theological discussion in recent times (a good survey can be found in David Fergusson's *The Cosmos and the Creator* [London: SPCK, 1998]). But the doctrine of a God who creates and interacts with his

can be seen in the work of so-called 'Openness' theologians who argue that God's knowledge cannot include knowledge of the future actions of (libertarianly) free creatures because presently there are no truths about that segment of the future that free will can affect. The future has yet to occur and God, like the created order, is in time. Even if God creates the world out of nothing, he does not know how much of it will transpire, and what choices free creatures will make. He can guess and form beliefs about what we will do, and his ability to approximate to the truth of what will occur is second-to-none. But because he is a time-bound entity as we are and cannot, as a consequence *know* the future, the scope of divine providence is more limited than Calvin conceived it, and is different in nature.[3]

An example of the latter, more radical readjustment to creation and providence can be seen in the work of the feminist theologian Sallie McFague, who thinks of the theological task as setting forth models describing, amongst other things, how God and his creatures interact. These models are inherently metaphorical, heuristic constructions that offer imaginative explanations of the God-world relationship, which McFague believes necessary in order 'to remythologize Christian faith through metaphors and models appropriate for an ecological, nuclear age'.[4] According to McFague, a panentheist understanding of God and

---

(cont.) world, such as Calvin (in common with other classical divines) envisaged, is a source of discomfort to some theologians.

[3] The *locus classicus* of this movement is Clark Pinnock, Richard Rice, John Sanders, William Hasker and David Basinger, *The Openness of God: A Biblical Challenge to the Traditional Understanding of God* (Downers Grove, IL: InterVarsity Press, 1994). The literature on this topic is large. But amongst the recent contributions Bruce McCormack's essay, 'The Actuality of God: Karl Barth in Conversation with Open Theism' in Bruce L. McCormack, (ed.), *Engaging the Doctrine of God: Contemporary Protestant Perspectives* (Grand Rapids: Baker Academic, 2008), pp. 185–242, offers an interesting critique of the doctrine of God Openness theologians assume in the context of wider criticism aimed at the sort of classical theism Calvin (amongst others) endorsed. See also James K. Beilby and Paul R. Eddy, eds. *Divine Foreknowledge: Four Views* (Downers Grove, IL: Intervarsity Press, 2001).

[4] Sallie McFague, *Models of God: Theology for An Ecological, Nuclear Age* (Philadephia: Fortress Press, 1987), p. 40. McFague takes a very strong *via negativa* approach to formulating doctrine. She thinks that 'we are prohibited from absolutizing any models of God' because 'when we try and speak of God there is nothing which resembles what we can conceive

creation is a most appropriate model for thinking about creation and providence in the contemporary world. That is, the world is somehow contained 'in' God, or – to change the metaphor – God's relation to the world is rather like the traditional way in which substance dualists have thought about the connection between the human soul and its body: God is the 'soul'; the created order is his 'body'. In which case, God 'needs' the creation in order to be fully himself, just as a soul 'needs' a body in order to live and move in the corporeal world.[6] Process theology is another influential contemporary school of theology that endorses a variant of panentheism and offers a different, though not unrelated, sort of criticism of traditional accounts of creation and providence such as Calvin defended. For process theologians, God is not omnipotent, and the creation is formed from some pre-existing chaotic matter which God shapes, and which he tries to keep from slipping back into disorder after he has fashioned it. This is in many ways an attempt to baptize a Platonic account of the creation, where the *Demiurgos* – or Craftsman god Plato conceived of in *Timeaus* – becomes assimilated to YHWH of the Old Testament (or, perhaps, where YHWH has been cut down to the size of a Demiurge).[7]

These examples illustrate several of the doctrines of creation and/or providence one can find in contemporary theology, which are quite different from the classical theological conceptions Calvin would have been familiar with. Much could be said about these

---

(cont.) when we say that word.' *Metaphorical Theology: Models of God in Religious Language* (Philadelphia: Fortress Press, 1982), p. 194.

[5] McFague, *Models of God*, 72. She explains that her panentheistic model of God and the world is a view 'in which all things have their origin in God and nothing exists outside God, though this does not mean that God is reduced to these things.'

[6] See McFague, *Models of God*, ch. 3 in particular for discussion of this. John Cooper offers trenchant criticism in *Panentheism: The Other God of the Philosophers* (Grand Rapids: Baker Academic, 2006), 294–297, as does Randal Rauser in 'Theology as a Bull-Session' in Oliver D. Crisp and Michael C. Rea, eds. *Analytic Theology: New Essays in The Philosophy of Theology* (Oxford: Oxford University Press, 2009), ch. 3.

[7] See Plato, *Timaeus*, § 30. For a serviceable introduction to Process Theology see John Cobb Jr. and David Ray Griffin, *Process Theology: An Introductory Exposition* (Philadelphia: Westminster John Knox Press, 1977). For a careful critical analysis of Charles Harteshorne's version of Process Theology, see Colin E. Gunton, *Becoming and Being, New Edition* (London: SCM Press, 2001 [1978]).

various attempts at revision in contemporary theology.[8] But I shall refrain from doing so here. Instead, this chapter gives a broadly sympathetic account of Calvin's theology of creation and providence. I shall argue that Calvin's view offers a robust description of God's relation to the creation that is both plausible and defensible in the current intellectual climate, despite those who think both creation and providence need to be re-thought for the contemporary world.

The chapter falls into three parts. The first offers some conceptual context for discussion of Calvin's contribution, which, given the constraints of space, can only be an overview of some of the most important dogmatic issues in creation and providence. This is followed by discussion of Calvin's doctrine, where our focus will be upon his understanding of the creation and conservation of the world. A final section sets out some constructive criticism of Calvin's view, as a contribution to the continuing discussion of these important dogmatic themes, in which Calvin's thought has played, and continues to play, an important role.

The dogmatic context

For the most part, Calvin was not a fan of speculative theology, which he often rails against. However, as several recent commentators on Calvin's thought have pointed out, he sometimes indulges himself in theological speculation when it suits his purposes.[9] Yet in order to get a sense of where Calvin's views on creation and providence sit in relation to other accounts of these twin doctrines, including the sorts of revisionist accounts already mentioned, some sort of philosophical

---

[8] Some theologians are deeply concerned by Calvin's doctrine of creation, which they think is perniciously anthropocentric, to the exclusion of important ecological considerations. See for example David Kinsley, *Ecology and Religion: Ecological Spirituality in Cross-Cultural Perspective* (Englewood, NJ.: Prentice Hall, 1995), p. 111. Randall Zachman responds to this sort of concern in 'The Universe as the Living Image of God: Calvin's Doctrine of the Universe Reconsidered' *Concordia Theological Quarterly* 61 (1997): 299–312. He argues, to my mind convincingly, that Calvin's view is precisely the opposite of that Kinsley imputes to him.

[9] See Paul Helm, *John Calvin's Ideas* (Oxford: Oxford University Press, 2004), pp. 22–29; Richard Muller, *The Unaccommodated Calvin: Studies in the Foundations of a Doctrinal Tradition* (Oxford: Oxford University Press, 2000), passim; and David Steinmetz, *Calvin in Context* (New York: Oxford University Press, 1995).

and dogmatic contextualizing is in order – in which a smattering of theological speculation might be permissible. This falls into two parts, corresponding to the two doctrines themselves as the two aspects of the *opera naturae*, although too strict a division between creation and providence is, as we shall see, artificial.

We begin with creation. Here two, or perhaps three, dogmatic components of this doctrine are important, depending on what is made of the third. The first constituent is the divine motive in creating the world; the second, the act of creating itself; and the third, the relation between creation and the sustenance of the created order thereafter.

As to the first, the divine motivation for creating the world is itself connected to at least two further dogmatic issues of importance.[10] The first of these subsidiary points concerns the doctrine of the divine decrees. The second and related issue has to do with the divine freedom in creating the world. The divine decrees touch upon matters that are sublime and difficult. Those classical theologians that think God is atemporal, maintaining that God's motivation in creation is logically but not chronologically first in the order of the external works of God (*opera ad extra*).[11] Some post-Reformation Reformed divines have

---

[10] I assume in what follows, as Calvin and all orthodox theologians would, that all the external works of God are triune works, even if some of these works terminate on a particular divine person, such as the Incarnation. See Calvin, *Institutes of the Christian Religion*, ed. John T. McNeill, trans. Ford Lewis Battles (Philadelphia: Westminster Press, 1960 [1559]), 1.13.20. hereinafter, cited as Inst. Followed by Book, Chapter and Section numbers, as here. Cf. Heinrich Heppe, *Reformed Dogmatics*, trans. G. T. Thompson (London: Wakeman Trust, n.d. [1950]), ch. IX.

[11] For Calvin's endorsement of divine timelessness, see Inst. 3. 21. There, in the context of setting forth divine 'fore' knowledge, Calvin says 'When we attribute foreknowledge to God, we mean that all things always were, and perpetually remain, under his eyes, so that to his knowledge there is nothing future or past, but all things are present. And they are present in such a way that he not only conceives them through ideas . . . but he truly looks upon them and discerns them as things placed before him.' See also similar comments with respect to the Trinity in *Inst.* 1.13.18. Calvin cautions against probing divine election (and, by implication, the divine decrees) out of intellectual curiosity. This will only result in entry upon a 'labyrinth from which' such persons 'can find no exit.' *Inst.* 3.21.1. There has been some recent dispute over whether Calvin did believe God is atemporal. See Henri Blocher 'Yesterday, Today, Forever: Time, Times, Eternity in Biblical Perspective' in *Tyndale Bulletin* 52.2 (2001) and the response by Paul Helm, 'Calvin on "Before All Ages"' in *Tyndale Bulletin* 53.1 (2002).

further distinguished the external divine works into those that are somehow 'internal' to God, being works conceived in the divine mind 'prior', as it were, to the act of creation, and other works that are 'external' to God, being works that are consequent to his 'internal' works, and which are directed towards the created order.[12] But in fact such distinctions are, on this way of thinking, merely intellectual devices by which human creatures can make sense of what is not literally distinguishable in the divine nature, because God is essentially metaphysically simple – that is, without any distinct 'parts' whatsoever.[13]

However one distinguishes the works of God, the motivation for creation is a matter intimately tied to the eternality of God. If God is atemporal then his motivation in creation is not something that *happens* at a particular moment in time, but something eternal in the divine nature. On the question of the nature of the divine motivation in creating the world theological opinions diverge, some opting for the union of the creation of human beings with the divine nature as the crowning glory of the created order, others opting for some weaker account of the reconciliation of fallen humans to God and the restoration of all creation to its former glory prior to the Fall of humankind. But these matters are surely subordinate to the overarching divine motivation in all God's works, namely, to bring glory to himself – a matter that received wide agreement in the post-Reformation period immediately after Calvin, from both Lutheran and Reformed dogmaticians.[14]

---

[12] The external works of God that are (paradoxically) said to be 'internal' in some sense, must be distinguished from the internal work of God as such, which has to do with things like the relations of origin, by which the persons of the Trinity are distinguished (e.g. the eternal generation of the Son; the eternal procession of the Holy Spirit). Traditionally, the doctrine of creation does not include this internal work of God, which is logically prior to any external work he undertakes in the creation.

[13] For an excellent discussion of the development of the doctrine of the divine attributes from the high Middle Ages through to the demise of post-Reformation orthodoxy, see Richard A. Muller, *Post-Reformation Reformed Dogmatics*, Vol. III (Grand Rapids: Baker Academic, 2003). For Calvin's endorsement of divine simplicity in the context of his discussion of the Trinity, see *Inst.* 1.13.2 and 19.

[14] See Heinrich Schmidt, *The Doctrinal Theology of the Evangelical Lutheran Church*, trans. Charles A. Hay and Henry E. Jacobs (Philadelphia: Lutheran Publication Society, 1875), chs. III–IV and Heppe, *Reformed Dogmatics*, chs. IX and XII.

Divine freedom in creation presents particular theological problems that have been, and continue to be, the source of some difficulty. Although most Christian theologians want to affirm that God is free to create or refrain from creating, precisely what this means is the subject of controversy. For instance, should divine freedom be construed as the freedom to choose to do other than he has in fact chosen? If so, how is this to be squared with an account of the divine nature where God is metaphysically simple, a perfect being without any passivity or unrealized potential? For most contemporary theologians this problem does not arise as it would have done in Calvin's intellectual *milieu*, where a kind of consensus on the divine nature had been handed on from the school theology of the high Middle Ages.

Today, there are other issues to be negotiated for those no longer enamoured with this classical picture of the divine nature. One such is how to make sense of the idea, found in Karl Barth amongst other modern divines, that God is free to determine who he will be, and (according to some commentators on Barth) in some eternal or primordial divine act decides he will be the God and Father of Jesus Christ, thereby freely choosing to be the sort of God we know him to be in and through Christ.[15] Other theologians and philosophers, objecting to what is sometimes called the 'Hellenization' of Christian theism, have objected to parts or the whole classical conception of the divine nature, opting instead for the idea that God is in time, is passible, mutable, and so on.[16] And besides these issues, the theological waters have been muddied by those who, as previously mentioned, have adopted some version of panentheism where the relation between creature and Creator is much closer than in classical theism,

---

[15] See Bruce McCormack 'Grace and being: The role of God's gracious election in Karl Barth's theological ontology' in John Webster ed., *The Cambridge Companion to Karl Barth* (Cambridge: Cambridge University Press, 2000), pp. 92–110. For a defence of Calvin against McCormack's reading of Barth on this score, see Paul Helm, 'John Calvin and the Hiddenness of God' in McCormack ed., *Engaging the Doctrine of God*, pp. 67–82.

[16] Two recent theological attacks on classical theism can be found in Colin E. Gunton, *Act and Being: Towards A Theology of The Divine Attributes* (Grand Rapids: Eerdmans, 2002) and Robert W. Jenson, *Systematic Theology* Vol. I. An influential critique from a philosophical perspective comes from Nicholas Wolterstorff, 'God Everlasting' in C. Orlebeke and L. Smedes (eds.), *God and the Good: Essays in Honor of Henry Stob* (Grand Rapids: Eerdmans, 1975).

to the extent that God must create a world, even if he may have some
freedom about the sort of world he creates.

We come to the second dogmatic question, concerning the act of
creation itself. Here there has been considerable discussion in the
modern period, with a number of theologians and philosophers
claiming that the opening verse of Genesis does not teach the traditional doctrine of creation out of nothing (*creatio ex nihilo*) but something closer to a Platonic doctrine of creation from chaos.[17] Much
depends on whether this verse should be translated 'In the beginning,
God created the heavens and the earth . . .' as per traditional discussions of creation out of nothing, the default option in the Christian
tradition, with which Calvin allied himself. Alternatively, Genesis 1:1
could be translated '*When God began to create* the heavens and the
earth . . .'.[18] The dogmatic difference between these views turns on
what is entailed by the divine fiat in the act of creation, not whether
God has, in some sense, created the temporal world. But closely related to this is the question of whether the cosmos is created in time,
or with time. For those modern theologians who think God is in time,
it is natural to suppose that the world is created in time, or at some
moment before which God existed. But for those, like Calvin, who

---

[17] Some theologians, notably St Thomas Aquinas, have discussed the possibility of creation being metaphysically contingent, but having no first
moment in time (although St Thomas dismisses this as contrary to
Scripture in *Summa Theologiae* I.46.1). To my knowledge, Calvin does not
discuss this at any length, and given his qualms about speculative theology, would probably have been reticent about doing so.

[18] Typical of those who defend the 'revisionist' reading of Genesis 1:1, the
Princeton philosopher Harry Frankfurt says: 'This is manifestly not an
account of creation *ex nihilo*. Whatever basis there may be for supposing
that the world was created out of nothing, these opening lines of Genesis
seem to be flatly inconsistent with that supposition' (Frankfurt, 'On God's
Creation' in *Necessity, Volition, and Love* [Cambridge: Cambridge
University Press, 1999], p. 119). But compare Robert Jenson's judicious
comments in defence of the traditional, creatio *ex nihilo* reading: 'The
recent preference for translations that make Genesis 1:1 a dependent
clause derives from residual prejudices of a now antique form of critical
exegesis that tended always to look for the "real" meaning of texts in
some stage of the tradition before and outside the structure of the canonical text and then to interpret the canonical text to fit' (Jenson, *Systematic
Theology Vol. 2, The Works of God* [New York: Oxford University Press,
1999], p. 3 n. 2).

follow the older way of thinking where God is atemporal, it is impossible to say this.[19]

There are problems explicating the very notion of a timeless creative act – what does it mean to say there is no time at which God brings about the world, and yet that the world begins to exist at a particular moment in time? One might think that the world is timelessly created 'in' time, where time somehow 'contains' the created order as the pan of water 'contains' the egg boiling in it. Then, God creates time and creates the world subsequently, so that the world begins to exist in a temporal series that has already been set in motion. But this is not how theologians like St Augustine of Hippo understood matters. In *Confessions* Book XI, he says God timelessly creates the world 'with' time: the divine creative fiat begins the whole of creation, time included. So there is no 'time' prior to the first moment of creation. And, as such, the questions 'What was God doing before he created the world?' or 'Why did God not bring about the creation sooner than he did?' are idle.[20]

What of the third dogmatic component to the doctrine of creation, concerning the Creator and the sustenance of his creation? For most Christian theists, God is distinct from his creation, exists *a se*, and, as a consequence, is free to refrain from creating this world or any other metaphysically possible world. But is the act of creating the world he does bring about distinct from his act of sustaining that world thereafter? In one sense, it is: if we think of the act of creation as creation from nothing then the sustaining of a world that has been called into existence by divine fiat must be something different from the act that calls forth that world. So there is a conceptual distinction between these two sorts of divine act.

Yet a number of classical divines have thought that there is no substantive difference between the two acts, because the created order is

---

[19] Susan Schreiner has recently observed that in his commentary on Gen. 1:5 'Calvin saw no need to insist that the creation of the world was free of temporality'. Schreiner, *The Theater of His Glory, Nature and the Natural Order in the Thought of John Calvin* (Durham, NC: The Labyrinth Press, 1991), p. 15. In other words, Calvin thinks God creates the world in phases, over six days, rather than all at once. But this is consistent with the claim that an atemporal God creates the world with time.

[20] Calvin echoes St Augustine's language in his *Commentary on Genesis*, trans. John King (Grand Rapids: Baker Books, 1979 [1554]), pp. 61–62, although, unlike Augustine, Calvin thinks such intellectual curiosity is reprehensible.

not merely dependent on God for its preservation in being once created, but is conserved in being by the divine will, without which it
would immediately cease to exist. For such theologians the reliance of
the creation upon its Creator implies a radical dependence. Consider
the act of thinking of the Mona Lisa. The first instant at which one
calls the thought to mind, it begins to exist. Every moment one thinks
of the painting thereafter, provided one continues to think of this
without interruption, and without being distracted by some other
thought, one is conserving that initial thought in the mind's eye. But
if one were to stop thinking of the Mona Lisa, the thought of the painting would cease to exist. So, we might say, the initial thought of the
painting perdures provided I continue to think it. But if, like Professor
Albus Dumbledore, one were able to take a thought from one's mind,
and deposit it in a magical thought-repository, or Pensieve, then the
thought would continue to exist without my continuing to think it. In
which case, the relation between my thought and me is much less radical, since the thought can persist without my consciously sustaining
it in being, once it is placed in the Penseive.[21]

This thought experiment should not be pressed too hard. It is only
intended to show something of the difference between the dependence of the creation upon the Creator where God preserves an existing creation in being, though, in some sense, the creation perdures –
that is, continues to exist under its own steam – and the idea of a radical dependence of the creation upon its Creator. The relation of radical dependence (call it, the *radical dependence view*) should be distinguished from what is sometimes called continuous creation, although
not all dogmaticians make this clear.[22] If, like Jonathan Edwards, one
thinks that God creates the world which, having no power independent of God to perdure momentarily ceases to exist, only to be replaced
by a numerically distinct replica of the first world, and so on seriatim,
then one has dispensed with the idea of divine preservation of the creation. There is no created entity to preserve because no created entity
has the power to exist for more than a moment. Continuous creation,
then, is a much stronger doctrine than even the robust version of the

---

[21] The Pensieve makes its first appearance in J. K. Rowling's novel, *Harry
Potter and the Goblet of Fire* (London: Bloomsbury, 2000).

[22] It does not help that scholastic theologians sometimes distinguish
between *creatio continua* (continuous or constant (re)creation) and *creatio
continuata* (a creative act that persists from one particular time to another).
I am grateful to Ben Myers for directing me to this.

divine preservation of creation, though both are often referred to as continuous creation doctrines.

This brings us to the doctrine of divine providence, even a cursory consideration of which should be sufficient to demonstrate the intimate connection between it and the doctrine of creation. Common in post-Reformation works of theology is the distinction between divine preservation of the creation (*conservatio*), his concurrent activity in upholding and sustaining the creation (*concursus*) and his government of it (*gubernatio*). Sometimes the first two of these are conflated, depending on the theory of divine preservation under consideration. Thus, if God preserves the cosmos via concurrently causing all things to occur alongside mundane causes, then God's concurrent activity is a function of his preservation of the created order.

This idea that God orders all things that come to pass, such that no event occurs without his concurrently bringing it about in conjunction with mundane creaturely causes, is usually referred to as *meticulous providence*, in order to distinguish it from those accounts of divine providence where God does not decree or otherwise bring about all that comes to pass.

But there is another distinction to be made, between general and specific divine providence. One might speak of God upholding and sustaining the world in being as a general act of God: he sustains all created things in existence, good and bad, for as long as seems good to him. But God's particular acts by which he ordains certain things that will take place, things of salvific importance – the election of some to life, and reprobation of others in eternal death – is often thought of as a specific act of providence. However, the distinction seems somewhat artificial, if, with Calvin, we think that God ordains *all* that comes to pass: 'For he is deemed omnipotent . . . because, governing heaven and earth by his providence, he so regulates all things that nothing takes place without his deliberation.'[23] If God deliberately decrees all things or events to occur, then all things or events are deliberate acts of God, and it seems that the difference between 'general' and 'specific' acts of providence evaporates. Still, it does serve to distinguish certain sorts of providential action, whereby God brings about salvation, from other sorts of providential action, whereby God sustains the creation as the 'the most beautiful theatre' of God's glory,[24] in which the narrative of salvation history is played out.

---

[23] *Inst*. 1.16.3.
[24] *Inst*. 1.14.20.

Provided we understand 'general' and 'specific' acts of providence in this way, as a means of separating out what, from the human vantage point appears to be different sorts of divine act in creation, rather than as a means of distinguishing different 'levels' of divine causal activity in creation, the distinction may be of some theological use.

Calvin on creation and providence

With some idea of the major dogmatic structures in the doctrines of creation and providence in place, we can turn to consider what Calvin contributes to these twin *loci*. Here two things are important. First, an understanding of where Calvin's views sit with respect to the spectrum of views just outlined. And, second, several ways in which Calvin introduces important theological nuances that make a considerable difference to how creation and providence are understood.

We begin with his doctrine of creation. Recalling our three dogmatic questions on creation outlined in the previous section, we can see that, under the topic of the divine motive in creating the world Calvin endorses the traditional view that the ultimate end of all God's works is his own self-glorification, albeit with a Calvinian twist. This is particularly evident in his metaphor of creation as the 'theatre' and 'mirror' of God's glory, tropes which recur in the *Institutes* and elsewhere in his *corpus*.[25] Thus, for example, in setting forth how the knowledge of God shines forth in the created order (though our sin-blind faculties are incapable of apprehending this without the spectacles of Scripture) Calvin says 'this skilful ordering of the universe is for us a sort of mirror in which we can contemplate God, who is otherwise invisible' (*Inst.* 1.5.1, pp. 52–53). And later in commending the spiritual lessons the doctrine of creation engenders, he says 'let us not be ashamed to take pious delight in the works of God open and manifest in this beautiful theatre.' He goes on to encourage his readers to be 'mindful that wherever we cast our eyes, all things they meet are works of God' and to 'ponder with pious meditation *to what end* God created them' (*Inst.* 1.14.20, p. 179, emphasis added). The 'end' in question is, of course, the glory of God.

It is true that Calvin also says things about the purpose of creation that sound at times alarmingly anthropocentric, such as this com-

---

[25] See for example *Inst.* 1.6.2; 1.14.20; 3.9.2, his Commentaries on Ps. 104: 31 and 138: 1 and on Heb. 11:3.

ment: 'God himself has shown by the order of Creation that he created all things for man's sake' (*Inst.* 1.14.22, pp. 181–182). But this must be tempered with what he says elsewhere in the *Institutes*, where he makes clear that human beings are themselves 'microcosms' that reflect the divine Artificer (*Inst.* 1.5.3, p. 54; cf. Inst. 1.5.6). Humanity is as much a work of God as any other created thing, with this important qualification: human beings bear the image and imprint of the Creator upon their souls (Inst. 1.15.3). It is this that sets human beings apart from the rest of creation, which is why Calvin labours the point about the world being created *for* human beings. But humans are a part of that creation, according to Calvin. Humans are, in a way, bearers of the glory of God (via the *imago dei*) that show forth God's ultimate end of bringing glory to his name in all his created works – humanity included. As Zachman points out, for Calvin

> [t]he creation of all good things in the world for the benefit and enjoyment of humans is not . . . an end in itself, but is rather the way God initially reveals to humankind that he is the author and fountain of every good thing. Our use and enjoyment of the good things of creation is not intended by God to be an end in itself, but is rather the way God allures and invites us to seek him as the source of every good thing.[26]

Although Calvin does not use the precise language of later Reformed scholastic theology, it is clear from a careful reading of his comments on the doctrine of election in *Inst.* 3.21–24 that he thinks God has eternally destined human beings to life or death according to the good pleasure of his will alone – a matter which is well-known. Was God free to choose to create or refrain from creating the world he did bring about? Calvin does not appear to address this question head-on. But it is clear that he has a high view of divine freedom. God has, he thinks, 'in his own hand and will the free disposing of his graces' (*Inst.* 2.21.14). What is more God's will is, he maintains, 'the cause of all things that are' (*Inst.* 3.23.2). 'When, therefore, one asks why God has so done,' says Calvin, 'we must reply: because he has willed it. But if you proceed further to ask why he so willed, you are asking for something greater and higher than God's will, which cannot be found' (*Inst.* 3.23.2). This apparent theological voluntarism is tempered by his appeal to the divine character: God wills as he does because his nature is perfect (*Inst.* 3. 23. 2). What is important for our

---

[26] Zachman, 'The Universe as the Living Image of God,' pp. 303–304.

purposes is that this suggests Calvin does think God could have created a world other than the one he did in fact create, although his
aversion to theological speculation means he does not pursue the
matter which, he thinks, is hidden from human scrutiny.[27]

Concerning the second dogmatic issue in creation – the act of creation itself – Calvin sides with the tradition in holding unambiguously to *creatio ex nihilo*. For instance, in commenting on Genesis 1:1,
he says that Moses 'teaches by the word "created," that what before
did not exist was now made; for he has not used the term . . . *yatsar*
. . . which signifies to frame or form, but . . . *bara* . . . which signifies to
create. Therefore his meaning is that the world was made out of nothing.' Interestingly, given the attempts of some recent theologians to
return to a more Platonic doctrine of creation from existing matter, he
goes on to say: 'Hence the folly of those is refuted who imagine that
unformed matter existed from eternity; and who gather nothing else
from the narration of Moses than that the world was furnished with
new ornaments, and received a form of which it was before destitute.'
To which he adds, 'for Christian men to labour . . . in maintaining this
gross error is absurd and intolerable.'[28] So Calvin is aware of the sort
of ideas that inform some modern revisionist discussions of creation.
And it is clear he has little patience with such ideas.[29]

For the modern reader there are curiosities in Calvin's understanding of the act of creation, typical of pre-critical exegesis. For instance,
he thinks the created order was brought about through six literal days

---

[27] Helm has a helpful discussion of this matter in the context of Calvin's use
of the medieval distinction between the absolute and ordained power of
God in *John Calvin's Ideas*, ch. 11.

[28] Calvin, *Com. Gen.*, p. 70.

[29] Calvin, writing before the widespread acceptance of the Copernican
understanding of the cosmos, still holds to the geocentric theory: 'We
indeed are not ignorant, that the circuit of the heavens is finite, and that
the earth, like a little globe, is placed in the centre.' *Com. Gen., Argument*,
p. 61. However, this should not be taken as an indication that Calvin was
a scientific luddite. Unlike contemporary 'creationists', Calvin is at pains
to align his own theological views with what he understood of the natural sciences. See, e.g., his *Comm. Gen.* 1:16 (praising astronomy), and his
remarkable comment on Ps. 136:7, where he says 'The Holy Spirit had no
intention to teach astronomy', *Comm. Ps.* Vol. V., trans. James Anderson
(Grand Rapids: Eerdmans, 1949), p. 184. Our understanding of the natural world has overtaken Calvin; but this is no judgment on Calvin himself,
or his theological method.

(*Inst.* 1.14.2). And he spends a considerable amount of time dealing with angelic beings and their place in the created order (e.g. *Inst.* 1.14.3–19), something which is seldom the subject of serious theological discussion today. But one of the important things Calvin's doctrine implies, in good Augustinian fashion, is that creation, like annihilation, is an act only God can perform. We creatures can make things, just as we can destroy them. But making is no more creating than destroying is annihilating. I make a clay statue; my daughter destroys it. But I cannot *create* a clay statue, because I am incapable of generating the matter of which clay is composed from nothing. Just so, my daughter is incapable of annihilating my statue because she cannot eliminate the energy/matter of which it is made. She can only redistribute it over a different area. This is an important consideration whereby the work of God as Creator is clearly distinguished from the 'creative' activity of his creatures – something which defenders of panentheism find much more difficult to do.

It might be thought that Calvin's understanding of creation, when taken together with what he says in *Inst.* 1.1–4 about the *semen religionis* (seed of religion) and the *sensus divinitatis* (sense of the divine) as well as his doctrine of the limited role natural theology plays in theology, yields the view that one can know God as Creator without Christian faith. The reasoning here would go something like this: Calvin holds that the natural order reflects the glory of its Creator, though, due to the noetic effects of sin, fallen human beings are no longer in a position to perceive this through the naked contemplation of creation. In this way, we may distinguish between the revelation of God in creation that is *offered us*, and the revelation that is (or is not) *received by us*.[30] Our intellectual equipment, including the sense of the divine with which we are endowed as human beings, is vitiated. At best fallen humans through exercising this malfunctioning belief-forming apparatus can arrive at some notion that there is a Maker of this world, but the revelation of God in nature cannot deliver a saving knowledge of God because of the effects of sin. We are sin-blind. So God has to provide the spectacles of Scripture in order for us to be able to 'read' this revelation in creation. But this still means that the heathen can know there is a Creator of some sort without the need for special

---

[30] Compare David C. Steinmetz, *Calvin in Context*, p. 32, who argues that this distinction between 'what is given' and 'what is received' informs Calvin's theology as a whole, not merely his natural theology. It is certainly present in his sacramental theology.

revelation. And the fact that fallen humans can know this much is a reason for their condemnation in not giving due glory to God.

This is true, as far as it goes. But Calvin does think the role Christian faith plays in human understanding concerning God the Creator is crucial. Take, for instance, what he says in commenting on Hebrews 11:3:

> It is by faith alone that we understand that the world was created by God . . . There has always been a certain supposition that the world was created by God among the heathen, but a vague one. Whenever they imagined some sort of God they quickly became vague in their thinking so that they groped uncertainly at a shadow of deity in the darkness rather than grasping the true God. Furthermore, since it was only a fleeting conjecture that flitted through their minds, it was far from any understanding.[31]

He goes on to say that only those with faith have more 'a firm conviction deep in their hearts' that enables them to behold the true Creator God.[32] This does seem to be in tension with other things he says in the *Institutes*, where it appears that fallen humans can really *know* that there is a god of some sort via the *sensus divinitatis*, absent special revelation. But perhaps what Calvin means to say is that the epistemic condition in which fallen humans find themselves is such that they have no way of rightly identifying God as Creator without divine assistance in the form of the renewal of the *sensus divinitatis*. This renewal comes about through the internal work of the Holy Spirit in regeneration, and a right reading of Scripture, which, in passages like Psalm 19, helps us through the eyes of faith to comprehend what we could only with faltering steps begin to see – vaguely, inchoately, and lacking understanding – without faith. If this is right, then there is an important epistemic role faith plays in Calvin's doctrine of creation, which is absent from some later works of Reformed dogmatics.[33]

---

[31] Calvin, *Commentary on The Epistle of Paul the Apostle to the Hebrews, Calvin's New Testament Commentaries*, Vol. 12 trans. W. B. Johnston, eds. David W. Torrance and Thomas F. Torrance (Grand Rapids: Eerdmans, 1963), p. 159. (Hereinafter cited as CNTC, followed by volume number.)

[32] Ibid.

[33] But not Barth, for whom the doctrine of creation is properly a piece of dogmatics that can only be understood by faith. See *Church Dogmatics* III/1, § 40 eds. G. W. Bromiley and T. F. Torrance (Edinburgh: T&T Clark, 1958).

Concerning the third dogmatic issue, namely, the relation between creation and the sustenance of the created order thereafter, Calvin takes the view that creation and conservation are not properly distinct, but two parts of one whole divine act, whereby God creates and thereafter conserves in being what he has brought about. In this way, Calvin's position is a species of the radical dependence view of the relation between the created order and its Creator.

Such a position implies a doctrine of meticulous divine providence. However, Calvin's doctrine is not quite as meticulous as that of his contemporary, Huldrych Zwingli, for whom secondary causes are not real causes. Zwingli thinks God directly causes everything to occur that does occur such that mundane causes are merely the occasions (or something very like the occasions) of God's activity. Calvin, by contrast, wants to uphold some version of concurrence: God causes or otherwise brings about all and every event in the created order, but in a way that is not inconsistent with real creaturely causation.[34] There is a nest of problems in the neighbourhood of this assertion, which are well known. For one thing, Calvin, like other theological determinists, wants to affirm significant moral freedom for at least some creaturely actions. He also wants to affirm that human beings are morally responsible for their sins. And, of course, he thinks that the conjunction of these two things is important: there is an intimate connection between moral responsibility and freedom; I am morally responsible for the actions I perform provided I am free to do them. One way of framing Calvin's response to this sort of problem is by appeal to levels of causal activity. God is the primary cause of every action I perform; but I am the secondary cause. However, there are real problems with this approach if God causes all things. He is not just a necessary condition, but a necessary and sufficient condition for any creaturely

---

[34] Although he does not call his view occasionalism, Huldrych Zwingli denied the reality of secondary causes in his doctrine of Providence – which is tantamount to occasionalism. See his Sermon on *The Providence of God in The Latin Works of Huldreich Zwingli Vol. II*, trans. Samuel Macauley Jackson, ed. William John Hinke (Philadelphia: The Heidelberg Press, 1922), p. 138. There Zwingli bluntly states, 'Secondary causes are not properly called causes. This is of fundamental importance for the understanding of Providence.' For comparison between Calvin and Zwingli on this, see Paul Helm 'Calvin (and Zwingli) on Divine Providence' in *Calvin Theological Journal* 29 (1994): 388–405.

action. In which case, talk of my causing a particular action seems otiose.[35]

What of human freedom and moral responsibility? A theological compatibilist like Calvin can say human agents are free to the extent that they act voluntarily: I make the moral choices I do, and provided I am not coerced into, or prevented from making those choices, they are voluntary. Moreover, one might think that I am morally responsible for such acts. Provided one thinks of human freedom in terms of voluntary actions of the sort just outlined, one can be morally responsible for such actions – even where there is no real alternative open to the human agent concerned (whether she knows that or not).[36]

To illustrate: I chose to stay in the study to work on my book, rather than watch television in the lounge, although (unbeknownst to me) my daughter had locked me into my study so that I could not have gone to watch television in the lounge even if I wanted to. Does this diminish my responsibility for choosing to stay in the study and work? This is a hoary philosophical conundrum. But, plausibly my responsibility for so acting is not diminished, given the compatibilist assumptions about what counts as a voluntary action. After all, I chose to stay. True, I could not have left if I had wanted to. But the point is that I did not *want* to. I wanted to stay in the study, and chose accordingly. If I had known that the door to my study was locked and I could not leave, then I would not have been able to choose to leave the room. But I would have been able to choose to choose to leave the room. The fact is, whether I knew I could leave the room or not, I still had that choice to make. Perhaps if I could only have chosen to choose to leave the room, I would still have chosen to stay where I was. So, one might think, provided I have the capacity to choose to choose between options before me, even if I am not in a position to act upon my choice, I am responsible for

---

[35] A point Paul Helm, amongst others, raises in *The Providence of God* (Leicester: Intervarsity Press, 1993), pp. 178–180.

[36] There is a large contemporary philosophical literature on this matter, which owes its impetus to Harry Frankfurt's paper, 'Alternate Possibilities and Moral Responsibility' reprinted in *The Importance of What We Care About* (Cambridge: Cambridge University Press, 1988), pp. 1–10, and his development of so-called 'Frankfurtian counterexamples' to the notion that moral responsibility presumes a choice between alternatives, such as the example given in the text above.

making the choice I do (even if it is not 'formalized' in action, so to speak).[37] And even where I have no obvious alternative, I may still refrain from making a decision (refraining from 'choosing to choose', as it were), thus preserving moral responsibility.

Of course, Calvin never takes this sort of line in his work. His thinking is much more 'concrete' than this.[38] But what I have just said is consistent with what Calvin does offer. He is set against what he calls 'bare permission', that is, the idea that God merely allows certain things to occur. Calvin wants a full-blooded determinism: God ordains all that comes to pass. This poses obvious problems for theodicy. But he is more concerned by the prospect of a world where things happen over which God has no control, than he is about a world where things happen which are evil. There is comfort in knowing that, behind the apparent mare's nest of circumstance, God is in control – even if we cannot always fathom his purposes. So, in essence, Calvin's response is the response of Job: trust in God, sometimes despite circumstances, in the knowledge that he works all things to the good, even though we cannot comprehend that from our limited epistemic vantage.

Interrogating Calvin

We are now in a position to scrutinize Calvin's position. In the first place, it is important to ask why contemporary evangelical theologians should prefer Calvin's thinking on creation and providence to alternatives offered from progressive evangelicals, e.g. openness theology, or theological revisionists, e.g. panentheists like McFague. Much here will depend upon what one makes of the doctrine of God.[39] Calvin's adherence to the main lines of a classical doctrine of God, including divine simplicity, aseity, immutability, and atemporality have implications for

---

[37] Intentional acts are a good case in point: I may choose to daydream about Gustav Klimt's *Danäe* when I should be concentrating on a committee meeting. My action is determined, but it is my choice; I do so voluntarily.

[38] This is not to say that Calvin does not think about divine providence in a rather philosophical manner, even appropriating the argumentative form of school theology in his treatise *A Defence of the Secret Predestination of God*, as Helm makes clear in John Calvin's *Ideas*, ch. 4.

[39] Much, but not all. Another important issue Calvin would have taken for granted is metaphysical realism, which is now the subject of dispute – as McFague's work makes clear.

his account of creation and providence. But these deliverances of a classical doctrine of God are increasingly the subject of dispute within the evangelical theological constituency. Disenchantment with the classical doctrine of God[40] will inevitably mean distance from the sort of notions, culled from this classical picture of God, that inform Calvin's understanding of creation and providence.

That said, a God who is in time, whose nature is strongly unified though not simple, strictly speaking (such that he has distinct properties, say), and who is capable of change may still be able to create the world from nothing and sustain it thereafter. So one could make changes to the classical doctrine of God and retain the core commitments that inform Calvin's understanding of creation and providence, that is, creation *ex nihilo* and a meticulous doctrine of providence. But some changes may be thought a bridge too far. Giving up a strong doctrine of divine aseity in order to endorse panentheism, on the grounds that a God who *must* create may not be said to exist *a se*, is, I imagine, one such. But even with respect to panentheism there are complications: at least one major theologian beloved of evangelicals embraced a seemingly traditional doctrine of God *and* panentheism.[41] The bottom line seems to have much more to do with whether or not one is convinced by Calvin's attempt to reason from Scripture to certain propositions about the nature of creation and providence, and the God who creates and sustains the world. For it is certainly beyond dispute that Calvin thought of himself as engaged in a theological project rooted in Scripture, as his commentaries, treatises and *Institutes* testify. So perhaps the important question is not whether we should adopt Calvin's specific interpretation of Scripture, but whether we should adopt Calvin's commitment to Scripture as a theological criterion, a *norma normans*, or norming norm, which stands behind and informs all other theological 'norms'.

---

[40] Disenchantment with the classical doctrine of God comes in theological and philosophical varieties, of course, as I have already indicated.

[41] See Jonathan Edwards, *End of Creation* in *The Works of Jonathan Edwards*, Vol. 8 ed. Paul Ramsey (New Haven: Yale University Press, 1989). I suppose most evangelical theologians will not want to follow Edwards in this matter because they think commitment to a robust doctrine of divine aseity precludes it. But Edwards endorses both panentheism and aseity. This does open up an interesting avenue for discussion about whether panentheism is beyond the bounds of evangelical theology.

Some contemporary theologians think that the classical picture of God with which Calvin, like so many others, was enamoured, is simply hopeless because it is not sufficiently *Christological* in character. Recently Bruce McCormack has taken this line, concluding that 'Abstract doctrines of God [viz. classical conceptions of the divine nature such as the one Calvin endorsed] have had their day. It is time for evangelicals to take more seriously their affirmation of the deity of Jesus Christ and begin to think about God on a thoroughly Christological basis.'[42]

Perhaps there is some truth in this criticism. But consider again Calvin's account of creation and providence in light of those aspects of his doctrine of God that bear upon these issues. Where does Christology fit in? In reading the *Institutes* one might be forgiven for thinking that Christology enters into the picture only once Calvin has thoroughly prepared the ground in the first book, concerned with the knowledge of God, where creation and providence are discussed. It is in the second book that the knowledge of God the Redeemer is set forth. But here familiarity with Calvin's commentaries is important because what he says in commentating on several New Testament passages throws a rather different light on matters. Thus, in his reflections on the Prologue to the Fourth Gospel, he says:

> So far, he [the Evangelist, In John 1: 4] has taught us that all things were created by the Word of God. He now likewise attributes to Him the preservation of what had been created; as if he were saying that in the creation of the world His power did not simply suddenly appear only to pass away, but that it was visible in the permanence of the stable and settled order of nature – just as Heb. 1.3 says that He upholds all things by the Word of command of His power . . . For did not His continued inspiration quicken the world, whatsoever flourishes would without doubt immediately decay or be reduced to nothing . . . It is God, therefore, who gives us life; but He does so by the eternal Word.[43]

And in his Commentary on Colossians 1:15 he goes as far as to say,

> The sum is, that God in Himself, that is, in His naked majesty, is invisible; and that not only to the physical eyes, but also to the human

---

[42] McCormack, 'The Actuality of God', 242. See also his 'Grace and Being' where he deals with Calvin's position directly.
[43] Calvin, *Comm. Jn.*, CNTC Vol. 4, pp. 10–11.

understanding; and that He is revealed to us in Christ alone, where we may behold Him as in a mirror. For in Christ He shows us His righteousness, goodness, wisdom, power, in short, His entire self. We must, therefore, take care not to seek Him elsewhere for outside Christ, everything that claims to represent God will be an idol.[44]

Finally, with regard to Colossians 1: 20, Calvin says that the Apostle,

declares accordingly, that we are blessed through Christ alone, inasmuch as He is the bond of our union with God (*vinculum nostrae cum Deo coniunctionis*), and, on the other hand, that, apart from Him, we are most miserable, because we are shut out from God.[45]

Seen in light of these passages, Calvin's doctrines of creation and providence appear much more Christologically focused. Taken together with what we have already seen of Calvin's understanding of these twin *loci*, we see that, for Calvin, only those with faith can apprehend what God is *really* doing in creating and preserving the world: how he glorifies himself in his created order by ensuring human beings can apprehend his perfections, at first in and through the natural order and the in-built divine sense of things, and then, after the Fall of humanity, in special revelation, applied to the heart of the believer by the secret working of the Holy Spirit. And only those of faith can see that God creates and sustains the world through Christ, the one who makes the divine nature perceptible to us, through whose work we may be united to God.

Other Calvinian themes could be co-opted here too. Christ is the supreme *divine accommodation* to human limitations, not merely lisping to us in Scripture, but entering into the creation as a creature.[46] Yet even when 'contracted to a span' as a human being, Christ is upholding and sustaining the universe he fashioned via the so-called *extra*

---

[44] Calvin, *Comm. Col.*, CNTC Vol. 11, p. 308.

[45] Ibid., p. 312.

[46] 'It is evident from this that we cannot believe in God except through Christ, in whom God in a manner makes himself little (*quodammodo parvum facit*), in order to accommodate Himself to our comprehension (*ut se ad captum nostrum submittat*)', in Calvin, Comm. I Pt. 1:20–21 in CNTC, Vol. 12, p. 250. Cf. *Inst.* II.VI.4 and Jon Balserak, *Divinity Compromised: A Study of Divine Accommodation in the Thought of John Calvin* (Dordrecht: Springer, 2006), especially ch. 6.

calvinisticum.[47] It should be tolerably clear from this that Calvin's Christology plays a fundamental role in his doctrines of creation and conservation, and that Calvin sees no tension between such commitment and adherence to a classical conception of the divine nature.[48]

Conclusion

In common with several recent commentators on Calvin's work I have tried to show that Calvin's account of creation and providence only makes complete sense when seen as part of the fabric of his theological project, which is an integrated and organic whole. We are created and conserved in being for the glory of God. But God's delight is to so fashion human beings that they (or at least, the elect) may be united to Christ. I have also highlighted Calvin's Christological development of these doctrines in his commentaries, which do seem to put what Calvin says in his *Institutes* in a rather different light. It turns out that on Calvin's way of thinking those who believe are not just spectators in this divine theatre; they are participants in this glorious work of creation, fashioned by God through the Son to be united via the work of Christ with the Father by the Holy Spirit, to the praise of his glory.

---

[47] *Inst.* 4.17.30, 'for the very same Christ, who, according to the flesh, dwelt as Son of man on earth, was God in heaven. In this manner, he is said to have descended to that place according to his divinity, not because divinity left heaven to hide itself in the prison house of the body, but because even though it filled all things, still in Christ's very humanity it dwelt bodily [Col. 2:9], that is, by nature, and in a certain ineffable way.' Cf. Helm, John Calvin's *Ideas*, ch. 3.

[48] Question: *Why* is it that Calvin's commentaries seem much more Christological on the doctrines of creation and providence than the *Institutes*? Perhaps the answer to this lies in the restructuring of this material in the 1559 *Institutes*, where Calvin separated out the material on providence and the material on election. Paul Helm suggests this move came about because Calvin came to see the need to distinguish human choice as such (part of God's providential rule) from human choice as bound in sin and freed by divine grace, which is properly treated in soteriology. If so, then perhaps structural and systematic considerations in the dogmatic arrangement of material in the final Latin form of the Institutes come into play in a way they do not in his commentaries. For discussion of this, see Helm, 'Calvin, The "Two Issues," and The Structure of the *Institutes*' in Calvin *Theological Journal* 42 (2007): 341–348.

CHAPTER TWO

Karl Barth on Creation

The heavens declare the glory of God; the skies proclaim the
work of his hands. Day after day they pour forth speech;
night after night they display knowledge. There is no speech
or language where their voice is not heard. Their voice goes
out into all the earth, their words to the ends of the world.

– Psalm 19:1–4 (NIV)

It is often claimed that Karl Barth is so consumed by Christology
that all other theological *loci* in his work are 'Christologized'. They
are re-forged (some might say, gerrymandered) in the shape of
some aspect of his overarching Christological vision. Whether this
is a fair representation of Barth or not, it is true to say that, for
Barth, Christ is the centre of all truly Christian theology.[1] In a similar fashion, there is some truth in the idea that, under Barth's eye,
the doctrine of creation is 'Christologized'. His rendering of this
doctrine involves placing Christ at the centre of the theological
agenda and working out from there. This is not to say that Barth's
Christologized doctrine of creation is just Christology under
another name, although it does represent an extension of the way
in which Christology has traditionally been applied to the doctrine.[2]

This chapter engages with several prominent aspects of Karl
Barth's account of creation as found in *Church Dogmatics* volume III

---

[1] Compare T. F. Torrance: 'The evangelical heart of Barth's theology is the
   doctrine of Christ as the divine Reconciler . . . Barth never ceased to insist,
   Christology gives us the determining centre from which all our knowledge of God and of creation must take its shape.' *Karl Barth: Biblical and
   Evangelical Theologian* (Edinburgh: T&T Clark, 1990), pp. 20–21.

[2] John Webster makes a similar point in *Barth*, second edition (London:
   Continuum, 2004 [2000]), 97.

(hereinafter, CD).[3] What Barth has to say on this matter, like much of the CD, is far too rich and theologically suggestive – not to mention prolix – to compress into one short chapter. And in any case, there are a number of very helpful accounts of CD III in the recent literature, which make another short exposition of Barth's treatment of this doctrine otiose.[4] Consequently, this chapter is not an exposition of, or commentary on, Barth's doctrine of creation as such, but a critical interaction with some of the more controversial issues involved in his treatment of the doctrine of creation proper, in CD III/1. I say this discussion is restricted to matters pertaining to 'creation proper', because there is much else in the third volume of *Church Dogmatics* that there is not the space to enter into here, including Barth's account of providence, evil, prayer, angelology, and the ethics of creation.[5] It is tempting in a treatment like this to say something about all of these important matters. I have resisted that temptation, in the belief that it would be more useful to the reader to have a critical discussion of several issues in Barth's doctrine of creation proper, than a rather more general attempt to touch upon, and highlight, a number of important matters in a cluster of related dogmatic issues included by Barth in CD III.

The focus of this essay is the relationship of Barth's doctrine of creation to that of the classical (western) theological tradition, particularly, the Reformed strand of that tradition. We shall begin by

---

[3] All references are to the English translation of the *Church Dogmatics*, (eds.) G. W. Bromiley and T. F. Torrance (Edinburgh: T&T Clark, 1957–1969). In what follows, I shall cite this in parentheses in the body of the text as CD, followed by volume, part-volume and pagination, e.g. (CD III/1, 30).

[4] See for example Eberhard Busch, *The Great Passion: An Introduction to Karl Barth's Theology* (trans.) Geoffrey W. Bromiley (ed.) Darrell L. Guder and Judith J. Guder (Grand Rapids: Eerdmans, 2004), ch. 11. 6; Joseph L. Mangina, *Karl Barth: Theologian of Christian Witness* (Louisville: Westminster John Knox Press, 2004), ch. 4; Caroline Schroeder, '"I See Something You Don't See": Karl Barth's Doctrine of Providence' and the response by Randall C. Zachman, both in *For the Sake of the World, Karl Barth and the Future of Ecclesial Theology* (ed.) George Hunsinger (Grand Rapids: Eerdmans, 2004); Kathryn Tanner, 'Creation and Providence' in *The Cambridge Companion to Karl Barth* (ed.) John Webster (Cambridge: Cambridge University Press, 2000) and John Webster, *Barth*, ch. 5.

[5] These are, arguably, the major themes in the first, third and fourth part-volumes of CD III. I have also omitted any discussion of the theological anthropology of CD III/2 due to constraints of space.

considering some areas in which Barth's doctrine of creation overlaps with classical theological accounts of creation. We then turn to some areas where his doctrine is at odds with the tradition, particularly that of his Reformed theological forbears. The discussion shows that, in several respects, Barth's account of creation offers some important and interesting theological insights, although not everything he has to say about the doctrine is entirely satisfactory. A concluding section offers some reflections on engaging with Barth on the doctrine of creation.

Four areas of overlap between Barth and the Reformed tradition on creation

The relationship of Barth's doctrine of creation to classical theology – particularly the scholastic theology of his own Reformed tradition – is rather complicated. There is some conceptual overlap, and even agreement, such as Barth's defence of *creatio ex nihilo* (creation out of nothing).[6] But there are also key areas in which Barth departs from the tradition, particularly in his 'christologizing' of the doctrine. It is important to understand this, in order to ascertain where Barth's doctrine is innovative, so that we may assess the extent to which what Barth is making an original and helpful contribution to this theological locus.

We begin with four areas of conceptual overlap between Barth's doctrine of creation and the Reformed tradition. First, Barth could certainly have endorsed the Reformed Orthodox notion that 'the triune God is the creator, but in such as way that the Father, as the "source of the Trinity" is also the proper source of the works of creation which he has executed through the Son and the H[oly] Spirit'.[7] Barth himself

---

[6] See CD III/1, pp. 16 ff. and 103. Barth is particularly keen to distance the creation narrative of Genesis 1 from any notion of God creating the world from some pre-existing chaotic matter. In this respect he stands with the tradition and against those modern theologians, such as Process thinkers like David Griffin and John Cobb, who have abandoned creation out of nothing for a more Platonic doctrine of creation from existing matter.

[7] From Heinrich Heppe, *Reformed Dogmatics* (trans.) G. T. Thomson (London: Wakeman Trust, n.d. [1950]), p. 191. Compare CD III/1, pp. 12–14. This should not be taken to mean that this way of thinking about the relation of the Trinitarian persons to the act of creation is peculiar to the Reformed Orthodox.

approves of the scholastic notion that the works of the Trinity in creation are indivisible (*opera trinitatis ad extra sunt indivisa*). He says that
although the Father is the Creator, to this must be added the qualification: with the Son and the Spirit. 'The proposition that God the
Father is the Creator and God the Creator the Father can be defended
only when we mean by "Father" the "Father with the Son and the
Holy Spirit"' (CD III/1, 49).[8]

Secondly, like classical Reformed theologians, Barth affirms that
the act of creation is a free act of God. There is, both Barth and the
Reformed Orthodox declare, nothing inevitable about creation as
such. God was not *bound* to create a world of some kind, nor was he
bound to create this particular world. To affirm that God was bound
to do either of these actions is to infringe divine freedom and make
creation into something necessary.[9]

Thirdly, like many, though not all, of the Reformed Orthodox, Barth
is supralapsarian in his doctrine of the divine decrees, although the
content of Barth's supralapsarianism is different from traditional con-
struals in important respects.[10] For one thing, he denies that divine

---

[8] Barth is sometimes accused of not having a robustly Trinitarian doctrine
of creation. If this is un-Trinitarian theology, then Barth is in the company
of a great cloud of witnesses in the Christian tradition!

[9] Compare Heppe, *Reformed Dogmatics*, 'above all it is fixed, that the creation of the world is a thoroughly free act of God, in fact an act of God free
libertate contradictionis . . . so that God could also refrain from creating',
p. 192. The Reformed Scholastics usually speak in terms of creation as necessary as a consequence of the divine decree (*ex necessitate consequentiae*),
not necessary in and of itself. Barth says similar things at times. For
instance, he claims that there is a genuine necessity involved in creation
by the fact that God loved the world (from eternity), and gave his Son for
it (cf. John 3:16) – see CD III/1, p. 51. But, although Barth does not make
this connection in this passage, what he says clearly does not concern any
absolute necessity. It something like the scholastic consequential necessity, since God's love for the world is a consequence of his free decision to
create it.

[10] Supra- and infralapsarianism are the two major views in Protestant
Orthodoxy, concerning the logical ordering of the divine decrees.
According to Barth (CD II/2, p. 142) supralapsarianism has to do with
God ordaining the salvation of some and damnation of others prior to
(usually understood in the tradition to mean conceptually or logically
prior to, not temporally prior to) his decision to create the world or
redeem it – hence the '*supra-*', which refers to the fact that the *decretum
absolutum* takes place 'prior to' the decree concerning the fall. By contrast,

decrees fork at the point where God elects some human beings and reprobates the rest. Instead, according to Barth, God elects and reprobates Christ, the Elect (and Reprobate) One, and derivatively elects all humanity 'in' Christ, whose sin is expiated by Christ who stands as 'the judge judged in our place'.[11] This has important ramifications for Barth's doctrine of creation, as we shall see.

It is nevertheless true to say that Barth's supralapsarianism overlaps with the traditional scholastic principle that, in the matter of the divine decrees, *what is first in divine intention is last in execution*. In this regard, Kathryn Tanner observes that for Barth, 'what is first in God's intention and what spurs God's relation with us from the very beginning – to be the loving Father of us all in Jesus Christ – comes last in execution. Therefore the history of God's relations with us, like the Bible, has to be read from back to front and only on that basis from the front in anticipation of the end.'[12] But this does raise a question about what Barth considers the first intention of all God's works to be. If, like Tanner, we say Barth thinks that it is the redemption of all humanity in and through the work of Christ, this would appear to mean that God's end in creation is not, or is not ultimately (as has often been traditionally thought) his self-glorification. It is instead the reconciliation of humanity to Godself.[13]

However, it might be argued that it makes better theological sense to say that even if there are several ends or goals of creation including the redemption of humanity, the ultimate end of all God's works is his self-glorification – to which even the redemption of humanity is subordinate. (In which case, the redemption of humanity is one subordinate end of creation, but not its ultimate end. There is, in other words, an ordered hierarchy of 'ends' of creation, on this way of thinking about God's divine decrees.) We can always ask why God has ordained the reconciliation of humanity (or some number of human beings less that the

---

(cont.) infralapsarianism, according to Barth, begins with the decree to create and preserve humanity despite the fall. Only subsequent to this decree does God ordain the election of some and reprobation of others, hence *'infra' lapsus* (after the fall) (CD II/2, pp. 143–144).

[11] For an insightful discussion of Barth's doctrine of election, see Bruce McCormack's essay, 'Grace and Being: The Role of God's Gracious Election in Karl Barth's Theological Ontology' in *The Cambridge Companion to Karl Barth*, ed. John Webster (Cambridge: Cambridge University Press, 2000).

[12] Tanner, 'Creation and Providence', p. 114.

[13] Barth does speak of the covenant (of grace) as the goal of creation at times. See CD III/1, p. 231.

totality of humanity). It makes sense to respond to such a question, 'God does this for his own glory'. And this implies that divine self-glorification is a more ultimate end of creation than the redemption of human beings. But it does not make a great deal of theological sense to ask why God seeks to glorify himself, if we expect a response which points to a more ultimate goal than his self-glorification. God glorifies himself, according to a number of classical theologians (sometimes dubbed 'perfect being theologians') because it would be an imperfection in God not to do so.[14] A *maximally* perfect being (that is, a being who has all possible perfections to a maximal degree) cannot, after all, seek to glorify something other than himself, for that would be to glorify something that is less than maximally perfect (assuming that God alone is maximally perfect). And giving glory to something less than maximally perfect would itself be an imperfect act. But God is maximally perfect, so he cannot glorify something less perfect than himself, the maximally perfect being. Does this offer a good reason for thinking that the ultimate end of creation is God's self-glorification? A number of classical theologians, including theologians in the Reformed tradition, have thought so. At the very least, this raises a question about the adequacy of Barth's understanding of the end or ends of creation (if Tanner is correct about Barth's views on the goal of creation[15]).[16] (It also raises questions about his understanding of the scope of reconciliation, but that is another matter.[17])

---

[14] This notion can be found in the work of Anselm of Canterbury, Thomas Aquinas and Jonathan Edwards, to name three. For a recent treatment of perfect being theology, see Katherin Rogers, *Perfect Being Theology* (Edinburgh: Edinburgh University Press, 2000).

[15] It is sometimes difficult to pin down exactly what Barth thinks on this matter. Although he makes much of the covenant as an (the?) end of creation, he also says things that seem to conflict with this. For instance, in CD III/1, 44, while commenting on Romans 11:36, he says that creation is 'through God', 'from God' and 'for God'. This sounds more like the traditional view.

[16] Perhaps the most sophisticated theological account of the ends of creation in the Reformed tradition can be found in Jonathan Edwards' dissertation, *The End of Creation*, in *The Works of Jonathan Edwards Volume 8: Ethical Writings*, (ed.) Paul Ramsey (New Haven: Yale University Press, 1989). The relationship between Edwards and Barth on this matter has been elucidated by Stephen R. Holmes in *God of Grace and God of Glory: An Account of the Theology of Jonathan Edwards* (Edinburgh: T&T Clark, 2000).

[17] See ch. 6 of this volume for more on this matter.

Fourthly, Barth takes considerable pains to show that there is an intimate connection between the divine act of creation, and the covenant of grace whereby God graciously ordains to elect Christ as the one through whom human redemption is brought about. He speaks of creation as *the external basis of the covenant* (CD III/1, § 41. 2) and of the covenant as *the internal basis of creation* (CD III/1 § 41. 3). On the one hand, creation is the means by which God ordains to bring about his covenant relationship with humankind through the agency of Christ. God will redeem human beings through Christ, the Elect One, and in order to do this, God will create the world. (This offers another window onto Barth's supralapsarian understanding of the divine decrees.) But on the other hand, or looked at from another point of view, the covenant is the internal meaning or basis of the creation. It is the reason why God creates the world.

John Webster thinks that Barth's two claims about the relation between creation and covenant amount to the same thing.[18] But, without some explanation, this is not obvious (if it were, we have a distinction without a difference). I suggest that at least part of what Barth is getting at is this: the creation should not be treated independently of the covenant of grace. The two things are not unrelated to one another, or merely doctrines running along parallel lines in the mind of God. They are both interconnected in the divine mind. God creates the world in order to bring about his covenant (the supralapsarian element to this claim). But Barth also wants to assert that the covenant is itself somehow the 'internal' basis of the creation. It is, we might say, the rationale for the creation: 'the covenant is the goal of creation and creation the way to the covenant' CD III/1, 97. It is rather like asking which of two pillars that support a house are more fundamental to the integrity of the structure. Is it the one on the left, or the one on the right of the portico? Such reasoning is futile because both are needed for the house to remain standing. And similarly, both the creation and covenant are needed for God's purpose in creation to stand, although it is the covenant that is the goal and purpose of creation, and which gives creation its rationale.

What I am suggesting is that Barth's distinction between the 'internal' and 'external' in his characterization of the relationship between the creation and covenant in the plans of God is nothing more than a

---

[18] John Webster, *Barth*, second edition, p. 98. Barth explicitly states at one point that the relationship between creation and covenant is not reversible. See CD III/1, p. 97.

device for emphasizing different aspects of their interconnectedness in the plans of God, and the logical, or conceptual, priority of the covenant in the divine plan. But this distinction relies upon his commitment to a supralapsarian view of the ordering of the divine decrees. It is the covenant that gives meaning to creation, not the other way around. Moreover, the 'internal basis' of creation can only be understood when we see that God uses creation as the means by which to redeem humanity through Christ (under the terms of the covenant in which Christ is the Elect One). So, what Barth has to say about the relationship between the covenant and creation implies a particular theological conception of the nature of creation and its rationale, or goal. And this rationale is connected in turn to his claim that creation can only be understood by faith – when we understand that Christ's work is the means by which the redemptive goal of creation is achieved.[19] It is to this matter that we now turn.

Four areas of disagreement between Barth and the Reformed tradition on creation

And so, via four areas of partial agreement and overlap between Barth and his theological forbears in the Reformed tradition, we come to four areas of disagreement between Barth and the Reformed tradition. And, following on from the foregoing, we begin with Barth's claim that a proper understanding of creation requires prior faith in Christ (CD III/1, § 40), without which creation cannot be understood. It is, he declares, an *articulus fidei* (article of faith), not a component of some theological prolegomena prior to dogmatic theology proper. However, most classical theologians agree that to some extent human beings are capable of understanding that the world was created. And this can be achieved in the absence of faith, and despite the noetic effects of sin. For instance, in his *Institutes* (1.1–5) John Calvin maintains that the creation is a natural revelation, and that, even in a fallen state, human beings are capable of seeing in the creation the hand of a creator (though not, it should be pointed out, a saving knowledge

---

[19] Of course, it may be that the internal logic of Barth's doctrine is consistent and yet his account of creation still fails if, say, his conception of the reconciliation of humanity as the (ultimate?) end of creation is wide of the mark. I have already given one good reason from the tradition for questioning Barth's position in this regard.

of God in Christ).[20] But Calvin also claims that the created order can only be seen for what it truly is by those with faith. Believers should, 'take pious delight in the works of God open and manifest in this most beautiful theatre', that is, the theatre of God's creation. He goes on to say that although the creation 'is not the chief evidence for faith, yet it is the first evidence in the order of nature'. So believers should 'be mindful that wherever we cast our eyes, all things they meet are works of God'. Such experiences of creation should leave the Christian ready to 'ponder with pious meditation to what end God created them [the world]'.[21]

Barth's account of creation in CD III/1 raises several issues with this sort of reasoning. The first has to do with the fact that creation is no evidence *for* faith, if this means, 'evidence *in support of*' or, alternatively, 'evidence *that grounds*' faith. Nature can offer no evidence for faith – no 'point of contact' between the creation and human beings. For there is no *analogia entis*, or analogy of being between the created order and human beings whereby the created order may act as a conduit, or catalyst for revelation apart from the special revelation of the Word of God.[22] Neither would Barth be entirely happy with discussion or reflection upon creation that did not draw attention to the fact that without a saving knowledge of Christ, one cannot truly be said to *perceive* and *understand* what it means to speak of a creation as such.

---

[20] Barth denied Calvin believed this in his infamous tract, *Nein!*, directed at his Swiss colleague, Emil Brunner – see *Natural Theology*, trans. Peter Fraenkel (London: Geoffrey Bles, 1946). However, most Calvin interpreters think Barth is mistaken in his reading of Calvin. See, for instance, Paul Helm, *John Calvin's Ideas* (Oxford: Oxford University Press, 2004), ch. 8, and the argument of the previous chapter.

[21] *Institutes* 1. 14, p. 20.

[22] Much is made of the analogy of being in literature on Barth, and Barth himself says, 'I regard the *analogia entis* as the invention of the Antichrist' in CD I/1, xiii. But, as George Hunsinger points out, Barth never really explains precisely what he means by this term. See Hunsinger, *How To Read Karl Barth: The Shape of His Theology* (New York: Oxford University Press, 1991), p. 283, n. 2. According to Hunsinger, a rough idea of what Barth has in mind would be this: a state of affairs by which human beings are inherently open to and capable of knowing God and a procedure whereby this inherent openness is exercised such that God becomes known (in some sense). But from this it is still not clear how this involves an *analogy* of being. Cf. Emil Brunner, *The Christian Doctrine of Creation and Redemption, Dogmatics Vol. II*, trans. Olive Wyon (London: Lutterworth Press, 1952), ch. 1, Appendix C.

Thus, at the beginning of his discussion of creation in CD III/1: 28, he says, 'Jesus Christ is the Word by which *the knowledge of creation* is mediated to us because He is the Word by which God has fulfilled creation'. He goes on to say,

> I believe in Jesus Christ, God's Son our Lord, in order to perceive and understand that God the Almighty, the Father, is the Creator of heaven and earth. If I did not believe the former, I could not perceive and understand the latter. If I perceive and understand the latter, my perception and understanding are completely established, sustained and impelled by my believing the former (CD III/1, 29).

In this respect, Barth goes beyond what Calvin and his successors amongst the Reformed Orthodox were willing to say in his 'christologizing' of creation, which he freely acknowledges:

> With . . . reference to the noetic connexion between Jesus Christ and creation we emphasise something which has been strangely overlooked and neglected, or at any rate not developed in any detail, either in more recent or even in earlier theology (CD III/1, 29).

Whereas Calvin and the Reformed Orthodox were willing to make space for natural revelation and (a limited) natural theology, such notions are anathema to Barth, for whom any concession towards natural theology of any description is tantamount to making God in our own image.[23]

According to Barth we may not presume to know what God is like from our own ratiocination, or on the basis of some putative natural revelation in the created order. We can only know what God is like where God breaks into our world in an event of revelation and makes himself known to us. Applied to his doctrine of creation, this means that human beings are incapable of knowing that this world is a creation as such (rather than, say, a cosmic accident, or a random occurrence, or a brute fact without any explanation), outside of revelation. And since the Word of God is the agent of revelation and the one who

---

[23] Elsewhere in CD III, when discussing theological anthropology, Barth argues that the *imago dei* is not some property possessed by human beings. It is Christ (cf. Col. 1:15), into whose image all the redeemed will be formed. This point is helpfully discussed by Mangina in *Karl Barth: Theologian of Christian Witness*.

is revealed to us in Scripture, it is through the Word of God that we come to understand that God has created the world. So Barth is entirely serious in his claim that creation cannot be made sense of apart from knowledge of Christ.[24] Barth believes that the history of dogmatic theology shows how, when this insight has been ignored, the doctrine of creation has become enslaved to a general account of creation that is 'naturalized'. That is, it becomes an account of creation that is not specifically Christian, whose principal purpose is to function as a bridge to those working in the natural sciences – whose sympathies lie with philosophical naturalism (roughly, the idea that all that exists is the material world), not the supernaturalism of Christian theology. Such an account of creation, according to Barth, can only end up surrendering what is distinctively Christian in the doctrine of creation, in order to make the theological account of creation palatable to a wider (and unsympathetic) audience.[25]

Related to this is a second area of disagreement between Barth and his Reformed forbears, to do with his denial of an apologetic purpose to the doctrine of creation. At the beginning of CD III/1, ix he

---

[24] At one point he offers the following argument against 'all science both ancient and modern' (presumably – although he does not say as much – he means here scientific *naturalism* not natural science *per se*) in CD III/1, p. 6: 'If the world is not created by God it is not. If we do not recognise that it has been created by God, we do not recognise that it is. But we know that it has been created by God only on the ground of God's self-witness and therefore in faith. Therefore we know only in faith that the world is.'

[25] Eberhard Busch spends some time explaining how Barth saw this declining trajectory of the theology of creation from the seventeenth century onwards. According to Busch, Barth saw the Enlightenment as the beginning of the gradual domestication of the doctrine, and its eventual assimilation to an entirely secular understanding of what 'creation' means: 'first the interpretation of the covenant of grace in terms of the creation, and then creation without reference to this covenant, and ultimately without reference at all to God; the understanding of "nature" as humanity's mass of manageable things and then its negatability by humans; the understanding of the human person without reference to the fellow person and then in terms of the animal – this entire pathway began, for Barth, in a theology that thought of God without the human and the world, saw him in relation to creation as one not essentially connected to it.' *The Great Passion*, p. 179. Cf. Thomas Torrance's comments on the 'Latin heresy' of Medieval and post-Reformation theology, in *Karl Barth: Biblical and Evangelical Theologian* (Edinburgh: T & T Clark, 1990), ch. 8.

declares, 'there can be no scientific problems, objections or aids in relation to what Holy Scripture and the Christian Church understand by the divine work of creation.' He does not pause to explain this in detail, but it seems Barth believed cosmology and theology are dealing with two very different, though perhaps complementary, accounts of the creation of the world.[26] According to Barth, once it is understood that the creation narratives of Genesis 1–3 are not to be read as a scientific textbook of what literally took place in creation, but as a story – or, as Barth puts it, a saga – which explains what went on in creation, much of the supposed conflict between cosmological and theological accounts of creation dissolve. (Compare the way in which a mechanic might offer to someone unversed in the workings of the combustion engine a story that explains why their motor car broke down, which, while not giving a technical account of the matter in all its facts, is nevertheless a way of explaining what the problem consisted in that is not untrue. Such a story might be a 'saga' in Barth's sense. It is clearly not a 'myth', which, as Barth makes clear, can have no basis in actual events.) Barth maintained that the biblical account of creation is a piece of dogmatics, not apologetics, which is quite different to the way this doctrine is often treated in modern theology. Because of this, Barth argued that the proper form this doctrine should take is theological, not apologetic. For this reason he felt free to leave the apologetic problems associated with creation to one side in CD III/1.

---

[26] Compare *Dogmatics in Outline*, trans. G. T. Thomson (London: SCM Press, 1949), p. 51 and Letter 181, to Christine Barth, where he says, 'The creation story is a witness to the beginning or becoming of all reality distinct from God in the light of God's later acts and words relating to his people Israel – naturally in the form of a saga or poem. The theory of evolution is an attempt to explain the same reality in its inner nexus – naturally in the form of a scientific explanation . . . Thus one's attitude to the creation story and the theory of evolution can take the form of an either/or only if one shuts oneself off completely either from faith in God's revelation or from the mind (or opportunity) for scientific understanding.' *Karl Barth, Letters 1961–1968*, trans. Geoffrey Bromiley (Edinburgh: T&T Clark, 1981), p. 184. This does not mean that Barth saw no place for a more apologetic account of creation. See CD III/1, x. Thomas Torrance, a pupil of Barth, was at pains to show how (for want of a better word) 'Barthian' theology has methodological parallels with modern natural science. See, for example, Torrance, *Karl Barth: Biblical and Evangelical Theologian*, pp. 145 ff. And his *Space, Time and Resurrection* (Edinburgh: T&T Clark, 1976).

This approach to the creation narratives and their relation to the natural sciences has been controversial and few have followed Barth's lead. The main point of contention has to do with whether or not Barth is right about the dogmatic, rather than apologetic, purpose of the creation narratives of Genesis 1–3. There has also been some criticism, even amongst Barth's allies, of the way in which he expounds the texts of the Primeval Prologue of Genesis 1–3 in CD III/1.[27] But for many evangelicals, the most serious problem with Barth's treatment of the creation narratives is his willingness to think of them as 'saga', rather than as broadly historical events. Much here depends on a complex of issues surrounding the nature of the creation narratives, their place in biblical literature and their status as revelation (or their status as the vehicle for revelation, on Barth's account of revelation).

I do not propose to enter into this morass here. However, several things should be borne in mind when tackling Barth on this issue. To begin with, he is very concerned to get to grips with the text, and what it says – there are literally pages of exegesis on the creation narratives in CD III/1. He is also somewhat wary of tying his own exegesis too tightly to particular historical-critical theories about some putative original sources for the canonical text.[28] He does not make the mistake of thinking that because a canonical text has a literary prehistory, this *ipso facto* undermines its status as revelation, or – for Barth – its status as the vehicle for revelation. Finally, as I have already indicated, his description of the creation narratives as saga should not be misunderstood. Barth's characterization of Genesis 1–3 as saga is not a thinly veiled way of saying 'Genesis 1–3 is a fairy tale', although the way he negotiates Genesis 1 and 2 is not always as clear as one might have hoped.[29] (However, and *ad hominem*, Barth is not alone

---

[27] See, for example, W. A. Whitehouse's friendly criticism in his short essay, 'Karl Barth on "The Work of Creation": A Reading of Church Dogmatics III/1' in *Reckoning with Barth: Essays in Commemoration of the Centenary of Karl Barth's Birth*, ed. Nigel Biggar (Oxford: A. R. Mowbray and Co., 1988). Mangina also refers to Barth's rather 'unusual' way of thinking about Genesis 1:2. See his *Karl Barth: Theologian of Christian Witness*.

[28] A point also noted by Mangina. See *Karl Barth: Theologian of Christian Witness*, p. 91.

[29] My concern here is just to defend Barth against certain common misunderstandings of what he is trying to say about the creation narratives, in the interest of fair play. I am not committing myself to what Barth actually says about Genesis 1–3.

amongst modern theologians in this regard. There is precious little theological discussion of the creation narratives in modern theology that does not treat the dogmatic implications of these passages rather like an embarrassing family secret. This, it seems to me, is a major dogmatic lacuna in modern theology, which has few exceptions).

A fourth area of disagreement between Barth and traditional Reformed theology has to do with the creative act itself. Unlike classical theologians, Barth does not believe creation is a timeless act of an atemporal God, whose essence remains unaffected by the utterance of the divine fiat, and bringing into being of the created order.[30] Barth believes that the fact of the Incarnation should 'control' what is believed about the relation of God to time in this respect, such that creation is understood as a temporal act of God. Let us focus on two claims made by Barth in this context. The first is that God is somehow in time, although a time very different from 'created time'. The second is his denial of Augustine's thesis that God atemporally creates the world 'with', rather than 'in' time.

On the question of God's relation to time, Barth says the following:

> Eternity is not merely the negation of time. It is not in any way time-less. On the contrary, as the source of time it is supreme and absolute time, i.e., the immediate unity of present, past and future . . . God Himself is temporal, precisely in so far as He is eternal, and His eternity is the prototype of time, and as the Eternal He is simultaneously before time, above time, and after time (CD III/1, 67).

Later in the same discussion, he speaks of God's time as 'absolute', as opposed to created time that is 'relative time' (CD III/1, 68). This is difficult to make sense of. It might be that Barth means God exists in some sort of exalted temporal state, where God is 'in time' but without an absolute past, present or future. One could claim that God exists omnipresently through time and that there is no 'God's eye' view from which we can say a particular moment is objectively past, present or future. Then, we could say that God is past, with reference to a particular circumstance, but that there is no past for God, objectively speaking. On such a way of thinking God does not, in one sense, have an objective past, present, or future without reference to

---

[30] For expositions of the classical view, see Augustine, *Confessions*, Bks. XI and XII; Boethius, *The Consolation of Philosophy*; Aquinas, *Summa Theologica* I. Q. 10.

particular circumstances, such as 'God created the world some time *before* this afternoon'. But God is temporal, nevertheless. Some recent metaphysicians have discussed this sort of view of time, and it does seem to correspond to Barth's notion of God's time as 'pure duration'.[31] The difference between this view of an exalted or 'pure duration' view of God's time and created time would be that, for the creature, there is an objective past, present and future. He or she experiences the present, recalls the past and looks forward to a future in a way that, on the 'pure duration' view of God's time, God does not. Perhaps this sort of distinction is what Barth means when he emphasizes the importance of history in creation: 'No less than everything depends upon the truth of the statement that God's creation takes place as history in time' (CD III/1, 69).

One of the problems with trying to make sense of Barth's understanding of God's relation to time is that what he does say on the matter is rather ambiguous at times, and difficult to get a handle on.[32] Still, this is one way in which Barth's claim that God is in time but not in 'created time' could be construed. But it is still a departure from the classical view that God is timeless, and creates the world with time. This brings us to the second aspect of his discussion of God and time that I want to mention. Barth takes issue with Augustine's account of divine atemporal creation in his *Confessions*, Books XI–XII.[33] There, amongst other things, Augustine says that God creates the world and time 'simultaneously' (if the reader will excuse the anachronism). He

---

[31] For more on recent metaphysical arguments in this area, see Thomas M. Crisp, 'Presentism', and Michael C. Rea 'Four Dimensionalism', both in *The Oxford Handbook of Metaphysics*, eds. Michael J. Loux and Dean W. Zimmerman (Oxford: Oxford University Press, 2003). Robert W. Jenson says 'He [Barth] describes the particular "eternity of the triune God" as "pure duration [reine Dauer]"' *Systematic Theology, Vol. 1: The Triune God* (New York: Oxford University Press, 1997), p. 217. His discussion of the way in which Barth's doctrine of divine eternity echoes elements of Gregory of Nyssa is interesting, although, I have argued elsewhere that Jenson's own account of divine eternity is unworkable. See Oliver D. Crisp, *God Incarnate: Explorations in Christology* (London: T&T Clark, 2009), ch. 3.

[32] This has hampered other interpreters of Barth too. See, for example, R. H. Roberts' rather tortuous essay, 'Barth's doctrine of time: Its nature and Implications' in *Karl Barth: Studies of His Theological Method*, ed. S. W. Sykes (Oxford: Oxford University Press, 1979).

[33] See the small print discussion in CD III/1, pp. 69–71.

denies what we might call the 'container' view of time, where God creates time, and then creates the world that sits 'in' time, like a ball might sit in a bowl or other container.[34] Barth replies that God may certainly create the world in time. God is not atemporal, as Augustine believes. He has 'pure duration'. So the created world begins in this 'pure duration' of God's eternity. Perhaps part of what he means is that, although 'created time' begins with the divine fiat to create, this does not mean that it is meaningless to speak of some period of time before creation. God exists before creation in his exalted time. Nevertheless, there is a sense in which the sort of time belonging to the creation does begin at the moment God creates the world. If this is what Barth is getting at, then he is really only objecting to Augustine's idea that there is no time prior to the creation because God is time-less. Yet, although there is time before the creation, it is not 'created time' but God's 'pure duration', which as we have already seen, is quite different from created time.

Once again this is a departure from the classical view of God's relation to time. But if one allows that God exists in some temporally exalted state as Barth does, it is a short step from there to the view that God creates the world in time. In fact, Barth ends up 'correcting' Augustine as follows: *mundus factus cum tempore, ergo in tempore* – the world is created with time, and [therefore] in time (CD III/1, 71).

Concluding remarks

An important theme in the New Testament doctrine of creation is the fact that Christ, the Word of God, is the agent through whom all things are created and sustained. Thus, John 1:3 states, 'through him [i.e. the Word of God] all things were made; without him nothing was made that was made'. Colossians 1:16 says, 'for by him all things were created; things in heaven and on earth, visible and invisible . . . all things were created by him and for him. He is before all things, and in him all things hold together.' And Hebrews 11:3 tells us that, 'by faith we understand that the worlds were framed by the Word of God'. This biblical affirmation of the centrality of Christ's work in the creation and conservation of the world lies at the heart of Karl Barth's doctrine of creation in *Church Dogmatics* volume III. As T. F. Torrance

---

[34] Cf. ch. 1. I owe this analogy to Paul Helm. See *Faith and Understanding* (Edinburgh: Edinburgh University Press, 1997), ch. 4.

points out, 'the evangelical heart of Barth's theology is the doctrine of Christ as the divine Reconciler . . . Barth never ceased to insist, Christology gives us the determining centre from which all our knowledge of God and of creation must take its shape.'[35]

But, as we have seen, Barth goes beyond the biblical affirmation that Christ is the agent through whom and for whom all things are created. For him the doctrine of creation can only be understood as an article of faith *in Christ*. The success of what I have called Barth's *christologizing* of the doctrine of creation can be seen in the hostility shown in some evangelical circles towards natural theology, often maligned as a way of cashing out the doctrine of creation in the absence of Christ. (Although, it should be said, not all evangelicals take this sort of view, and not all of those evangelicals sympathetic to Barth's account have taken this view as a result of reading Barth.) The influence of Barth's doctrine of creation can also be seen in the insistence by some contemporary theologians that the doctrine of creation must be connected with Christology. (See, for instance, Colin Gunton's book, *Christ and Creation*[36]). To my mind, discussion of the interconnections between Christian doctrines is welcome, and Barth's treatment of creation lends itself to such a way of thinking. But I am less enthusiastic about his treatment of natural theology. It seems to me that there is a right use of natural theology to which Calvin and his successors in the Reformed Orthodox tradition point (*pace* Barth). This may lead back to the dreaded *analogia entis* (whatever this is exactly). But it need not. The recent development of Reformed Epistemology from philosophical theologians like Alvin Plantinga, Nicholas Wolterstorff and William Alston signals one way in which Calvin's legacy may be usefully appropriated for the theological task without ceding ground to ways of thinking that are not profoundly shaped by the person and work of Christ.[37]

I am also not sure that Barth's attempt to tell a consistent supralapsarian story about the relationship between creation and covenant is entirely successful, because I am not convinced that Barth grasps the importance of the ultimate end of creation viz. divine self-glorifica-

---

[35] *Karl Barth: Biblical and Evangelical Theologian*, pp. 20–21.

[36] Colin E. Gunton, *Christ and Creation* (Carlisle: Paternoster, 1992).

[37] The *locus classicus* of Reformed Epistemology is *Reason and Religious Belief*, eds. Wolterstorff and Plantinga (Notre Dame: University of Notre Dame Press, 1983). The most sophisticated development of this position to date is Alvin Plantinga, *Warranted Christian Belief* (New York: Oxford University Press, 2000).

tion. If, as Barth's doctrine suggests, the covenant is the end of creation, is it the only end or one of several ends? And if it is one of several ends, is it the ultimate end, or a subordinate one? This question does not seem to be adequately answered in Barth's discussion.

Fewer evangelicals will be disturbed by Barth's way of thinking about God's relation to time as it bears upon the doctrine of creation, because many contemporary evangelical theologians do not believe that God is timeless.[38] But, at the very least, those who wish to reject the unanimous voice of the classical theological tradition would do well to think carefully about why they feel the greatest minds in Christian theology were so wrong on this matter. It does not seem to me that the old Harnackian thesis that classical theology was hopelessly tangled in a philosophical web of Platonic presuppositions holds water on close examination. Yet a number of theologians deeply indebted to Barth continue to reiterate this thesis without sufficient regard being paid to the arguments of those who dissent from this view.[39]

Barth's account of creation is a theologically sophisticated piece of Christian dogmatics that intersects with several key concerns in his larger *corpus*, such as his polemic against natural theology and his Christology. Theologians of all stripes, evangelicals included, would benefit from availing themselves of the important insights he brings to this doctrine. I suppose that no theologian will find everything Barth says to his or her taste. But this is hardly a reason to neglect Barth: I know of no single theologian with whom I agree on every single theological matter – and I do not suppose myself to be unusual in this regard. If Barth were dismissive of the authority of Scripture or the importance of the tradition in his doctrine of creation,[40] there might be good reason for being wary of what he says on creation. But

---

[38] See, for example, the views represented in *God and Time: Four Views* (ed.) Gregory Ganssle (Downers Grove: IVP, 2001).

[39] See, for example, Colin E. Gunton, *Act and Being: Towards A Theology of The Divine Attributes* (Grand Rapids: Eerdmans, 2002) and Robert W. Jenson, *Systematic Theology, Vol. 1.* One might also compare the work of Openness theologians like Clark Pinnock, although their reasons for rejecting the traditional view of the divine nature are quite different from either Gunton or Jenson.

[40] Some evangelicals think that Barth's account of revelation means he does fail to take Scripture as seriously as he should and, as a consequence, we should be very wary of what Barth has to say on any given theological topic. I think this is a mistake. Although Barth's doctrine of revelation is

this is hardly the case. What Barth offers is a biblically informed and theologically robust doctrine of creation in which those who align themselves with classical Reformed, or, more broadly, evangelical, theology will continue to find a rich seam of ideas and careful reflection – even if, in the final analysis, one has to disagree with him in a number of important areas. And that, I suggest, is surely a reason to engage with Barth.

(cont.) theologically innovative and could be taken in unhelpful directions, in practice, the way he uses Scripture is very conservative. It would certainly not be fair to Barth to say that he has a low view of the status and place of Scripture in his doctrine of creation, as I hope I have already indicated.

PART II

SIN AND SALVATION

CHAPTER THREE

Jonathan Edwards on the Imputation of Sin

> Wilt Thou forgive that sin where I begun,
> Which was my sin, though it were done before?
> Wilt Thou forgive that sin through which I run,
> And do run still, though still I do deplore?
> When Thou hast done, Thou hast not done;
> For I have more.
> — *John Donne, A Hymn to God the Father*

Jonathan Edwards' most sustained treatment of the doctrine of original sin in general and imputation in particular is laid out in his treatise on *Original Sin* (hereinafter *OS*).[1] The argument he lays out there has both theological and philosophical axes. The substance of the treatise is theological, being a trenchant defence of the coherence of the Calvinistic concept of depravity and its roots in the (as Edwards sees it) biblical doctrine of original sin. But in so doing, Edwards is drawn into controversy over the nature of imputation, and it is this issue that is of interest in the present chapter.

Edwards' thinking in this area is notoriously difficult to understand, and has generated a number of conflicting interpretations. What follows is an assessment of the theological nature of Edwards' doctrine of imputation from the perspective of systematic and historical theology. The burden of this essay is that Edwards' position is misunderstood if, in approaching his exposition of the doctrine, the expectation is that he is simply reiterating Calvinistic orthodoxy. He

---

[1] *Original Sin: The Works of Jonathan Edwards, Volume 3*, ed. Clyde Holbrook (New Haven: Yale University Press, 1970). All references are to this edition cited as *YE3*, followed by colon and pagination.

is not. Instead, his treatment of the issue represents a critical analysis of both Augustinian realism, and Calvinistic federalism, reformulating aspects of both in a *via media*, which he believed better represented the biblical picture of imputation.

Edwards' argument for original sin

The context of the debate into which Edwards wrote is now largely a matter for the history of ideas.[2] At the time of writing his treatise, Edwards believed that he was contributing to a battle being waged over the integrity of the Calvinistic doctrine of depravity. His antagonist was Dr John Taylor, whose volume entitled *The Scripture Doctrine of Original Sin*[3] sounded a note of what Edwards perceived to be 'Arminianism' in New England.[4]

Axiomatic to his discussion are the pre-critical assumptions of the plenary inspiration of Scripture, and in particular, the historicity of the creation and fall narratives of Genesis 1–3. Edwards chose to deal with the threat posed in Taylor by approaching hamartiology through experience and Scripture before adducing metaphysics in defence of key areas of dispute. As a consequence of this, *OS* follows an inductive structure, which falls into four parts. The first section lays out the evidence from observation and experience which tends to support the biblical doctrine he goes on to delineate. The Scriptural data supporting original sin are analyzed in section two of the treatise. In the third section, Edwards deals (rather briefly) with the application of original sin to soteriology in redemption. Finally, in section four he lays out several refutations of common objections to original sin on metaphysical grounds, including his discussion of imputation.

Robert Jenson has observed that the whole edifice of this work rests upon two theses which were responses to the 'Arminian' perspective

---

[2] Clyde Holbrook's Editor's Introduction to *YE3* is invaluable on the historical background to the context of Edwards' writing of *OS*. See especially pp. 1–26.

[3] The full title of Talyor's work was *The Scripture-Doctrine of Original Sin, Proposed to Free and candid Examination*. It is not clear whether it was published in 1738 (the traditional date) or 1740. See *YE3*: 2, n. 5.

[4] To my knowledge Edwards only makes one passing remark about Taylor's Arminianism (YE3: 375). But it is tacitly assumed throughout *OS* that Taylor's position is Arminian.

represented by Taylor: The defence of the Calvinistic understanding of innate depravity and the defence of imputation, each of which – according to Taylor – were separate theological offences which needed to be abandoned. These two theses stand at the beginning of *OS* as the Edwardsian points of departure for what follows in the treatise:

> By original sin, as the phrase has been most commonly used by divines, is meant the innate sinful depravity of the heart. But yet when the doctrine of original sin is spoken of, it is vulgarly understood in that latitude, as to include not only the depravity of nature, but the imputation of Adam's first sin.[5]

Conrad Cherry has noted that Taylor's attack upon the tenets of New England Calvinistic orthodoxy, to which Edwards was responding, devolved upon the difference between the effects of the fall and the imputation of the guilt accrued by the fall. According to Taylor, Adam's posterity were subject to the effects of the fall including physical frailty and death, but were not subject to eternal death or personal guilt simply on account of the imputation of Adam's guilt to his progeny. 'For Taylor, not only is grace conditional upon the self-determining natural human faculties; when Scripture speaks of the imputation of righteousness, it refers to the person's own act in itself, operating according to the exercises of the natural faculties, as righteous.'[6] It was the view of Taylor and his sympathizers that the position to which Edwards clung was fatally pessimistic in its perspective on human nature, whereas, in Cherry's view, what Edwards actually intended to do in *OS* was offer a version of Calvinism which endorsed a kind of 'tragic optimism', sometimes overlooked by his detractors.[7]

The inherent optimism of Taylor's doctrine led to a replacement (or displacement) of confidence in God's redemptive power with confidence in man's power to fulfill the moral law himself. This meant that the Reformation doctrine of *sola fide* was in danger of being undermined.

---

[5] *YE3*: 107. The importance of these two points has also been noted by Holbrook in his editorial introduction in *YE3*: 27, 'According to Edwards, there are two parts to the doctrine of original sin: the depravity of the human heart and the imputation of Adam's first sin to his posterity.'

[6] Conrad Cherry, *The Theology of Jonathan Edwards: A Reappraisal* (Indianapolis: Indiana University Press, 1966), p. 198.

[7] Ibid., p. 197.

It was because of this that Edwards felt the need to act. Hence the direction Edwards' thinking took in *OS*, namely, to outline and correct Taylor's doctrine from scripture and experience before dealing with the metaphysical issues. For Edwards, what was at stake was more than a dogmatic quibble: the entire evangelical legacy of his Puritan forebears was in question. Thus Cherry notes,

> The abandonment of the Calvinistic doctrine that all men are totally corrupt *coram deo* has as its counterpart that abandonment of the doctrine of justification by grace through faith. For the depravity of man and the glorious majesty of God's saving grace mutually illuminate each other. That is why Edwards insists that sin is a fall of the race in Adam (the continuity of guilt being maintained by the direct power of God) and not simply a series of separate human acts. It is a corruption of heart that reaches deep into the human subject, a corruption to be estimated primarily by comparing the selfishness of man with the overflowing love of the infinite God.[8]

Clearly, Edwards' rationale in completing *OS* was primarily an apologetic one, as had been the case with his treatise on the *Freedom of the Will*.[9] But here, even more than in *Freedom of the Will*, Edwards directed his thinking along apologetic lines.

Edwards' theology of imputation

Thus far we have seen that Edwards' doctrine in *OS* is directed to the goal of defending the traditional dogma of original sin as it has been classically construed. That is to say, the idea that Adam passed on to his progeny some terrible vitiation of moral nature due to the fall, resulting in its propagation to his posterity. However, there are two broad streams of thinking regarding the *means* by which this original

---

[8] Ibid., p. 201.

[9] Edwards' position in apologetics has been charted by Michael McClymond, in Chapter 6 of *Encounters with God: An Approach to the Theology of Jonathan Edwards* (Oxford: Oxford University Press, 1998), where he places him firmly in the mainstream, 'Edwards fits into the Augustinian or Anselmian pattern of "faith seeking understanding," hence there was no contradiction in his reliance on reason combined with his assertion that reason is no substitute for revelation' (p. 95).

sin is imputed to Adam's children, (that is, each of these two positions outlines the kind of *union* that is established by God in imputing Adam's sin to his progeny). The question of the union established by God in original sin is clearly related to, but separate from, the problem of the *nature* of the imputation involved in the transmission of original sin.

Whereas the problem of the union established by God in imputation deals with the way in which God sees the relationship between Adam-plus-his-progeny, the nature of that union deals with how the resulting original sin is passed on to Adam's posterity; either *immediately* in virtue of some metaphysical unity that is established between Adam and his posterity, or *mediately*, through some hereditary corruption which is passed down the generations from Adam onwards. It is the union established by God in original sin that is of primary interest to Edwards in his discussion of imputation in *OS*. His views on the nature of imputation arise out of his thinking on precisely how God establishes a union between Adam and his progeny that is a just reflection of the holiness of his character. We shall outline each of the two views involved in the question of union first, before moving to comment on the nature of the union that has been established.

The union established by original sin

The first conception of this metaphysical union is the realist view of the Augustinian school. Adam is seen here as the concrete universal of humankind, and humanity are dealt with 'in him'. This means that Adam's nature, while individual, in some way can also comprise the whole race in a metaphysical unity where they are dealt with by God as a corporate unity. Adam's progeny are somehow present in Adam at the point of original sin; according to the traditional interpretation of Augustinian realism, this presence is to be understood seminally.[10] Thus Augustine in *City of God* comments on the natures of Adam and Eve that,

---

[10] I have deliberately sidestepped this issue of the mechanism of imputation, which has caused not a little embarrassment to some theologians after Augustine. This pertains to the material cause of imputation (how the condition was passed on), whereas we are concerned with the formal cause (why it was passed on in the first place).

because of the magnitude of that offence, the condemnation changed
human nature for the worse; so that what first happened as a matter of
punishment in the case of the first human beings, continued in their
posterity as something natural and congenital...the whole human race
was in the first man, and it was to pass from him through the woman
into his progeny, when the married pair had received the divine sentence of condemnation.[11]

This realist position had something of a revival of interest in the nineteenth century when William G. T. Shedd defended it as the classic
theological and biblical model for articulating a doctrine of original
sin.[12] Thus, in his *Dogmatic Theology*, he writes,

Scripture is clear that the sin of Adam is the sin of us all, not only by
propagation and communication (whereby not his singular [individ-
ual] fault, but something of the same nature [with it] is derived unto
us), but also by an imputation of his actual transgression unto us all, his
singular [individual] transgression being by this means made ours.

He goes on to clarify this position,

The grounds of this imputation are: 1. That we were then in him and
parts of him. 2. That he sustained the place of our whole nature in the
covenant God made with him. When divines affirm that by Adam's sin
we are guilty of damnation, they do not mean that any are damned for
his particular act, but that by his sin and our sinning in him, by God's
most just ordination we have contracted that exceeding pravity and
sinfulness of nature which deserveth the curse of God and eternal
damnation.[13]

---

[11] *City of God*, XIII: III, trans. Henry Bettenson (Harmondsworth: Penguin,
    1984), p. 512. Augustine's doctrine is not always easy to discern, and it is
    not always clear that he advocates an unambiguous version of realism as
    John Murray points out, in his volume on *The Imputation of Adam's Sin*
    (Grand Rapids: Eerdmans, 1959) p. 31. For our purposes, it is sufficient
    that Augustine has traditionally been regarded as an exemplar of realism,
    though perhaps this is not as clear cut as is sometimes thought.
[12] This position was also taken by, amongst others, the Baptist theologian
    Augustus Strong in his *Systematic Theology* (Westwood: Fleming H. Revell
    Co., 1963, reprinted from 1907 edition), pp. 619 ff.
[13] Shedd, *Dogmatic Theology, Vol. III* (New York: Charles Scribner's Sons,
    1894), pp. 348–349.

The central idea here is that human nature for the purposes of imputation is treated generically and numerically as one metaphysical unit, that is as Adam-plus-progeny. This means that Adam and his posterity are not separate individuals but participate in one common substance. Therefore, if this human nature is corrupted by Adam in an act of original sin, then it is corrupted in the subsequent individualization of that nature in an infralapsarian state. Consequently, all humanity actually or really sinned in Adam, since all humanity actually or really share in this one substance of human nature.[14]

The second view is the Reformed, or federal view with which Edwards was familiar through his Puritan heritage. Here Adam is regarded not so much as in mystical union with humanity in one substance, as a federal representative of his race, just as Christ was a federal representative of mankind before God on the cross. Indeed, the whole federal tradition in theology turns on the identification of Adam and Christ as the two 'Adams' (see Romans 5 and 1 Corinthians 15:20–28). One is the father of humanity whose actions as representative led to the imputation of original sin; the other is the saviour whose actions, culminating in his death and resurrection, led to the proffering of salvation upon Adam's race, by a similar federal, and covenantal relationship.[15] Thus Calvin says,

> the beginning of corruption in Adam was such that it was conveyed in a perpetual stream from the ancestors into their descendants. For the contagion does not take its origin from the substance of the flesh or soul, but because it had been so ordained by God that the first man should at one and the same time have and lose, both for himself and for his descendants, the gifts that God had bestowed upon him.[16]

---

[14] For a standard theological recapitulation of this point, see Louis Berkhof, *Systematic Theology* (Edinburgh: Banner of Truth, 1988), p. 241.

[15] For a recent and illuminating account of the Biblical data pertaining to the federal position, especially Romans 5, see Henri Blocher's *Original Sin: Illuminating the Riddle* (Leicester: IVP, 1997), chapter 3. Here he outlines two positions on Romans 5, which roughly correspond to the realist and federalist interpretations, before trying to put forward a *via media*. However, his view appears to be more like a soft-federalism than a true third option.

[16] *Inst.* 2:1:7, Vol. I, ed. John T. McNeill, trans. Ford Lewis Battles (Westminster: Philadelphia, 1960), p. 250.

This embryonic federalism in Calvin's thought was developed into a full-blown covenantal theology during the so-called Protestant Scholastic period following the Reformation in the late sixteenth to seventeenth centuries.[17] Francis Turretin, a scholar of this period and theologian with whom Edwards was familiar, expressed the federalist position on original sin in these terms,

> For the bond between Adam and his posterity is twofold: (1) natural, as he is the father, and we are his children; (2) political and forensic, as he was the prince and representative head of the whole human race. Therefore the foundation of imputation is not only the natural connection which exists between us and Adam (since, in that case, all his sins might be imputed to us), but mainly the moral and federal (in virtue of which God entered into covenant with him as our head.) Hence Adam stood in that sin not as a private person, but as a public and representative person – representing all his posterity in that action and whose demerit equally pertains to all.[18]

Federalism went hand in hand with covenantal theology, the idea here being that God made several covenants with humanity down through the ages by which means biblical and church history was divided up.[19] Adam stood as the natural head of the race as the first man and father of his progeny, but he also stood in a covenantal relationship to his posterity, instituted by God, whereby Adam was deemed the federal representative of the whole race. This supralapsarian covenant was called the Covenant of Works, and the terms of the covenant were that Adam would continue as the steward of the Garden as long as he did not eat of the fruit of the tree of the knowledge of good and evil in

---

[17] In more recent literature a distinction is usually made between covenantal theology pertaining to federalism, and Protestant Scholasticism as a whole. The former tends to be seen as a more strictly biblical theological construct, whereas Scholasticism tended towards abstraction and casuistry (in a logical rather than pejorative sense of that word).

[18] Turretin, *Institutes of Elenctic Theology, Vol. I*, trans. George Musgrove Giger, ed. James T. Dennison, Jr. (Phillipsburg, NJ: P&R Publishing, 1992), p. 616.

[19] This covenantal theology lies behind what Edwards says in works like *The History of the Work of Redemption*, in *The Works of Jonathan Edwards Vol. I* (Edinburgh: Banner of Truth, 1990), pp. 532 ff, and the Appendix to *Observations Concerning the Trinity and the Covenant of Redemption in Treatise on Grace*, ed. Paul Helm (Cambridge: James Clark, 1971).

Genesis 2:16–17. (Eve was clearly aware of the terms of the covenant although she herself was not present when they were set, as evidenced in her response to the serpent in Genesis 3: 2–3.) Hence Adam's sin was imputed to all his posterity on the basis of this second, covenantal relationship. For if Adam was the divinely inaugurated representative of the whole race, then when Adam sinned God would be covenantally bound to impute his vitiated state to all members of his race (this thought is taken up by Paul in Romans 5:12).

The nature of the transmission of original sin

On this federalist view, the means by which original sin is imputed is usually construed as being immediate. That is, Adamic sin passes *immediately* to all his posterity in such a way that all his posterity are born with the inherited condition of a vitiated nature. But there is another possible view of the nature of the union achieved in imputation, known as *mediate* imputation.

This view was first propagated at the French Saumur school of Theology in the seventeenth century by Placaeus (Josue de la Place, 1596–1655).[20] Placaeus claimed that Adam's progeny were not born cursed with Adam's sin. Instead, his posterity inherited only Adam's corrupt nature and it is this nature alone, and not the imputation of Adam's original sin itself, which is the ground of the subsequent condemnation of humanity by God. Hence, there is no immediate imputation of Adam's sin to his posterity as with traditional Calvinism. Imputation is only mediate, and indirect, located in the fact that we share the same moral nature as Adam, which since the fall, has been vitiated. His progeny are not born corrupt because they are guilty in Adam; rather, they are guilty because they are corrupt. Philip Quinn makes this point clear when he says, 'According to the theory of

---

[20] The theological intricacies of this debate are convoluted and not always clear. Placaeus, on being charged with the mediate view at the Twenty-Eighth Synod of the Reformed Churches in France, apparently declared that this condemnation did not represent his own views, and that he did not deny immediate imputation. Instead, he believed that the imputation of Adam's first sin was mediate not immediate. (See Murray, *The Imputation of Adam's Sin*, p. 43 on this.) What is important for the present purpose is a clear understanding of the doctrine of mediate imputation. We may leave the historical problems concerning the specifics of Placaeus' views to the church historians of the period.

immediate imputation the guilt of Adam's first sin is directly imputed to his posterity, and in them guilt logically precedes and is the
ground of inherent sin or corruption. Adam's descendants are corrupt
because they are guilty. According to the theory of mediate imputation . . . the order is reversed; corruption in Adam's descendants logically precedes and is the ground of imputed sin or guilt. They are
guilty because they are corrupt.'[21]

Although this view had a vogue in the seventeenth century, it
failed to establish itself as an effective alternative to the immediate
way of understanding the nature of imputation.

Having outlined the different theological views on the union
involved in imputation and the nature of that union, we may now
consider which of these views best represents Edwards' thinking on
the subject in *OS*.

There are those who have taken the view that Edwards does not
adhere to federalism in his doctrine of imputation. Paul Helm is
among these: his position, recently outlined in *Faith and Understanding*,[22] does not incorporate elements of a federalist reading of this
aspect of Edwards' doctrine. Others have taken the view that
Edwards was more orthodox in his Calvinistic understanding of
imputation and that what he says on this subject can be squared with
apparently federalist elements in his thinking elsewhere. Others have
claimed that Edwards was substantially federalist in his thinking on
original sin, but that his discussion of imputation represents a kind of
hiatus in this federalism; an internal inconsistency upon Edwards'
part which remained unreconciled within the argument of *OS*. There
was considerable debate on these issues, particularly in relation to
where Edwards stood on the union and nature of imputation in the
nineteenth century, which centred upon Princetonian Calvinism and
its appropriation of Edwards' thought.[23] In particular, Charles Hodge

---

[21] 'Disputing the Augustinian Legacy: John Locke and Jonathan Edwards on
    Romans 5:12–19', in *The Augustinian Tradition*, ed. Gareth B. Matthews
    (Berkeley: University of California Press, 1999), p. 239.

[22] (Edinburgh: Edinburgh University Press, 1997), ch. 7.

[23] For more on the relationship between the Princetonian theologians and
    Edwards see Mark Noll's essay, 'Jonathan Edwards and Nineteenth
    Century Theology' in Nathan O. Hatch and Harry S. Stout (eds.), *Jonathan
    Edwards and the American Experience* (Oxford: Oxford University Press,
    1988), pp. 260–81. He concludes his argument with the observation that
    the close of the nineteenth century marked the passing of Edwards as a
    serious theological force. Thereafter, theological interest in his corpus was

took issue with the consistency of Edwards' federalism in his doctrine of imputation, while B. B. Warfield defended Edwards as consistently federalist even in his exposition of imputation. Other divines were also drawn to take issue with Edwards, including Robert Dabney and William Cunningham.[24]

It is important to be clear where Edwards stands on the nature of the theological question under consideration, given these competing interpretations of his views. To this end, we shall examine three ways in which Edwards has been understood in the literature, with a view to assessing which, if any of these actually represents Edwards' position.

The realist-mediate interpretation

Charles Hodge maintained that Edwards' view of imputation was unclear, vacillating between federalism, which was Edwards' considered view in the majority of his work, and realism, which Edwards takes up in his defence of imputation in *OS*, coupled with a mediate view on the nature of imputation.[25] From the Saumur school (Placeaus), Hodge traced the influence of this mediate doctrine through Stapfer to Edwards,[26] claiming that it was an *'excrescence'*, not part of the body of Edwards' work in general and not affecting the other parts of his work on original sin in particular. However, on closer examination, Hodge believed that Edwards' view of imputation apart from his explicit endorsement of Stapfer's mediate position, appeared instead to be more consistent with a peculiar version of the realist view of imputation. What is more, Hodge maintained that Edwards defended an orthodox view of federalism in one of the

---

(cont.) more historical than dogmatic. Hence the time-frame for the theological discussion of Edwards' position on imputation in this essay.

[24] See Hodge, *Systematic Theology, Vol. II* (London: James Clarke, 1960), pp. 205–8 and pp. 216–221; Warfield, *Works Vol. IX, Studies in Theology* (New York: Oxford University Press, 1932), chapter XVIII; Dabney, *Lectures in Systematic Theology* (Grand Rapids: Zondervan, 1972 (reprint)) p. 338 ff.; Cunningham, *The Reformers and the Theology of the Reformation* (Edinburgh: Banner of Truth, 1989 (reprint)), pp. 384 ff.

[25] What follows utilizes Vol. II of Hodge's *Systematic Theology*, pp. 205–8 and 216–221.

[26] Edwards himself cites Stapfer with approval at one stage of his discussion in *YE3*: 391–393, n. 1. It is this extended footnote to which Hodge was referring.

earlier sections of his treatise. In a citation I have been unable to trace, he claims that Edwards teaches federalism in the context of his exposition of Romans 5:12–21:

> In his exposition . . . he expressly teaches the common doctrine [meaning federalism], and says, "As this place in general is very full and plain, so the doctrine of the corruption of nature, as derived from Adam, and also the imputation of his first sin, are both clearly taught in it. The imputation of Adam's one transgression, is indeed most directly and frequently asserted. We are here assured that by one man's sin death passed to all; all being adjudged to this punishment as having sinned (so it is implied) in that one man's sin. And it is repeated, over and over, that all are condemned, many are dead, many are sinners, etc., by one man's offence, by the disobedience of one, and by one offence.[27]

Moreover,

> This is the current representation throughout the work on Original Sin. It is only when in answer to the objection that it is unjust that we should be punished for the sin if Adam, that he enters in an abstruse metaphysical discussion on the nature of oneness or identity, and tries to prove that Adam and his posterity are one, and not distinct agents. It is, therefore, after all, realism, rather than mediate imputation, that Edwards for the time adopted.[28]

A similar reading of Edwards was also taken by William Cunningham who believed that Edwards had imbibed a version of mediate imputation from Stapfer, and that his view was inconsistent with other remarks elsewhere in his writings which endorsed 'the common Calvinistic doctrine'.[29]

The idea that Edwards' argument for imputation appears to be internally disordered, vacillating between some form of mediate and realist view, while elsewhere in *OS* Edwards defends a traditional version of federalism seems rather fantastic. However, Hodge *does*

---

[27] Hodge, *Systematic Theology*, Vol. II, p. 208.

[28] Ibid.

[29] Cunningham, *Theology of the Reformation*, p. 384. His explanation for this lapse in Edwards' thinking was that Edwards had simply not investigated this topic of imputation carefully enough!

raise serious questions about the consistency of Edwards' doctrine, which require a considered response. Such a response has been provided in outline by B. B. Warfield, and in detail by John Murray in his study of original sin, *The Imputation of Adam's Sin*, to which we now turn.

The federalist-immediate interpretation

Unlike his erstwhile mentor, B. B. Warfield evidently believed that Edwards' view of imputation was consistent with his other writings; that is, Edwards maintained a consistently federalist view of imputation which was immediate. In his *Studies in Theology* he has this to say of Edwards' position:

> in answering objections to the doctrine of Original Sin, he appeals at one time to Stapfer, and speaks, after him, in the language of that form of doctrine known as "mediate imputation". But this is only in order to illustrate his own view that all mankind are one as truly as and by the same kind of divine constitution that an individual life is one in its consecutive moments. Even in this immediate context he does not teach the doctrine of "mediate imputation," insisting rather that, Adam and his posterity being in the strictest sense one, in them no less than in him "the guilt arising from the first existing of a depraved disposition" cannot at all be distinguished from "the guilt of Adam's first sin"; *and elsewhere throughout the treatise he speaks in the terms of the common Calvinistic doctrine.*[30]

John Murray, who explicitly endorses Warfield over and against Cunningham and Hodge, has taken this up in more recent times.[31] His particular interest is in whether Edwards maintained mediate imputation, which, with Warfield, he denies categorically, for several reasons. First, in *OS* Edwards makes clear and unambiguously federalist statements that can only be understood in the context of an immediate view of imputation. Thus,

> God, in each step of his proceeding with Adam, in relation to the covenant or constitution established with him, looked on his posterity

---

[30] Warfield, *Studies in Theology*, p. 530, emphasis added.
[31] See John Murray, *The Imputation of Adam's Sin*, pp. 52 ff. The following argument is indebted to Murray's account.

as being one with him . . . And though he [God] dealt more immediately with Adam, yet it was as the head of the whole body, and the root
of the whole tree; and in his proceedings with him, he dealt with all the
branches, as if they had been existing in their root.

From which it will follow, that both guilt, or exposedness to punishment, and also depravity of heart, came upon Adam's posterity just as
they came upon him, as much as if he and they had all coexisted, like a
tree with many branches; allowing only for the difference necessarily
resulting from the place Adam stood in, as head or root of the whole,
and being first and most immediately dealt with, and most immediately acting and suffering.[32]

Elsewhere in the earlier discussion of *OS*, Edwards makes even
stronger federalist claims as part of his defence of his doctrine against
his protagonist, Dr Taylor. In light of an exposition of the creation and
fall narratives of Genesis 1–3, Edwards says,

It may be proper in this place also to take some notice of that objection
of Dr. Taylor's against Adam's being supposed to be a federal head of
his posterity . . . I think, a very little consideration is sufficient to shew,
that there is no weight in this objection [.]

And later in the same discussion,

And the honour of these two federal heads arises not so much from
what was proposed to each for his trial, as from their success, and the
good actually obtained; and also the manner of obtaining: Christ
obtains the benefits men have through him be proper merit of condig-
nity, and a pure purchase by an equivalent: which would not have been
the case with Adam, if he had obeyed.[33]

Furthermore, in light of what Edwards' sees as Taylor's misunderstanding of the key passage on imputation in Romans 5:12, Edwards
has this to say, 'in the eye of the Judge of the world, in Adam's first
sin, all sinned; not only in some sort, but all sinned so as to be exposed
to that death, and final destruction, which is the proper wages of
sin.'[34] These passages, taken together, constitute a considerable body

---

[32] *YE3*: 389.
[33] *YE3*: 259 and 260 respectively.
[34] Ibid.

of evidence that Edwards was defending some kind of federalist interpretation. To derive from this the notion that Edwards' view of the transmission of original sin was mediate rather than immediate would require a considerable argument, and the burden of proof appears to lie with those who claim that Edwards' view is other than immediate federalism.[35]

Secondly, it is clear that Edwards was aware of, and endorsed the distinction between the union involved in original sin and the nature of that union in imputation which we have already drawn. In referring to the whole passage of Romans 5:12–19, he says,

> As this place in general is very plain and full, so *the doctrine of the corruption of nature*, as derived from Adam, and also *the imputation of his first sin*, are both clearly taught in it. The imputation of Adam's one transgression, is indeed most directly and frequently asserted. We are here assured, that "by one man's sin, death passed on all"; all being adjudged to this punishment, as having sinned (so it is implied) in that one man's sin.[36]

This is important since, as noted earlier, those who defend a mediate view of imputation believe that the whole nature of original sin consists in that corruption which is hereditary to all humanity because of the fall, and that alone. It denies the actual imputation of Adam's sin to all men. In so doing, it affirms only one of the two aspects to original sin which Edwards here enunciates, viz., the 'corruption of nature' resulting from the fall, and 'the imputation of Adam's first sin' to all humanity.

But, thirdly, there is a difficulty over one passage where Edwards appears to conflate this corruption of nature derived from Adam with the imputation of his first sin to his posterity, which could be construed as an endorsement of some form of mediate view of imputation, or at least an inconsistency in his view, which is expressed in quite different, federal terms elsewhere as we have already noted.[37]

---

[35] Murray comments, 'the most conclusive evidence in support of a doctrine of mediate imputation would have to be presented if the prima facie import of such statements is to be ruled out; the account given is altogether similar to that which we might expect in an exponent of immediate imputation.' *The Imputation of Adam's Sin*, pp. 55–56.

[36] *YE3*: 348, emphasis added.

[37] *YE3*: 390.

In the passage in question Edwards argues that the notion that Adam's progeny are all born with a *double guilt* is false. This double guilt ostensibly stems from the conjunction of the imputation of original sin with the additional guilt each person accrues by being in possession of a corrupt heart from the moment they are born (as a result of bearing the marks of original sin.) Edwards opposes this bifurcation of guilt, but in so doing appears to be rescinding upon his earlier comments regarding the distinction between the corruption of nature as a result of Adamic sin and the imputation of that first sin. In fact, as Murray argues, Edwards manages to maintain that humans *are* doubly guilty, but only as a result of their forensic status subsequent to birth (they are *not born* with this double guilt. That is the crucial distinction that he is here making). Moreover, they are only doubly guilty on grounds which distinguish between the corruption of the heart as *'first existing of a depraved disposition'* and the corruption of heart which becomes a *'confirmed principle'* through acting upon it inclinations. Edwards' maintains that on the grounds that individuals continue in having corrupt hearts and acting upon them after their birth, this 'confirmed principle' of a corrupt heart represents reasonable grounds for additional guilt to be imputed to humanity. However, this is to be carefully distinguished from the initial corruption of heart which, along with the imputation of original sin, is treated *as one* for the purposes of guilt. Two crucial passages make this plain:

> Indeed the guilt, that arises from the corruption of the heart, as it remains a confirmed principle, and appears in its consequent operations, is a distinct and additional guilt: but the guilt arising from the first existing of a depraved disposition in Adam's posterity, I apprehend, is not distinct from their guilt of Adam's first sin.

And,

> The depraved disposition of Adam's heart is to be considered two ways. (1) As the first rising of an evil inclination in his heart, exerted in his first act of sin, and the ground of the complete transgression. (2) An evil disposition of heart continuing afterwards, as a confirmed principle, that came by God's forsaking him; which was a punishment of his first transgression. This confirmed corruption, by its remaining and continued operation, brought additional guilt on his soul.[38]

---

[38] Ibid.

It is this second citation which is the foundation for what he goes on to say about the theological nature of the transmission of sin from Adam to his posterity. Later in the same discussion Edwards says that the evil disposition of heart in man is prior to any charge of guilt by God, 'the evil disposition is first, and the charge of guilt consequent; as it was in the case of Adam himself.'[39] It was largely as a result of this passage that Hodge charged Edwards with defending a Placaean (that is, mediate) view on transmission of sin.[40] But this is to misunderstand Edwards' distinctive contribution to the discussion on the means of transmission.

Edwards was actually saying that in the imputation of Adam's sin to his posterity, the two elements which apply to Adam's sin viz. the evil disposition of heart which gave rise to the act and the act itself are distinct elements in time, but are treated as parts of one action. Thus, 'The first evil disposition or inclination of the heart of Adam to sin, was not properly distinct from his first act of sin, but was included in it.'[41] Similarly, where Adam's sin is imputed these two elements are present, such that the evil disposition to sin comes first (as it did with Adam) and the charge of guilt consequent upon that disposition comes after as the person continues in that disposition which becomes a confirmed principle. As Adam was charged on the basis of the initial disposition plus the act (which is treated as one action which deserves punishment), so this is imputed to his posterity in such a way that they too are charged as a consequence of having an evil disposition which is part of the vitiation of original sin. As that disposition becomes a confirmed principle that is worked out in the life of the person, they are liable to accrue additional guilt. But that additional guilt is subsequent to the initial charge of guilt which incorporates both the disposition given in Adam as well as the vitiation of the person in original sin.

This is not mediate, since Edwards is nowhere denying the immediate imputation of Adam's sin, he is merely distinguishing the succeeding elements that make up the original action of Adam, which are also transposed onto his posterity in original sin and as such result in condemnation. Sinful actions after the original condemnation are treated as separate grounds for further condemnation and guilt giving rise to his peculiar understanding of double guilt. So, this whole exer-

---

[39] *YE3*: 391.
[40] See Hodge, *Systematic Theology*, Vol. II, p. 207.
[41] *YE3*: 390.

cise in distinguishing the elements which make up Adam's sin and the means by which it is propagated is a judicial, or forensic analysis of the parts of original sin which make up the whole action of Adam, and the whole imputation of the state which follows from that action along with the penal consequences of Adam's sin for his posterity.[42]

Murray contends that although this appears superficially to be rather similar in tone to a mediate view of imputation, on closer examination of the distinctions which Edwards is employing it is evident that he is not guilty of endorsing a mediate view, nor of inconsistency with regard to his distinction between the union of Adam and his progeny on the one hand, and the means of imputation on the other. And, on the basis of the foregoing analysis, that verdict has been sustained. Edwards' view on the means by which imputation occurs can now be summarized as follows,

1. Adam's disposition to sin and the (original) sin itself are treated by God as one forensic unit.
2. Adam's ongoing evil disposition subsequent to his original sin (Edwards' 'confirmed principle') is a consequence of that first

---

[42] It may still be asked how Edwards can apparently endorse the view of Stapfer in his discussion of the means of imputation if his view does not support a mediate position, as Stapfer is traditionally thought to have done. To this several things can be said by way of response. First, it is not entirely clear that Stapfer did endorse the mediate view. Murray maintains that such a judgement is at least uncertain, (see Murray, *The Imputation of Adam's Sin*, p. 63, n. 114). Second, although Edwards does endorse Stapfer's views, it is not clear that in so doing he is endorsing a mediate view. In the context of the passage, Edwards' use of Stapfer is primarily as a means to bolster his contentions about the identity between Adam and his posterity in imputation. Even when Stapfer does deal with immediate and mediate views, his view in Edwards' citation is not clearly or categorically mediate: '" The whole of the controversy they have with us about this matter, evidently arises from this, that they suppose the mediate and immediate imputation are distinguished one from the other, not only in the manner of conception, but in reality. And so indeed they consider imputation only as immediate, and abstractly from the mediate; when yet our divines suppose, that neither ought to be considered separately from the other"' (*YE3*: 393). At most this is confused, and one may legitimately ask why Edwards chose to cloud his own careful exposition of the matter with this apparent obfuscation of the issues. But that is not the same as calling Edwards' entire exposition of this aspect of the doctrine into question.

sin and constitute grounds upon which God imputes additional guilt (since the 'confirmed principle' is a distinct, subsequent action from his first sin).
3. This twofold understanding of the forensic nature of Adam's sin
   has application through imputation to his posterity such that,
4. Adam's posterity all partake of the original sin of Adam, and
5. the participation of Adam's posterity in Adam's sin involves
   both Adam's disposition to sin and his sin itself, which are
   treated as one forensic unit by God, and
6. this initial disposition to sin is temporally prior to the charge of
   guilt which accrues to the whole forensic unit of imputed original sin as it did with Adam.
7. In addition, Adam's posterity all continue in sin as a 'confirmed
   principle' leading to further condemnation and double guilt.

It should now be clear that Edwards' position with regard to the
nature of imputation was not mediate, but immediate. Moreover,
Murray has made a strong case, *contra* Hodge and Cunningham for
the coherence of Edwards' position as a unified presentation of a federalist position.

However, although Edwards stood within the federal tradition of
Puritan covenantal theology, his federalism was not conventional. Nor
did he find traditional federal arguments sufficient to the purpose of
defending the justice of the union instituted in imputation. Although
Murray's discussion of Edwards' position on the immediacy of imputation is clear and insightful, he fails to make any mention of the way
in which Edwards found himself compelled to revise his federalism in
dealing with the metaphysical unity established between Adam and
his progeny in imputation. Edwards did retain aspects of federalist
residue even here, but his apologetic purpose in establishing the rea-
sonableness of imputation was not served by the bald represent-
ational premise underlying the traditional federal argument. Edwards
felt that more was needed by way of metaphysical arguments to
defend the traditional understanding of the unity established by God
in the act of imputing Adam's sin.

A nonfederalist-immediate interpretation?

In contrast to the foregoing, Paul Helm's recent work in this area of
Edwards' thinking does not take seriously any federalism in his
thought on imputation. He believes that Edwards' worked out his

view in conscious opposition to what he perceived to be the failings of the traditional realist and federalist understandings of imputation. Helm maintains that it was the perception that neither of these traditional alternatives satisfactorily explained the metaphysics of imputation that led Edwards to develop his own view, which falls into neither traditional formulations of the problem. Helm comments,

> [a]s a result of the deep conviction he had about the immediate dependence of the creation upon the Creator, Edwards did not accept either of these views, the realist or the federal view. Instead he developed an account of the relation between Adam and his progeny in a different direction as part of his overall defence, both philosophical and theological, of the Christian doctrine of original sin.[43]

It is the conviction of the present author that this understanding of Edwards is wrong in its denial of any federalist elements in Edwards' view of imputation, but right in pointing out that Edwards' solution to the problem of imputation did not fall into either traditional federalism or realism. The reason why this whole area of Edwards' thought has caused such controversy and misunderstanding is because his proposal was so subtle in its reorientation of a traditional theological issue along new metaphysical lines. Edwards was driven to formulate a view which did not follow the traditional alternatives because he was aware, through his reading of Taylor and others, that the traditional options on imputation did not adequately explain why God imputed Adam's sin to all his posterity, given that his posterity were not one and the same as Adam. For this reason, the subject of *OS* IV: III, is the great objection that 'imputation is unjust and unreasonable, inasmuch as Adam and his posterity are not one and the same'.

Thus far, Helm appears to be correct. But it is not the case that in his search for an alternative solution, Edwards jettisoned all the material from both alternatives available to him. Instead, it seems that he took up elements of both and fused them together with his own occasionalistic reading of Adam and his posterity's persistence through time, to provide a novel solution to the problem.[44] From realism he

---

[43] *Faith and Understanding*, p. 161.

[44] Occasionalism involves a continuous creation doctrine, coupled with the denial of secondary causation. God is the sole cause of all things, and nothing persists through time for more than a moment. God recreates all things *ex nihilo* at each moment.

appropriated the notion that there must be some ontological reality behind the idea of Adam and his progeny being treated as one, and that this reality must have a metaphysical explanation. From federalism he took the idea that Adam stands in a particular relationship to his posterity as the first man, and that it is by virtue of being *homo primus* that God treats Adam and his posterity for the purposes of imputation, as one.[45]

But his solution to the ontological problems underlying the doctrine of imputation went beyond both federalism and realism, since he felt that the metaphysics underpinning realism was false and the representationalism of federalism failed to take sufficiently seriously the ontological union which God institutes in imputation. Edwards rejected both alternatives as they stood, choosing instead to reformulate elements of each in his own answer to the problem, with the addition of an occasionalistic understanding of the metaphysics of creation and conservation (and, indeed, imputation).[46] He was determined to show that, *contra* Taylor *et al.*, the doctrine of imputation was not only theologically as well as philosophically coherent, but also eminently reasonable. To this end, he sought to establish his apologetic in *OS* (IV: III) on grounds independent of authority so as to force the burden of proof on to detractors from the traditional doctrine of imputation.[47]

Summary

I have argued that Edwards' work on the nature of imputation has been misunderstood by the nineteenth-century divines who sought to understand Edwards, and has also been misrepresented by more

---

[45] See *Miscellany* 717 in *The "Miscellanies" 501–832, The Works of Jonathan Edwards Vol. 18*, ed. Ava Chamberlain (New haven: Yale University Press), pp. 348–349. There, Edwards speaks of why Adam's first sin is imputed to humanity in a way that is commensurate with seeing Adam as *homo primus*.

[46] Thus Jenson's contention that Edwards method in *OS* was 'first to establish a *prima facie* case for an Augustinian doctrine of original sin, from scripture and experience' (*America's Theologian*, p. 144) is erroneous. While Edwards saw himself as an inheritor of the Augustinian-Calvinistic legacy of his Puritan fathers, he did not, as we have shown, develop his doctrine along entirely traditional lines.

[47] It may be thought that this reading of Edwards' eclecticism in his doctrine of imputation is inconsistent with what has been already said

recent, twentieth-century commentators like Murray and Helm. The subtlety with which Edwards picks his way through the complexities of this doctrine seems to have been the chief source of confusion, coupled, perhaps, with the diffuse nature of his *corpus*. However, on re-examining his theory of imputation, we have seen that Edwards took the notion of the union of Adam and his posterity from Augustinian realism, and the notion of Adam's place as the first man from federalism, to forge a *via media* between these two traditional views on this matter. This, coupled with Edwards' occasionalism in *OS* (IV:III) yields a theory of imputation in which Adam and his posterity are united together by God for the purposes of imputation, such that Adam's sin becomes the sin of his posterity. They form one metaphysical unity for this purpose. All of which offers an intriguing response to the oft-cited criticism of imputation: that it is unfair that I am punished for another's sin. In response to this question Edwards can claim that it is not *his* sin, but *ours*.

(cont.) about the considerable evidence of Edwards' federalism. However, it must be emphasized that the point here is to do with the nature of the ontological union established in imputation rather than the means of transmission, which has been dealt with in the previous argument. Edwards was a federal theologian in his conception of the covenant and in his acceptance of an immediate understanding of the nature of imputation. It is on the matter of the precise nature of the union established in imputation that he took a new approach, and one which owed much to both federalism and realism, but went beyond both into occasionalism. That is the point being made here and it is consistent with what has already been argued.

CHAPTER FOUR

Francis Turretin on the Necessity of the Incarnation

> And if you want to know what the true necessity was
> behind all the things which he did and had done to him,
> know this: all these things of necessity were, because he
> himself so willed it. Indeed, no necessity is antecedent
> to his will.
> – *St Anselm of Canterbury*, Cur Deus Homo, II. 17.

One longstanding dispute in Christology has to do with whether the Incarnation was a necessary or contingent matter. On the face of it, it seems mistaken to think that God must bring about the salvation of some human beings via the Incarnation – as if God is compelled to offer salvation to some of his fallen creatures, and required to do so by the particular means offered in the Incarnation. For, on the one hand, salvation is surely the outcome of divine grace, which, by its very nature is not an act that can be coerced. And on the other hand, if God is omnipotent as well as graciously disposed towards fallen human beings, it seems intuitive to think that some means of salvation was open to the Deity other than the costly one presented in the prospect of the Incarnation. In which case, the Incarnation does not appear to be necessary to salvation. It is simply the means by which God deigned to bring about salvation, though he could have brought it about by some other design. And, since God does no thing without good reason, he must have a good reason for ordaining the Incarnation as the means by which salvation was obtained rather than some other, less costly method, or, indeed, rather than withholding salvation altogether, or creating a world which was not populated by creatures who were in need of salvation in the first place.

A moment's reflection is sufficient to see that there are several distinct but related issues here. One concerns what we might call the question of *the necessity of salvation*: Must God save any of his fallen human creatures? The other has to do with the *necessity of the Incarnation*: Must God bring about salvation by this particular means (i.e. the Incarnation of God the Son)?[1] We shall not concern ourselves with the necessity of salvation, or even whether God could have brought about a world of human creatures that did not require salvation in the first place. The main concern of this chapter will be to ascertain whether the Incarnation is somehow necessary (in some sense it cannot not have occurred) or contingent (it might not have occurred). Questions concerning what, if any, metaphysical options were open to God at the 'moment' at which he ordained to bring about the world he did bring about are beyond the purview of what follows.[2]

The argument falls into three parts. First, we shall consider the case for the necessity of the Incarnation put forward by the Genevan Reformed Orthodox theologian, Francis Turretin. He was one of Calvin's successors in the Academy of Geneva, where he taught for the majority of his professional life. Turretin's major work is his *Institutes of Elenctic Theology*.[3] It is to this work that we shall turn to ascertain what he thought about this important matter. Then, in a second section, I shall consider several objections to this reasoning. These are the unjustifiable cost of the Incarnation objection, the objection from divine freedom to the necessity of the Incarnation, and the objection based on the modal implications of Turretin's account of the necessity of the Incarnation. I will argue that Turretin's account has the resources to rebut the first two of these objections, but that in

---

[1] I suppose there are other questions in the neighbourhood of this one. For instance, whatever the *de facto* mode of reconciliation was, was it necessary in some sense? But I shall pass over this question in what follows.

[2] For more on this matter, see for example William E. Mann, 'The Best of All Possible Worlds' in Scott MacDonald, ed. *Being and Goodness, The Concept of the Good in Metaphysics and Philosophical Theology* (Ithaca: Cornell University Press, 1991), pp. 250–277.

[3] Francis Turretin, *Institutes of Elenctic Theology*, 3 Vols., trans. George Musgrave Giger, ed. James T. Dennison, Jnr. (Phillipsburg, NJ: Presbyterian and Reformed, 1992–1997). All references are to this translation of Turretin's work, cited in the body of the text as '*Inst.*' Followed by the topic number, question number, and page reference in the Giger translation, e.g. '*Inst.* XIII.III.299'.

order to deal with the third some changes will have to be made to Turretin's understanding of the sort of world God can bring about. Although it transpires that this does place a restriction upon Turretin's account of the hypothetical necessity of the Incarnation (as he terms it), it does not undermine the central features of his reasoning. Thus, by 'correcting' certain modal features of his reasoning, one can preserve a broadly Turretinian argument for the necessity of the Incarnation.

Turretin on the necessity of the Incarnation

Turretin considers the question of the necessity of the Incarnation in three parts. As he conceives it, these are,

a. Whether it would have been necessary for the Son of God to become incarnate if human beings had not sinned.
b. Whether the mode of salvation was necessary. That is, whether there was some other mode of salvation possible apart from the incarnation of the Son of God.
c. Whether it was necessary for the mediator of salvation to be a God-man (*Inst.* XIII.III.299).

Let us take these in reverse order. The third consideration is, in several important respects, dependent upon the central argument in St Anselm of Canterbury's *Cur Deus Homo*. Turretin adopts some of the key motifs of Anselm's reasoning. But he interpolates into his argument the *munus triplex* (three-fold offices of Christ) introduced into Reformed theology from Calvin's Christology in the *Institutes* as well as a number of biblical tropes that apply to Christ, such as his being the *go'el* or kinsman redeemer of his people. He also sets to one side the Anselmian device of framing his discussion *remoto christo*, that is, without recourse to divine revelation, assuming (for the sake of the argument) only the deliverances of sanctified reason. Thus for Turretin:

> The work of redemption could not have been performed except by a God-man (*theanthropon*) associating by the Incarnation the human nature with the divine by an indissoluble bond. For since to redeem us, two things were most especially required – the acquisition of salvation and the application of the same; the endurance of death for satisfaction

and the victory over the same for the enjoyment of life – our mediator ought to be God-man (*theanthropos*) to accomplish these things: man to suffer, God to overcome; man to receive the punishment we deserved, God to endure and drink it to the dregs . . . This neither a mere man nor God alone could do . . . Both natures, therefore, should be associated that in both conjoined, both the highest weakness of humanity might exert itself for suffering and the highest power and majesty of the divine might exert itself for the victory (*Inst*. XIII.III.302–303).[4]

The dialectical strategy Turretin adopts in order to explain the need for a God-man *sounds* Anselmian. But it is interesting to note that there are a number of key Anselmian claims he omits from consideration. There is no explicit commitment to the idea that the God-man must have a human nature that is morally upright and unfallen, although he certainly affirms this notion elsewhere in the *Institutes*.[5] And he only mentions the concept of divine justice motivating his reasoning in passing, saying that in his divine nature, the God-man satisfies divine justice, abolishing sin and bringing about everlasting righteousness, 'which no mortal can do'. What is more, the God-man must be more than human to 'add an infinite weight and merit to the truth of his sufferings' (*Inst*. XIII.III.303). But given what he does say about divine justice in his doctrine of God earlier in the *Institutes* it is clear that he thinks an act of atonement for human sin must have a value sufficient to offset the disvalue of the human sin for which it atones; the disvalue of human sin is infinite; so, the satisfaction Christ offers must be correspondingly infinite in value. God cannot accept as atonement some act that has a value less than this. In which case, it would appear that he cannot accept the putative act of atonement

performed by any *merely* human being.[6] Hence, the need for a person

---

[4] Compare *Inst*. XIV.X.418, where Turretin defends the absolute necessity of the atonement against those who claim that no atonement was necessary for salvation (i.e. the Socinian position expressed in *De Iesu Christo Servatore* Pt.I.1); and against those who say the atonement was only hypothetically necessary, that is, that God could have ordained some other means of salvation, but did not, decreeing the atonement as the means of salvation (the position of St Augustine in *De Trinitate* 13.10).

[5] See *Inst*. XIII.V.310 where he affirms that 'although Christ sprang from Adam, a sinner, still he did not draw from him sin either imputed or inherent'.

who is wholly human, but not merely human; and wholly God but not just divine: only a God-man is able to do the job.

Now, suppose Turretin is right and the work of salvation requires a God-man to perform it. This still does not demonstrate that there were no other avenues open to God which would yield the same result, the salvation of fallen humanity, without the same cost, or without the act in question being the sort of atonement Turretin envisages.

This brings us to the second issue in Turretin's characterization of the necessity of the Incarnation, which had to do with whether there was some other mode of salvation possible apart from the incarnation of the Son of God (i.e. whether the particular mode of salvation was necessary). On this question Turretin maintains that, given the divine decree to redeem some number of fallen humanity, it was 'not only suitable, but necessary . . . that the Son of God should become incarnate' (*Inst.* XIII.III.301). The sort of necessity he has in mind here is not absolute, but depends on the following hypothetical: *granted that God deigns to save some number of sinners, could he have brought this about by some means other than that by which he did bring it about?* Turretin thinks he could not. In keeping with many Reformed theologians, he sees no obstacle to thinking that God need not have performed any given act of salvation. God may have deigned to save fewer than the number he did save; perhaps he might have ordained that no human beings be saved, for 'God could (if he had wished) leave man no less than the Devil in his destruction' (*Inst.* XIII.III.301). The supposition seems to be that, presuming salvation is an act of divine grace, God cannot be required to perform it.[7] Nor can there be a difficulty with the divine decree itself, as if God's ordaining a given thing were not necessary

---

[6] Turretin's discussion of divine retribution in *Inst.* III.XIX includes commitment to the idea that divine retribution must be satisfied. God cannot accept some act of atonement that has a value less than that required to make up the disvalue accruing to a given act of sin. For more on this, see Crisp, 'Salvation and Atonement: On the Value and Necessity of the Work of Jesus Christ' forthcoming in Ivor Davidson and Murray Rae, eds. *The God of Salvation: Essays in Systematic Theology* (Aldershot: Ashgate, 2010).

[7] However, (and contrary to Turretin) although I concede that the Incarnation and atonement of Christ are acts of divine grace, such that God did not have to save any given fallen human, I do not think that it was possible for God to save no fallen human being, given the fact that God is essentially gracious and merciful. He had to act in a way consistent with his divine character. But this, as I conceive it, is a constraint that is

and sufficient for that thing obtaining. Turretin is, after all, committed to a version of theological compatibilism: God ordains all that comes to pass; nothing can frustrate the divine will; and nothing comes to pass without God willing it.[8] The problem concerning the modality of the means of salvation arises, as he sees it, only when one assumes that the divine design includes the salvation of some number of fallen humanity.

Once that is assumed, the issue becomes a matter of what modality is in view. In other words, what sort of requirement does he have in mind when he says the Incarnation was necessary? Turretin says that it cannot be a matter of the 'necessity of fitness' because 'all confess' that the Incarnation was 'in the highest degree fitting to the divine majesty' in order that 'his precepts might not be said to have been violated with impunity' (*Inst.* XIII.III.301).[9] The modality in question is the *necessity of justice*: 'that in no other way could the jus-

---

(cont.) consistent with divine freedom and aseity since no entity can act in a way inconsistent with its nature. I have discussed this at greater length in 'Salvation and Atonement: On the Value and Necessity of the Work of Jesus Christ'.

[8] See *Inst.* X.III.665–683.

[9] It is not entirely clear to me what Turretin means by the 'necessity of fitness' or a 'necessity of fittingness'. The notion that the Incarnation is supremely fitting has a long theological pedigree and can be found amongst the medievals (see, e.g. Anselm, *Cur Deus Homo* I.12, where he discusses whether it is fitting for God to forgive sin without satisfaction). I suppose some act might be necessary and fitting. But the context of Turretin's remarks suggests he has in mind an act that is necessary by its fitness, or on account of its fittingness, which is rather a different matter. In discussing St Anselm's argument for the necessity of the Incarnation, Brian Leftow comments, 'To claim that God should have become incarnate is to claim that the Incarnation is positively fitting to God, that God ought to become incarnate. So in this context, to say that God could have become incarnate is to say that the Incarnation is not unfitting to God, that it is not the case that God ought not to be incarnate.' Leftow, 'Anselm on the Necessity of the Incarnation' in *Religious Studies* 31 (1995): 174. Perhaps Turretin could be read to mean something similar to this. In which case, the necessity of fittingness has to do with deontic, not alethic or metaphysical, necessity, since it pertains to moral, not metaphysical, considerations. For further discussion of this issue with reference to Anselm's *Cur Deus Homo*, see David Brown, 'Necessary and Fitting Reasons in Christian Theology' in William J. Abraham and Stephen W. Holtzer, eds. *The Rationality of Religious Belief* (Oxford: Oxford University

tice of God have been satisfied and our deliverance brought about' (ibid). This is a metaphysically robust response to the question in view – some might think too robust. Yet there is an internal logic to his understanding of the modality of the Incarnation and atonement.

Turretin thinks the Incarnation must obtain because of the nature of divine justice 'As God cannot deny his own justice, he could not free men without a satisfaction being made first' (*Inst*. XIII.III.302). Furthermore, the atonement must obtain because it is in God's nature to act in accordance with his divine justice – God cannot act in a way inconsistent with his perfect character, which includes his justice. 'Verily, the wisdom and goodness of God will not suffer us to believe that this was free to him, but a certain ineluctable necessity must have intervened.' And later in the same passage, 'Nor is it to be supposed that in holding this, we wish to limit the omnipotence of God or to define what he can do with supreme right toward the creatures. We only show from Scripture what God can or cannot do according to the ordinate power and right tempered by virtues' (*Inst*. XIII.III.302).[10] So God *must* act justly. Once God has ordained the salvation of some number of fallen human creatures, he is committed to acting in accordance with the deliverances of his own holy nature, which is to say, he must act in accordance with his own just character. The Incarnation includes the necessary exercise of such divine justice because it is only via the Incarnation that some number of humanity can be reconciled to God.

To put it somewhat differently, Turretin's reasoning here seems to be something like the following:

1. God must act in accordance with his divine nature; it is impossible for God to act contrary to his divine nature.
2. His divine nature is essentially just.

(cont.) Press, 1987), pp. 211–30; Brian Leftow, 'Anselm on the Cost of Salvation' in *Medieval Philosophy and Theology* 6 (1997): 73–92; and Sandra Visser and Thomas Williams, *Anselm* (Oxford: Oxford University Press, 2009), pp. 214–223.

[10] Language of 'supreme right' seems to sit rather ill alongside talk of 'ineluctable necessity'. But the two are not necessarily inconsistent. God could have a supreme right to dispose of his creatures as he sees fit, according to his divine nature, which is essentially just.

Hence,

3. Any divine act is one that is essentially just, or (at least) is one that is consistent with his essential justice (from (1) & (2)).[11]

So God cannot set aside the requirements of justice in bringing about the salvation of fallen human beings.[12]

4. Justice must be satisfied in the punishment of sin, either in the person of the sinner, or in some suitable equivalent (e.g. a mediator who is a God-man).[13]

Previously, we noted that, according to Turretin, *only* a God-man is able to offer an atonement that satisfies divine justice for the sin of all humanity. This implies:

5. If God could have brought about salvation via some other, less onerous means than that of the Incarnation, he would have brought about salvation via such means.[14]

That is, he does not think it credible that God would have brought about reconciliation to God via the atoning life and death of the

---

[11] Given Turretin's adherence to a classical doctrine of divine simplicity, the divine act (for there is only one if God is a simple pure act) is essentially just, and has numerous temporal effects in time. But I leave aside this complication here.

[12] This is the burden of *Inst.* III.XIX.234–241, where Turretin defends the essential 'vindictive' (i.e. retributive) justice of God against his Socinian opponents.

[13] '[A]s God cannot deny his own justice, he could not free men without a satisfaction being made first. Satisfaction could not be made to infinite justice except by some infinite ransom (*lytron*); nor could that infinite ransom (*lytron*) be found anywhere except in the Son of God' (*Inst.* XIII.III.302).

[14] 'If it could have been done in any other way, it is not credible that the most wise and good God would have entered upon this counsel, which seemed to be most suitable to his wisdom and goodness. For if he could free men by word alone, was it becoming to his wisdom to accomplish so easy a thing with so much labor and as it were to move heaven and earth? Would he have done by more, what he could have done by fewer?' (*Inst.* XIII.III.302).

God-man if, say, God could have brought about the same result by some much less costly means, such as by simply releasing human beings from their moral obligation to satisfy divine justice by divine fiat. Turretin is clear that only a God-man has the qualifications necessary in order for him to be the mediator of human salvation. This is because,

6. Only a fully human entity can atone for the sin of other human entities.

(Turretin seems to think justice requires that a human atone for the sin of other humans.)

7. Only a divine person can perform an act that has an infinite value, sufficient to atone for the infinite disvalue of human sin.

Hence,

8. Only an entity that is both fully divine and fully human (one person subsisting in two distinct natures) can atone for human sin.

To accept some lesser act as an act of atonement for human sin would be to violate these two requirements for the salvation of human beings. So:

9. The Incarnation is required in order to bring about the salvation of (some number of) fallen human beings.

However, Turretin is aware that not all the ancients or Scholastics agree that God could not bring about salvation via some means other than Incarnation. He claims St Athanasius, St Anselm, and St Ambrose as allies in this respect. But he has to concede that St Augustine, St Thomas Aquinas, Peter Lombard, and St Bonaventure are all lined up against him.[15] He even admits that this is an issue

---

[15] Or, at least, so he thinks. Brian Leftow has recently argued that the views of St Anselm and St Thomas on this matter are, in fact, compatible. See Leftow, 'Anselm on the necessity of the Incarnation' in *Religious Studies* 31 (1995): 167–185. Whether that is the case, all we need to see here is that there clearly is a difference of view on this matter in the tradition, and opinions are divided amongst some of the most important divines in the western tradition.

overwhich the Reformed Orthodox are divided, William Twisse being one of the most prominent opponents of Turretin's view. Of course, the fact that some important Doctor of the Church holds a given view is not, in and of itself, and without further argument, a reason to think that the view in question is the truth of the matter.[16] But it is surely not theologically insignificant when important sources of authority in the tradition are divided on a particular doctrinal matter. By raising the fact that there is significant theological disagreement about this issue, Turretin is registering this. Yet he thinks that the position he adopts is 'the truer and safer' (*Inst.* XIII.III.302).[17] Assuming that (i) divine justice must be satisfied, (ii) that the atonement has an infinite value and is therefore sufficient to off-set the disvalue of human sin, and that (iii) only a God-man is qualified to atone for fallen human creatures, Turretin's position on the necessity of the Incarnation naturally follows.[18] Those authorities whom he cites as disagreeing with him in this regard take issue with one or more of these three assumptions – typically, the first and/or third, although there are some theologians in the tradition who think Christ's work does not necessarily have an

---

[16] Doctors of the Church are usually (with the possible exception of St Thomas Aquinas for Roman Catholics) accorded a certain authority, voicing theologoumena, or theological opinions on matters that are not dogma, or officially sanctioned catholic teaching. Such theologoumena are not necessarily binding upon all catholic Christians. Turretin appears to assume that the precise modality of the Incarnation is one such theologoumenon. I have discussed the authority of theologoumena relative to other sources of testimony in the Christian tradition elsewhere. See Crisp, *God Incarnate: Explorations in Christology* (London: T&T Clark, 2009), ch. 1.

[17] This is an interesting epistemological concession on Turretin's part, viz. the claim that his own position is preferable. It shows that there are important epistemological as well as metaphysical modalities in play here.

[18] Turretin's position seems to require that human sin has an infinite disvalue, or, at least, a disvalue of such magnitude as to require an atonement of infinite value in order to 'balance off' this disvalue in the scales of divine justice. But things are a little more complicated than this. Does he mean to say that any given act of human sin carries an infinite disvalue (or disvalue of sufficient magnitude so as to require an atonement of infinite value)? Or is it that (somehow) the totality of human sin for which the God-man atones has this disvalue? He does not appear to commit himself one way or another on this question. For further discussion of these issues (with reference to the Anselmian position), see Crisp, 'Divine Retribution: A Defence' in *Sophia* 42 (2003): 35–52.

infinite value, Duns Scotus among them.[19] Whether the sort of objections mounted on the basis of (i)–(iii) pose a serious threat to Turretin's argument is a matter to which we shall return.

Thus far we have seen that on the assumption that God creates this world of fallen human beings that require salvation, coupled with the notion that God graciously deigns to save some number of fallen humanity, Turretin believes that it was necessary for the mediator of salvation to be a God-man and that there was no other mode of salvation consistent with the nature of divine justice that was metaphysically possible apart from the Incarnation of the Son of God. But what of his answer to the first issue he highlights under the heading 'the necessity of the Incarnation', to wit, whether it would have been necessary for the Son of God to become incarnate if human beings had not sinned? Turretin's response is unequivocal: 'the Son of God became incarnate only on account of sin'. Furthermore, 'it would not have been necessary for him to become incarnate if man had not sinned.' In this he is 'opposed to the old Scholastics, who rashly and without Scripture authority asserted it (as Alexander of Hales, Occam, Bonaventure and others)' (*Inst.* XIII.III.299).

His reasons for defending this view are several and can be divided into two halves: those concerned to offer positive biblical-theological support for his own position; and those which are more apologetic in nature, aimed at rebutting objections brought by those who take an 'incarnation anyway' position.[20] The most important biblical-theological consideration is this: 'In one word, he was incarnated that he might be a Mediator. And yet there would have been no need of a mediator, if there had been no sin' (*Inst.* XIII.III.300). There is 'no other

---

[19] As Richard Cross puts it, 'On Scotus's account, an act is meritorious if and only if God assigns a reward for it'. Cross, *Duns Scotus* (Oxford: Oxford University Press, 1999), p. 104. I discuss this doctrine of *acceptilatio* or acceptilation and its close relation acceptation in more detail in 'Salvation and Atonement'.

[20] 'Incarnation anyway' arguments claim that the Second Person of the Trinity would have become incarnate irrespective of human sin. There are a number of theological reasons that might motivate such a claim, such as that God would want to confer on the creation as much goodness as he could, whether or not human creatures sinned. This is taken up by Marilyn McCord Adams in *Christ and Horrors: The Coherence of Christology* (Cambridge: Cambridge University Press, 2006), ch. 7. See also Edwin Chr van Driel's recent monograph, *Incarnation Anyway: Arguments for Supralapsarian Christology* (New York: Oxford University Press, 2008). We shall return to this matter presently.

end of the advent of Christ and of his incarnation' that is 'ever proposed' in Scripture. 'If he is promised, it is only after the fall (Gen. 3.
15) and to bruise the head of the serpent.' Thus, it is clear from
Scripture that 'his office is occupied only with sinners.' In addition to
this biblical-theological argument, Turretin appeals to the Fathers for
confirmation of his position, citing Irenaeus, Augustine and Gregory
the Great in support (*Inst*. XIII.III.300).[21]

Turretin's apologetic arguments are several. First, he argues that
Colossians 1:15, a passage where Christ is called 'the firstborn of
every creature', does not imply that Christ is somehow the prototype
of human beings such that all humans were 'produced after his
model' (*Inst*. XIII.III.300). It is in respect of Christ's eternal generation
and dominion over creation that the author of Colossians speaks as he
does. All things are created by the Second Person of the Trinity and
for him as God, not as a human. He is the first in all things 'in digni-
ty, not in time.' Even the image of God in human beings is not, thinks
Turretin, the image of Christ (*qua* God-man) but the wisdom and holiness with which God has imbued humanity. All of which makes sense
if Turretin is responding to an objection based on Colossians 1 as a
means to showing that without Christ, humanity could not have been
formed because human beings are made in his image, or are, at least,
'produced after his model'. And this sort of objection fits with an
'incarnation anyway' argument: An Incarnation is necessary in order
for human beings to exist since humans are made in the image of the
firstborn over all creation, namely the God-man. On this way of thinking, the necessity of the Incarnation is independent of any considerations touching redemption. God must bring about an Incarnation if he
is to create a world of human beings, since Christ is the model for
such human beings, the template for humanity. Turretin's first apologetic resists this line of argument.

The second apologetic also turns on the right understanding of a
passage in the Pauline corpus, this time in Ephesians 5: 31. There, St
Paul is speaking of the Church as the body of Christ with whom she
is united, as in Genesis 2:24 we are told that God instituted marriage
so that the two might become 'one flesh'. To which Paul adds the
rather cryptic phrase in verse 32, 'This is a profound mystery—but I

---

21 To give just one example, Irenaeus says 'For if the flesh were not in a posi-
tion to be saved, the Word of God would in no wise have become flesh.'
Against Heresies 5.14 in Alexander Roberts and James Donaldson, eds.
Ante-Nicene Fathers, Vol. 1 (Grand Rapids: Eerdmans, 1981 [1887]), p. 541.

am talking about Christ and the church.' Turretin glosses this passage so as to foreclose the possibility that it might be used as ammunition for an 'incarnation anyway' argument. He says 'It is one thing for the marriage of Adam and Eve to have been a sign and type of the marriage of Christ with the church (according to the secret intention of the Holy Spirit); another for it to have been known by Adam and to be set forth by him as a prophecy of such wedlock' (*Inst.* XIII.III.301). As one schooled in a pre-critical approach to the biblical texts, Turretin worries that one who objects to his argument that the Incarnation is consequentially necessary only if God has already ordained the redemption of (some number of) fallen humanity might find some justification for their views here in Genesis 2 and Paul's use of it in Ephesians. The idea seems to be that an unfallen Adam might have been aware of the fact that his marriage to Eve was not merely a type of Christ's marriage to the Church, but was prophesying of the fact that Christ would be wedded to the Church *before* any fall had taken place. As Marilyn McCord Adams has recently put it (in commenting on an 'incarnation anyway' construal of Ephesians 5:31–32):

> Incarnation-anyway advocates understand *marriage* to be a sacrament of the indissoluble *one-flesh union* between Christ and the Church and of the indivisible hypostatic union of Christ's humanity and Christ's Divinity. Identifying Adam as the speaker, they take Genesis 2.24 to be a prophecy. They assume that, because Adam did not foresee his own fall, the content of this prophecy – Christ's marriage to, His one-flesh union with the Church – was not conditioned upon it and so would have come true even if humankind had never sinned.[22]

It is this that (so it might be thought) Paul takes up in his reference to Genesis 2 in Ephesians 5. But not so, says Turretin. It is too much to press St Paul's meaning into such service. Nothing in the Ephesians text (or the Genesis text for that matter) implies that Adam was prophesying, or that Paul thought Adam was prophesying about the relationship between Christ and the Church prior to, and independent of, any fall.

A third apologetic argument has to do with inappropriate theological speculation. Turretin thinks that 'Scripture proposes no other end of the mission of Christ than the salvation of sinners, nor it is right to push our inquiries further, since Scripture is silent' (*Inst.* XIII.III.301).

---

[22] Adams, *Christ and Horrors*, pp. 177–178.

So claiming that becoming incarnate without respect to human sin and becoming incarnate in order to expiate human sin are not options that Turretin thinks should be the subject of serious theological interest, since the resolution of this difficulty is a matter on which Scripture is silent.

Turretin also rejects the idea that 'incarnation anyway' might be motivated by the self-communicative goodness of God. At least some medieval divines took the view that divine self-communicative goodness is sufficient to warrant an incarnation irrespective of human sin. But Turretin is adamant that although the goodness of God 'could be a sufficient motive to influence him to the production of creatures' nevertheless it is not sufficient motivation 'for the incarnation of the son of God (which extended further to their restoration)' (*Inst.* XIII.III.301).

This completes our outline of Turretin's position. We are now in a position to consider several important objections to the arguments he offers.

Objections to Turretin's argument for the necessity of the Incarnation

There are several concerns that could be raised in connection with each part of Turretin's argument. To begin with, as was mentioned in the preamble to this chapter, there is something counterintuitive in thinking that God could not have brought about salvation by any other means than the Incarnation, given the great cost it incurs. It seems strange to think that it is not even *possibly* true that God could have offered humanity salvation via some less costly means than the Incarnation, since he has the power to bring about any logically possible state of affairs (we might suppose), as well as the perfect wisdom necessary to know which option is optimal, all things considered.[23] But Turretin must deny that some other, less costly option could have been (or could be) open to God in bringing about salvation from human sin if his argument is to go through. Note that the objection here is not that the Incarnation is *unavoidable*, but that it is *unjustified*. Turretin clearly does think that the Incarnation (and atonement) is

---

[23] Compare, for example St Thomas Aquinas, who claims regarding the Incarnation that 'God of his omnipotent power could have restored human nature in many other ways,' *Summa Theologiae* IIIa.1.2.

avoidable because God is not bound to save any fallen human. He could let every fallen human being be damned and remain just. What is more, there is nothing in the divine nature that compels God to act in a gracious fashion (on Turretin's way of thinking). Yet God graciously deigns to save some number of humanity via the Incarnation and atonement of Christ. Nevertheless, this means the Incarnation seems unjustified if God could have brought about the salvation of some number of fallen humanity via some less costly means. Call this *the unjustified cost objection* to the necessity of the Incarnation.

The objection can be finessed. Taking a leaf out of Brian Leftow's book, we could offer the following, more sophisticated version of the unjustified cost objection:[24]

10. God is perfectly wise and omnipotent.
11. If God is perfectly wise, God pays no unjustified costs to save (some fraction of) humankind.
12. If God is omnipotent, then (if it is possible that p, then God can bring it about that p).
13. Possibly, p.
14. If God can bring it about that p, then if God becomes incarnate or atones, God pays an unjustified cost to save (some fraction of) humankind.
15. If it is possible that p, then God can bring it about that p.
16. God can bring it about that p.
17. If God becomes incarnate or atones, God pays an unjustified cost to save (some fraction of) humankind.
18. God pays no unjustified cost to save (some fraction of) humankind.
19. God does not become incarnate or atone.

The most promising line of counterattack against this more formal version of the unjustified cost objection as far as Turretin is concerned, involves taking issue with (14).

---

[24] Adapted from Brian Leftow, 'Anselm on the Cost of Salvation', pp. 75–76. See also Sandra Visser and Thomas Williams, *Anselm*, pp. 214–218. Leftow's version of the argument, which he calls the Divine Cost Argument, does not distinguish between whether the Incarnation is unavoidable or unjustified. (This is a deliberate move on his part, which he makes clear as the argument progresses.) Since Turretin clearly does think the Incarnation is avoidable, I have adjusted the argument accordingly, so that it applies to Turretin's argument for the necessity of the Incarnation.

Assume the sort of theological compatibilism envisaged by Turretin, according to which God can bring about any logically possible state of affairs.[25] If it is logically possible for God to bring about the reconciliation of (some fraction of) humankind via some means less costly than becoming incarnate, then on the basis of the unjustified cost objection it would appear that God has a good reason to actualize such an alternative. The reason for this is not hard to ascertain. Such an alternative is less costly than the Incarnation, and, *ex hypothesi*, God does not pay any unjustified cost to save (some fraction of) humankind.

As we have already seen, Turretin's response to this objection relies on two theological assumptions. The first is that God is essentially just and that his essential distributive justice (that aspect of divine justice according to which God distributes rewards and punishments) includes a retributive element. God must act in a way consistent with his character; so he must act in a way that is essentially just. As Turretin puts it, divine justice 'is founded in the very nature of God and even identified with it' (*Inst.* III.XIX.236); 'the orthodox maintain that this justice is an essential property of God and not merely the effect of his free will' (*Inst.* III.XIX.237). He goes on to say, 'the question comes to this – whether the vindictive justice of God is so natural to him that he cannot but exercise it (the sinning of creatures being granted)', which is a position that, he says, 'we defend' (*Inst.* III.XIX.237). 'Hence', he concludes, 'if the hatred of sin is necessary in God, justice is equally necessary because the hatred of sin is the constant will of punishing it, which cannot fail in him who is not destitute of power . . . Therefore, if he hates sin necessarily, he must necessarily punish it' (*Inst.* III.XIX.237).

What is more, since divine justice includes retribution, he must visit just deserts upon sins committed. The 'fit' between punishment and crime is an important consideration here. Turretin is convinced that God *must*, not merely *may*, punish sin. Either the sinner himself is punished because culpable, or a suitable substitute takes upon himself the penal consequences for human sin:

---

[25] I take it that a theological compatibilist can claim that God can bring about all logically possible states of affairs because there are no logically possible worlds that are infeasible on account of the libertarian free choices of human agents. No creaturely free choice can in any way 'limit' what it is feasible for God to bring about.

> Justice demands necessarily that all sin should be punished, but does not equally demand that it should be punished in the very person sinning or at such a time and in such a degree. The Scholastics expressed this properly when they said that impersonally punishment is necessarily inflicted upon every sin, but not personally upon every sinner (*Inst.* III.XIX.236).

In this way, Turretin ensures in his discussion of divine justice that he has left open a door between the necessary exercise of divine retribution and the possibility that some suitable substitute might assume the penal consequences for the sin of some number of humanity.

The second, closely related assumption has to do with the Anselmian component to Turretin's reasoning. Not only must God punish sin given his divine nature. He must ensure that any means by which satisfaction for sin can be had apart from the punishment of the sinner is a suitable equivalent.[26] It is here that Turretin's appeal to the notion of a God-man and the logic of the overarching scheme of Anselm's *Cur Deus Homo* comes into play. (That is, only a divine person with a human nature is capable of offering up a suitable satisfaction for human sin that can act as atonement for that sin, etc.)

So in response to premise (14) of the unjustified cost objection, Turretin can answer that although God can bring about any logically possible state of affairs, it is not possible for God to act in a way inconsistent with his nature. Since he is essentially just and must punish sin, God cannot pass over or forgive sin without punishment. And since there must be a 'fit' between crime and punishment (given his adherence to a notion of divine retribution), and human sin incurs an infinite demerit that only a God-man can atone for, the cost involved in the Incarnation is not unjustified. Not only is God 'constrained' by

---

[26] I am assuming, for the sake of argument, that the notion of a suitable substitute for human sin is viable. In fact (as Turretin was well aware) this is a contested notion. The Socinians to whom Turretin is implacably opposed, maintained that no one can act as a penal substitute for sin because the penal consequences for one person's sin cannot be transferred to another: culpability as well as guilt are properties that can only be exemplified by the agent whose actions have engendered them. For recent discussion of the Socinian scheme of salvation, see Alan W. Gomes, '*De Jesu Christo Servatore*: Faustus Socinus on the Satisfaction of Christ' *Westminster Theological Journal* 55 (1993): 209–231. Turretin speaks at one point with approbation of arguments that will lead to the 'strangling' of 'that most pestilent heresy' of Socinianism! (*Inst.* III.XIX.237).

his nature to act as he does, if he is to bring about salvation at all, given the sort of world he brings about. He is also 'constrained' to save (some fraction of) humankind via the work of a God-man if he does bring about such a world with the intention of reconciling (at least) some fallen human creatures, since only a God-man is a suitable candidate for atonement.

But this raises a second sort of objection to Turretin's argument for the necessity of the Incarnation, having to do with the sort of 'constraint' upon the divine nature envisaged here. We might put it like this: how can God, who is supremely free and exists *a se*, be said to be constrained by anything without this infringing his divine aseity and freedom? How can he be constrained to bring about the Incarnation – in what sense is it necessary for God to act in this way? Call this *the objection from divine freedom.*

One line of response to this sort of objection is to deny that divine freedom is inconsistent with his being determined to act in a particular fashion. In other words, one could simply claim that some version of theological compatibilism applies to God just as it applies to his creatures. Then, God's being 'constrained' to act as he does turns out to be innocuous, provided what divine freedom denotes merely being free from external constraint, and acting in accordance with what one desires. God must act in accordance with his nature, but this does no violence to divine freedom because all entities must act in accordance with their natures – it would make no sense to claim otherwise. But there is also a cost involved in this sort of response. Assuming some form of compatibilism applies to God his acting to bring about this world and reconcile some number of fallen humanity is just the natural egress of the divine nature in his works. In which case, divine freedom means that God could actualize some world other than the one he does actualize if he so chose, but he cannot so choose, given his essential nature.[27]

---

[27] The classic example of a Reformed theologian who does appear to adopt the idea that God is only compatibilistically free is Jonathan Edwards, who maintains that God acts are morally necessary, given his power and wisdom. Thus Edwards: ''Tis the glory and greatness of the divine sovereignty, that God's will is determined by his own infinite all-sufficient wisdom in everything; and in nothing at all is either directed by any inferior wisdom, or by no wisdom; whereby it would become senseless arbitrariness, determining and acting without reason, design or end.' What is more, 'It no more argues any dependence of God's will, that his

Turretin resists this option. Instead, he maintains that God has libertarian freedom. Unlike his creatures, it appears that, from Turretin's point of view, for any given divine act, God could have done otherwise than he did. Not only does he have the power to bring about all logically possible states of affairs. He could have brought about states of affairs other than the state of affairs he did bring about. That is, he has a liberty of indifference when it comes to choosing which state of affairs obtains.

> When it is asked whether God wills some things freely, not only the will of spontaneity is meant (for so the things which God wills most necessarily, he wills also freely, i.e., without coaction), but properly the liberty of indifference (i.e., whether he so wills that he could have nilled them) (*Inst.* III.XIV.219).

But a distinction needs to be observed at this juncture. Turretin is clear that when speaking of whether or not God does certain things necessarily or freely, we should observe that there is an absolute necessity, which pertains to the divine nature. But there is also a second, hypothetical sort of necessity, which pertains to the effects of God's willing certain things to be. As to the first sort of necessity, God himself cannot be other than he is. His nature is such that it is, on Turretin's reckoning, 'absolutely necessary' that God is (say) good, or just (*Inst.* III.XIV.218). As he puts it at one point, 'I say that God wills himself necessarily, not only by a hypothetical necessity, but also by an absolute necessity.' God is 'the ultimate end and highest good which he cannot but will and love, not only as to specification (that he can will and love nothing contrary), but also as to exercise (that he never ceases from willing and loving himself), for he cannot nil his own glory or deny himself (*Inst.* III.XIV.219).

That God must will himself according to an 'absolute' necessity sounds rather like the modern claim that God's nature is metaphysically necessary. It cannot be other than it is; there are no possible worlds at which God has even one attribute different from the attributes he has at this possible world, the world that obtains. But this is consistent with the claim that God wills the creation freely and yet

_____

(cont.) supremely wise volition is necessary, than it argues a dependence of his being, that his existence is necessary.' *Freedom of the Will: The Works of Jonathan Edwards Vol. 1*, ed. Paul Ramsey (New Haven: Yale University Press, 1957), pp. 380 and 381, respectively.

according to a certain sort of necessity, different from this 'absolute' necessity. God freely ordains the world he does – nothing external to God constrains his choosing to create, or his choosing to create the world he does. But once he has ordained the creation of this world, it must obtain of necessity. This is Turretin's 'hypothetical necessity'. On this basis he distinguishes the hypothetical necessity of the creation from the absolute necessity of the divine nature itself: 'God wills created things necessarily from hypothesis because (supposing he has once willed) he can no more will them on account of the immutability of his will; by speaking absolutely he wills them freely because he is influenced to will them at first by no necessity, but my mere liberty and could abstain from their production' (*Inst.* III.XIV.219). Once God has ordained a certain course of events, he cannot renege on his willing it, because his will is immutable. Yet at the moment logically prior to his decision to bring about the world he does bring about, he could have refrained from so creating.

So in answer to the objection from divine freedom, Turretin can say that God is libertarianly free in his decision to act as he does in creating the sort of world he brings about. And, from what we saw earlier in the previous section of Turretin's views about the necessity of the Incarnation it is clear that he thinks the plan to bring about the salvation of some number of fallen humanity via the Incarnation of Christ is entirely a matter of divine grace. But given that God wills to bring about the world he does (a world where human beings require salvation), and given that God wills to bring about the salvation of some fraction of fallen humanity, the Incarnation must obtain. Its occurrence, like the obtaining of the created order itself, is only hypothetically necessary. God is not constrained to bring it about, either by some external agency, or by his own divine nature. But once he has ordained that he will create this world and will save some number of fallen humanity, the Incarnation becomes inevitable. It cannot but obtain.

This brings us to the final objection, having to do with the modal implications of Turretin's argument for the hypothetical necessity of the Incarnation. Let us designate this, *the modal implication objection*. From what we have seen of his views, Turretin is committed to the counterfactual claim that God could have brought about a world very like this one, populated by sinful human beings, but where no Incarnation takes place. In such a world the sinful human beings in question would all perish; divine retributive justice would be meted out upon them and they would all suffer the penal consequences for their own sin, and (presumably) for bearing original sin. But this seems inconsistent with other claims Turretin makes, concerning the end of God's work in creation and concerning the divine nature.

It is feasible for Turretin to claim that God brings about a world where no human sinner is saved via the Incarnation of the God-man. If the ultimate end of creation is the glorification of God, then God would be glorified in the damnation of the whole mass of fallen humanity. But how is this consistent with the notion that God is merciful and gracious? Both divine mercy and divine grace are essential to God, since, for Turretin, like other classical, orthodox Christian theologians, God is essentially simple.[28] All God's attributes entail each other and all God's attributes are essential to the divine nature, including his mercy and grace. Still, the exercise of mercy or grace might be different from the exercise of divine justice. Whereas the exercise of divine distributive justice is inexorable, on Turretin's way of thinking, divine mercy is not. Its exercise is at God's discretion. He need not exercise his mercy upon any given creature (see *Inst.* III.XX.241–244). Yet if God is fully actual, as Turretin also claims,[29] having no potential and no metaphysical 'room' for further exercise of his divine nature, it would appear to be inconsistent to assert both that God may create a world where no human sinners are saved and yet that in such a world the divine nature is fully exercised.[30] Since divine mercy or grace is only exercised when lavished upon some fitting created object (no divine person in the immanent Trinity requires the exercise of divine grace and mercy!) in the sort of world we are envisaging here, this divine attribute remains dormant, or is merely dispositional. It is not even that God can exercise his divine mercy upon the human nature of Christ alone (making Christ the only object

---

[28] '[T]he divine nature is conceived by us not only as free from all composition and division, but also as incapable of composition and divisibility.' *Inst.* III.VII.191.

[29] 'God is a most pure act having no passive admixture and therefore rejecting all composition (because in God there is nothing which needs to be made perfect or can receive perfection from any other, but he is whatever can be and cannot be other than what he is.)' *Inst.* III.VII.191–192.

[30] But suppose divine grace and mercy are *necessarily* discretionary. Even if this is the case, where God is a simple pure act it makes little sense to say his necessarily discretionary grace and mercy remains unexercised, even dormant or merely dispositional, since, if God is a pure act, there is no unrealized potentiality in the divine nature – God is fully actual and fully in-act, as it were.

of his mercy and grace by assumption), since, by Turretin's own reck-oning, in such a world there would be no Incarnation.[31]

This, I submit, reveals a real shortcoming in Turretin's argument. If grace and mercy are essential elements of the divine nature, and God is a simple pure act that has no passivity and no unrealized potential, then divine mercy and grace must have some created object upon which they may be exercised. Yet Turretin's reasoning countenances the possibility of a world at which this does not obtain. To make this a little clearer, let us put the objection in numbered propositions:

20. God is a simple pure act.
21. God has libertarian freedom.
22. God can bring about all logically possible states of affairs.
23. The creation of the world is only hypothetically necessary [con-junction of (21) & (22)].
24. The Incarnation only obtains at worlds where (a) there is at least one human sinner in need of salvation, and (b) God ordains that the God-man brings about the salvation of that sinner or sinners.
25. Possibly, God brings about a world, W_1, populated by human sin-ners none of whom are the objects of his saving grace.
26. At W_1, no Incarnation obtains [conjunction of (24) & (25)].
27. At W_1, there is no created object upon which God can lavish his mercy and grace.

In which case, it would appear that:

28. At W_1, divine mercy and grace remain unexercised.
29. But it is metaphysically impossible for any divine attribute to remain unexercised, given (20).
30. So, it is metaphysically impossible for God to create W_1.

It might be thought that this objection does not really damage Turretin's reasoning. After all, it concerns a purely counterfactual sce-nario: God has created a world of sinful human beings at least some

---

[31] This also raises a vexed question concerning the identity of Christ and the Second Person of the Trinity, if there are worlds at which no Incarnation takes place. I shall not pursue this matter here, although useful discussion can be found in Alfred Freddoso, 'Human Nature, Potency and the Incarnation,' *Faith and Philosophy* 3 (1986): 27–53 and van Driel, *Incarnation Anyway*, especially chs. 6–8.

of whom are the objects of his grace and are saved through the work of the God-man. But this fails to take seriously enough the implications of this sort of modal objection. Turretin is committed to the idea that a world like W$_1$ is metaphysically possible. The Incarnation is only hypothetically necessary and at least part of the reason for this is that there are worlds like W$_1$ where no Incarnation obtains. If it turns out that such worlds are not metaphysically possible because of considerations to do with the divine nature (being a simple pure act), then to that extent the force of Turretin's appeal to the hypothetical necessity of the Incarnation is diminished.

This does not show that Turretin cannot appeal to some sort of hypothetical necessity, because he can still claim that God could have refrained from creating any world. In which case, there would have been no Incarnation, because there would have been no creation. But this is rather a pyrrhic victory. It means that the hypothetical necessity of the Incarnation obtains just in case God creates a world, rather than refraining from creating any world. Far better to claim something like the following principle is true: *for any given created theatre, God's glory must be exercised in such a manner as to display all his divine attributes.* Taken together with a commitment to a pure act account of the divine nature, this principle means that worlds where one or more divine attributes are not, as it were, exercised, are not feasible. Appealing to such a principle is not without metaphysical cost, of course. But it does have the advantage of making sense of much of what Turretin wants to say. It preserves his account of the divine nature, although it tweaks his understanding of the exercise of divine grace and mercy. But it also retains a place for a broadly Turretinian understanding of the hypothetical necessity of the Incarnation, given God's decision to create a world of human creatures in need of salvation. On this view we can affirm that God might have refrained from creating. In which case, there would have been no Incarnation. And, presumably, God was free to create a world of human creatures that never sinned and were not in need of a redeemer either.[32] But where God creates a world of human creatures in need of redemption, his divine nature constrains him to act in a way that displays his justice and his mercy – and that requires an Incarnation.

---

[32] Since the objective here is to remain 'Turretinian', I shall not explore the possibility opened up by 'incarnation anyway' arguments at this juncture. See van Driel, *Incarnation Anyway, passim.*

CHAPTER FIVE

John McLeod Campbell and Non-penal Substitution

> He indeed consummated penitence in himself, before the eyes,
> and before the hearts, of men who were not penitent themselves.
> — *Robert C. Moberly*[1]

In his miscellaneous remarks on *Satisfaction for Sin*, the eighteenth-century American divine, Jonathan Edwards, remarked,

> it is requisite that God should punish all sin with infinite punishment;
> because all sin, as it is against God, is infinitely heinous, and has infinite demerit, is justly infinitely hateful to him, and so stirs up infinite abhorrence and indignation in him. Therefore, by what was before granted, it is requisite that God should punish it, unless there be something in some measure to balance this desert; either some answerable repentance and sorrow for it, or some other compensation.[2]

Edwards went on to argue that there can be no 'answerable repentance and sorrow' for sin equal to the infinite heinousness of sin that could be offered by a human being. The suggestion seems to be that no *mere* human being can offer an adequate satisfaction for sin by an act of vicarious penitence because no penitential act offered up by a mere human being is sufficient reparation for sin that is infinitely heinous. Instead, God must punish sin in the person of the sinner, or in the person of a vicar, able to offer perfect satisfaction for sin. But curiously, Edwards did not pause to consider in detail the possibility that Christ, as the God-man, might offer this 'answerable repentance and sorrow' in the place

---

[1] *Atonement and Personality* (London: John Murray, 1907), p. 283.

[2] From *The Works of Jonathan Edwards, Vol. II*, ed. Edward Hickman (Edinburgh: Banner of Truth, 1974 [1834]), p. 565.

of human beings. In the nineteenth century, the Scottish theologian John McLeod Campbell seized upon this lacuna in Edwards' reasoning. In his work, *The Nature of the Atonement*,[3] Campbell urged that two alternatives were open to 'the Mediator'. First, he could endure for sinful human beings an equivalent punishment for sin (Edwards' preferred option). Second, he could experience 'in reference to their sin, and present to God on their behalf, an adequate sorrow and repentance.'[4] This insight provided by Campbell regarding the vicarious penitence of Christ – that is, Christ offering a perfect confession of sins on behalf of all humanity that is somehow redemptive – is the linchpin of his non-penal, yet substitutionary, understanding of the atonement.[5]

Campbell is not alone in having developed this particular approach to the atonement. R. C. Moberly, at the beginning of the twentieth century, echoed Campbell's doctrine of the vicarious penitence of Christ in these words: 'the perfect sacrifice of penitence in the sinless Christ is the true atoning sacrifice for sin.'[6] And, in the same period P. T.

---

[3] John McLeod Campbell, *The Nature of the Atonement*, 6th Edition (London: Macmillan, 1895 [1856]). All references hereinafter are to this edition of Campbell's work, unless otherwise stated.

[4] This relationship between the theologies of Edwards and Campbell is the subject of Michael Jinkins' book, *A Comparative Study in the Theology of the Atonement in Jonathan Edwards and John McLeod Campbell: Atonement and the Character of God* (Lewiston, NY: Edwin Mellon Press, 1993).

[5] For discussion of this matter, see J. B. Torrance, 'The Contribution of McLeod Campbell to Scottish Theology', in *Scottish Journal of Theology* 26 (1973): 295–311, esp. p. 309; George M. Tuttle, *So Rich A Soil: John McLeod Campbell on Christian Atonement* (Edinburgh: Handsel Press, 1985), chs. VII & VIII; and Leanne van Dyk, 'Toward A New Typology of Reformed Doctrines of The Atonement' in *Toward The Future of Reformed Theology: Tasks, Topics, Traditions*, eds. David Willis and Michael Welker (Grand Rapids: Eerdmans, 1999). Benjamin Warfield characterized this aspect of Campbell's thinking, rather unsympathetically, as 'a theory of sympathetic repentance [by Christ on behalf of humanity]'. See Warfield, 'Modern Theories of the Atonement' in *The Works of Benjamin B. Warfield, Vol. IX, Studies in Theology* (Oxford: Oxford University Press, 1932), p. 290.

[6] R. C. Moberly, *Atonement and Personality* (London: John Murray, 1901), p. 130. Cf. p. 129. Moberly was not uncritical of Campbell, however. See pp. 396 ff. Some theologians, notably John Stott, class Campbell and Moberly along with Horace Bushnall, as exponents of a broadly Abelardian 'moral influence' view of the atonement. For reasons that should become clear presently, I think this is a mistake. See John Stott, *The Cross of Christ* (Leicester, InterVarsity Press, 1986), p. 142. Cf. Robert Letham, *The Work* of

Forsyth developed a position that, while distinct from Campbell's, nevertheless shared with Campbell the notion that Christ's atonement includes a confessional, or penitential, dimension.[7] More recently James and Thomas Torrance have defended versions of Campbell's approach to the atonement.[8] In this paper, we shall consider the internal logic of this way of thinking about the atonement. I call it non-penal substitution despite the fact that this view is often referred to as vicarious penitence, for two reasons. First, as we shall

---

(cont.) *Christ* (Leicester: IVP, 1993), pp. 169 ff. McLeod Campbell's influence on subsequent atonement theory in Anglo-Saxon Protestant theology was considerable. For an account of this, see Tuttle, *So Rich A Soil*, chs. IX and X.

[7] Forsyth summarizes his own view in relation to penal substitution in this way, 'I should, therefore, express the difference between the old view and the new by saying that one emphasizes substitutionary expiation and the other emphasizes solidarity reparation, consisting of due acknowledgement of God's holiness, and the honouring of that and not of His honour.' *The Work of Christ* (London: Hodder and Stoughton, 1910), pp. 164–165. According to Benjamin Warfield, Forsyth's position is that human redemption rests ultimately on Christ's work, but proximately on our own repentance. This happens in the following way. Christ's confession of sin and his death elicit a response of penitence in human beings that God accepts as adequate satisfaction for sin. See Benjamin Warfield, 'Modern Theories of the Atonement', p. 292. This is not non-penal substitution, but, as Forsyth's writings show, there is a considerable debt owed to Campbell's thinking about the nature of the atonement. See also Trevor Hart, 'Morality, Atonement and the Death of Jesus: The Crucial Focus of Forsyth's Theology' in *Justice the True and Only Mercy: Essays on the Life and Theology of Peter Taylor Forsyth*, ed. Trevor Hart (Edinburgh: T & T Clark, 1995).

[8] See J. B. Torrance, 'The Contribution of McLeod Campbell to Scottish Theology' and 'The Vicarious Humanity of Christ' in *The Incarnation*, ed. T. F. Torrance (Edinburgh: Handsel Press, 1981). There is substantial overlap between these two papers. For Thomas Torrance's views on Campbell, see *Scottish Theology: From John Knox to McLeod Campbell* (Edinburgh: T & T Clark, 1986). He also makes use of the notion of Christ's 'vicarious humanity' (of which, more presently) in *The Mediation of Christ* (Edinburgh: T & T Clark, 1992), p.41, but without explaining from whence he derives this concept. Daniel P. Thimell also defends Campbell in 'Christ in Our Place in the Theology of John McLeod Campbell' in *Christ in Our Place, The Humanity of God in Christ for The Reconciliation of the World*, eds. Trevor Hart and Daniel Thimell (Exeter: Paternoster, 1989).

see in due course, vicarious penitence is only one aspect of this doctrine of the atonement. Second, it seems to me that the central insight of defenders of this sort of view is that it offers a doctrine of the atonement that preserves the substitutionary character of penal substitution beloved of the Reformed tradition, while avoiding some of the problems associated with the penal aspect of the penal substitutionary view.[9] To put it bluntly, penal substitution is often criticized for requiring that divine justice be met by a substitute able to take upon himself the penal consequences for the sin of human beings (or some number of human beings less than the totality of humanity). Some think this paints God as an uncaring and bloodthirsty tyrant; one who demands that justice is satisfied when it was within his gift to exercise grace and mercy instead.[10] Others think that this view of the atonement does not adequately reflect the complex of biblical images used to explain the atonement.[11] Still others question the coherence of claiming that one person can take upon himself the penal consequences of the sin of another.[12] What defenders of non-penal substitution maintain is that Christ's work might involve a substitutionary element – particularly, though not exclusively, vicarious

---

[9] Leanne van Dyk in 'Toward A New Typology' pp. 231–233 maintains that Campbell's doctrine is a version of satisfaction theory, rather than a substitutionary theory. I think this is a semantic, rather than substantive disagreement for the most part, although Van Dyk's definition of satisfaction theories of atonement (p. 232) is, I think, misleading. She appears to think satisfaction is a genus of atonement theory, with penal substitution just one species belonging to it. I think that although there is conceptual overlap between satisfaction and penal substitution, they are distinct atonement theories. One could believe in satisfaction without holding to penal substitution, and *vice versa*. But there is not space to develop this point here.

[10] Kathryn Tanner's recent treatment of redemption could be taken in this way. See *Jesus, Humanity and the Trinity: A Brief Systematic Theology* (Edinburgh: T & T Clark, 2001), p. 88. But this complaint is widespread and is often tied to a particular postmodern thesis about the intrinsically violent nature of punishment – a matter into which I shall not delve here. Hans Boersma offers a defence of penal substitution against this sort of criticism in his book, *Violence, Hospitality and the Cross* (Grand Rapids: Eerdmans, 2004).

[11] This is an issue that motivates some of what Colin Gunton has to say about the use of different 'metaphors' for the atonement in his *The Actuality of Atonement* (Edinburgh: T & T Clark, 1988).

[12] This criticism is often associated with Socinianism.

penitence – without assumption of the penal consequences of human sin that is so repugnant to some, and so baffling to others. If a version of this argument can be found that makes sense, then those committed to a substitutionary doctrine of the atonement might be able to avoid those aspects of penal substitution that have caused problems. And they may be able to do so without relinquishing a robust doctrine of the atonement that is substitutionary in nature.[13] All of which raises the central question of this chapter, which is: *Can non-penal substitutionary theories of the atonement offer a more plausible account of the atonement than penal substitutionary theories do?*

With this in mind, the chapter is divided into three sections. In the first, we shall lay out two versions of the non-penal substitutionary view commensurate with an Edwardsian understanding of the need for satisfaction equal to the heinousness of sin committed against God. This is, as far as I know, a novel way of construing the doctrine. It also offers, I suggest, an important insight into this way of thinking about the atonement because it shows a defender of non-penal substitution need not follow Campbell in rejecting a traditional Reformed picture of the divine nature. The second section of the chapter fleshes this out by examining what distinguishes a Campbell-inspired version of non-penal substitution from an Edwards-inspired one. The third section of the chapter considers three of the most serious objections to non-penal substitutionary theories of the atonement. I

---

[13] The term 'robust' in 'robust doctrines of the atonement' is a term of art. It stands in for the more common theological term, 'objective' as in 'objective doctrines of the atonement' (as opposed to 'subjective doctrines of the atonement'). I think that the use of 'objective' or 'subjective' with respect to the atonement is a source of some confusion. For one thing, it perpetuates the misunderstanding that 'objective' views of the atonement, like penal substitution, are lacking in a more 'subjective' aspect (that is, an aspect that pertains to the experience of the Christian). It seems to me that 'robust' does not have this unhelpful connotation and still preserves the idea that certain doctrines of the atonement are stronger than others, in the sense of offering an account of the atonement in which there really is some act committed by Christ that brings about the reconciliation of human beings (or some number of humans less that the total number of human beings) with God. Theories of atonement that claim Christ is merely a moral exemplar, (such as that offered by John Hick, or nineteenth-century liberal theology) have no place for such a notion of reconciliation and would not, on my understanding, count as 'robust' accounts of the atonement.

contend that, unlike the Campbell-inspired doctrine, one of the Edwards-inspired versions of non-penal substitution can overcome all three of these problems.[14] Thus, at least one version of non-penal substitution – and an Edwardsian version at that – is able to offer a coherent, robust doctrine of the atonement.

Edwardsian non-penal substitution

To begin with, let us consider some central issues pertaining to the logic of non-penal substitutionary views of the atonement. Although the versions of the doctrine favoured by McLeod Campbell and those who have followed his lead involve a revisionist account of the divine nature, this is not necessary to a doctrine of non-penal substitution. As Edwards suggests, a doctrine of non-penal substitution could be given on the basis of a traditional, Reformed understanding of the divine nature and the requirements for redemption from sin. Edwards does not offer such an argument, so I offer one here on his behalf.

Let us assume, with many in the Christian tradition, that divine justice is essentially retributive in nature.[15] There are two ways this might be understood. First, it might be that divine justice *does not permit* forgiveness (without satisfaction). Second, it might be that divine justice *does not require* forgiveness (without satisfaction).[16] Clearly, the latter account of divine retribution is weaker than the former. For on the latter, God may forgive a sinner without reparation, whereas, on the former view such an action would be unjust.

---

[14] Note that, on my understanding of atonement theories, both non-penal substitution and satisfaction are species of robust atonement doctrine, as is penal substitution. Yet all three are distinct doctrines (that may share a number of ideas in common, such as that divine justice is essentially retributive). In this respect I am in entire agreement with Trevor Hart who points out that Anselm and McLeod Campbell share a number of ideas about the atonement in 'Anselm of Canterbury and John McLeod Campbell: Where Opposites Meet?' In *Evangelical Quarterly* 62 (1990): 311–333. What is baffling, as Hart observes, is that anyone should think Anselmian satisfaction is the opposite of non-penal substitution.

[15] Those unwilling to concede this assumption will find little of what follows appealing.

[16] For a relevant recent discussion of divine retributive justice see Oliver D. Crisp, 'Divine Retribution: A Defence' in *Sophia* 42 (2003): 35–52.

It seems to me that most theologians in the tradition who defend divine retribution, do so according to the stronger of these two views, that is, on the understanding that God may not forgive sin without some act of reparation being made, either by the sinner, or, perhaps, by some substitute on behalf of the sinner. Of course, if it turns out that the weaker of these two views obtains, then, in any particular instance of sin committed against God, it would be perfectly possible for God to forgive the sinner without demanding reparation of any kind, as an act of sheer grace. But, if this is possible, it does raise the question of why it is that God does not do this in the case of every sin committed against him. If God can forgive sin without punishment, as an act of sheer grace, and remain just, why does he not forgive all human beings without demanding satisfaction for sin? He does not have to act in this way, on this weaker view. God would be just were he to punish all sinners and just if he forgave all sinners. But it might be thought that the world would be an objectively morally better place if God were to exercise divine grace and forgive all sinners instead of punishing them (or punishing a vicar in their place). One might be forgiven for thinking that a world where there was significantly less suffering than this one, where God forgives sin and all are redeemed and none suffer an infinite punishment in hell, would be a world with less suffering and, as a consequence an objectively morally better world, than one where only some are saved, the rest being punished (infinitely in hell), or where none are saved, and all are punished (infinitely in hell).

So the weaker view of divine retribution has the following unfortunate consequence: God could have created an objectively morally better world than this one, where all human beings are saved by an act of divine forgiveness without the need for a prior act of reparation. And this is surely intolerable. It is, I suggest, for this reason (or for reasons very like this with similarly unpleasant theological consequences) that most defenders of divine retribution in the tradition have opted for the stronger of the two views of divine justice that we began with, which was that divine justice does not permit forgiveness without reparation being made to God. Following the lead of such theologians let us assume the stronger view of divine justice obtains. Hereinafter, I shall refer to this as *the strong view of (divine) retribution* or just *the strong view*, for short.

According to the strong view, crime must be punished and the punishment must fit the crime. Furthermore, God cannot act in a way that is unjust, since this would be to act in a way inconsistent with his own divine nature. It is sometimes asserted that on such a way of thinking about divine justice, divine freedom is compromised. If God must ensure justice is done and if this means that he must punish the sin committed against him (in the person of the sinner, or a vicar), then this seems to mean God is not free to forgive the sinner if he so desired. But it should be clear from what has already been said that this sort of objection betrays some confusion about the nature of divine justice and about the divine nature, more broadly construed. Regarding divine justice: this objection only has purchase if the weaker construal of divine justice (call it, *the weak view of (divine) retribution* or just *the weak view*) obtains. But, as we have just seen, there are good reasons for rejecting the weak view, to do with the implications this has for theodicy. And on the matter of the divine nature more broadly construed, it is no restriction on God that he has to act according to his nature (if he has a nature), any more than it is a restriction upon a monkey that he has to act according to his nature as a monkey, and not according to the nature of some other kind of creature. It would hardly make sense to say the monkey was not free if he has to act in a simian fashion, rather than in a human fashion. And in a similar way, it is hardly an objection against the strong version of divine retribution to say that if God has to act according to his nature, that is, in a way that is just (where divine justice is understood to be retributive in nature) then he is somehow un-free in so acting.[17] One could object that divine justice is not essentially retributive. But then the objection would not be about divine freedom, but about the nature of divine justice, which is quite another matter.[18]

There are several other aspects of the strong version of divine retribution that need to be touched upon before coming to a non-penal way of understanding the atonement consistent with this account of divine justice. Edwards' argument assumes just such a strong version of divine retribution, for, recall, he states that there must be some

---

[17] Similar reasoning could be applied, the relevant changes having been made, for those defenders of divine simplicity who might deny that God has a nature in the Aristotelian sense of a set of properties that make up a divine essence.

[18] But, why think that divine justice is essentially retributive? Well, classical theologians who have thought this (and all classical theologians I know of thought this) did so because they believed it reflected Scripture – a matter that is now disputed. Nevertheless, this view can rightly be called the traditional view of divine justice, even if it is not the most fashionable view. Whether it is also the biblical view I cannot go into here.

'compensation' which balances out the 'infinite heinousness' of human sin against God.

Now, this sort of thinking presumes that (a) for a punishment to be just there must be proportionality between the crime committed and the punishment allotted (i.e. the punishment must fit the crime), (b) that every human being since the Fall (excluding Christ) has a sinful human nature for which they are culpable quite apart from any actual sins they may commit, and (c) possession of such a sinful human nature incurs an infinite demerit quite apart from the demerit incurred by any actual sin, on account of the fact that possession of a sinful human nature is an affront to a being of infinite glory and honour, and any affront to a being of infinite glory and honour generates an infinite demerit, for which there are infinite penal consequences. These conditions are controversial, but there is not space to go into these matters here.[19] It seems to me that it is at least plausible to think that every human being is in a state of sin post-Fall, which is an affront to God. What is more, it also seems plausible to me that sin against a being of infinite glory and honour should incur an infinite demerit, and put the sinner in a position of needing to make reparation of infinite worth in order to compensate for the sin committed against God – and that this is proportional, in the relevant sense.[20] And, if Edwards is right, possession of a sinful human nature is itself a sin requiring just such reparation. Let us, in a spirit of Christian charity, grant these assumptions to the defender of a strong version of divine retribution, for the sake of the argument.

With the strong version of divine retribution made tolerably clear, we may proceed to consideration of its application to a non-penal but substitutionary account of the atonement. Since the objective here is to provide a doctrine of atonement which, while not a version of penal substitution, is nevertheless a properly substitutionary account of the atonement that stands foursquare upon a strong version of divine retribution, and since it was Edwards who suggested this sort

---

[19] For more on this matter, see, Oliver D. Crisp, 'Divine Retribution: A Defence' and 'Did Christ have a fallen human nature?' in *International Journal of Systematic Theology* 6 (2004): 270–288.

[20] Ibid. See also, William Wainwright, 'Original Sin' in *Philosophy and the Christian Faith*, ed. Thomas V. Morris (Notre Dame: University of Notre Dame Press, 1988), and Wainwright, 'Jonathan Edwards and the doctrine of Hell' in *Jonathan Edwards: Philosophical Theologian*, eds. Paul Helm and Oliver D. Crisp (Aldershot: Ashgate, 2003), pp. 13–26.

of argument might be made (giving McLeod Campbell his initial inspiration), let us call this the *Edwardsian argument for non-penal substitution*. (*Caveat Lector*: This is not to suggest Edwards endorsed this doctrine, only that it is consistent with his reasoning.)

According to the Edwardsian argument for non-penal substitution, divine justice must be satisfied, but there is more than one *manner* in which divine justice may be satisfied. First, God could punish sin in the person of the sinner, or in the person of a vicar. If in the person of the sinner, then, presumably, the sinner is punished in hell. If in the person of a vicar, then the vicar offers the requisite punishment in place of the sinner. And that, according to some Christian theologians, is what happens in the atonement: Christ is our vicar, taking upon himself the penal consequences of our sin, suffering in our place on the cross, thereby satisfying divine justice. If the vicar is able to offer reparation by taking upon himself the penal consequences of human sin (or the sin of some number less than the totality of humanity), then we have a version of penal substitution, which Edwards endorses.[21] But what if a vicar were to offer some other means of reparation that also satisfied divine justice? One such means, according to Edwards, would be 'some answerable repentance and sorrow' for the sin committed. A vicar would have to offer up a perfect repentance on behalf of human sinners and a perfect sorrow for the sin these sinners have committed. Were an argument for such a vicarious penitence forthcoming, we would have a version of substitutionary atonement that was non-penal. But what would such an argument look like? I suggest, like this:

Christ is the God-man, that is, a divine person possessing a complete human nature. Hence, he is fully divine and fully human. As the God-man, he is able to offer up a perfect penitence on behalf of fallen human beings (or on behalf of some number of fallen human beings

---

[21] A closely related, but distinct account of the atonement is Anselmian satisfaction, according to which Christ volunteers to die a blameless (sinless) death on behalf of human beings. This act of supererogation generates an infinite merit (Christ's life being of infinite value, because he is the God-Man), which Christ is then able to offer to God the Father as an adequate satisfaction for the affronted divine honour. Christ's merit may then be substituted for the infinite debt owed to God by sinful human beings on account of their sinful condition that generates an infinite demerit because it is a sin committed against a being of infinite worth and honour. See Anselm, *Cur Deus Homo*.

less than the totality of fallen human beings[22]). He is able to satisfy (the strong version of) divine retributive justice in this act because his penitence has a worth sufficient to the purpose (or, perhaps, of infinite worth). And it has a worth sufficient to the purpose because it is a perfect act of vicarious penitence offered by a being that is both fully divine and fully human (in virtue of the hypostatic union).

Only a morally blameless human being could offer perfect penitence, because only a morally blameless human being would be free from the stain of sin and its penal consequences. That is, only such an individual would be able to offer up vicarious reparation on behalf of other human beings blighted by original sin in a way that he was not. It would not be sufficient to the purpose if a morally blameless individual were fully but merely human. For then, the penitence offered would not be of *infinite* worth. (And that, I take it, is why Edwards rejects this option in his discussion of the atonement.) So, the individual concerned would have to be fully but not merely human as well as being morally blameless. In fact, he would have to be *fully divine* and fully human, as Christ is. For only a God-man could bring about a vicarious penitence that has an infinite worth and can thereby satisfy (strong) divine retributive justice. If it were asked how such an act of vicarious penitence could atone for sin, the answer would have a similar form to a traditional argument for penal substitution. That is, Christ is able to act as a substitute for human beings, Christ performs some atoning act that is of sufficient worth to expiate the infinite demerit of human sinfulness, and this satisfies divine retributive justice, thereby providing the means by which fallen human beings might be saved. (This says nothing about the means by which the atoning work of Christ is appropriated by fallen human beings, but we are concerned with the nature of the atonement, not the means by which the benefits of the atonement are appropriated by fallen human beings.)

Like penal substitution, the Edwardsian non-penal doctrine presumes that God will allow a certain sort of vicarious act performed by Christ to count as reparation for the sin committed by fallen human beings. And, like traditional versions of penal substitution, this involves a sort of substitutionary 'fiction' (a moral, rather than – as with penal substitution – a legal, fiction). By that I mean God treats

---

[22] Alternatively, his act of vicarious penitence is of such worth that it is sufficient to satisfy divine justice on behalf of all humanity, but may be efficient for some number less than this – those God elects to eternal life.

Christ's act of vicarious penitence *as if* it were an act offered by fallen human beings, such that Christ's act may be *imputed* to fallen human beings who may thereby benefit from Christ's vicarious action.

This still leaves the nature of the act itself. In traditional doctrines of penal substitution, Christ's atoning work involves him taking on the penal consequences of human sin and being punished in the place of fallen human beings. God treats Christ as if he were guilty of my sin, although he is not guilty, strictly speaking. In the Edwardsian version of non-penal substitution the penal element is set aside. Christ's vicarious act does not involve his being punished in place of another. Instead, it involves his apologizing, or committing some penitential act, on my behalf. The problem is that this does not seem sufficient to warrant satisfaction of divine retributive justice.

This point becomes clearer if we consider the nature of an atoning act. Richard Swinburne maintains that atonement involves four components: repentance, apology, reparation, and penance.[23] This seems plausible to me. I suggest that in the normal course of things we think that in order for a person who has perpetrated a crime to atone for their sin, he or she needs to show remorse and apologize for that crime, and should offer some sort of reparation and penance (taken here to mean some act that demonstrates that the sinner is truly penitent). The more serious the crime, the more we would insist on the satisfaction of all of these components for atonement to take place. So, for example, if Jack the Ripper had turned himself in to London's Bow Street Police station in the 1880s and expressed real contrition for his crimes, offering to apologize to the families of his victims, we would hardly think this sufficient to atone for his sins. Reparation and penance would have to follow for this to occur, and normally, in the case of a mass murderer, this involves a long custodial sentence, or, in Victorian London, the death penalty.

Apply this sort of reasoning to the Edwardsian doctrine of non-penal substitution. It might be thought to include the first three of these requirements for atonement, if, and only if, repentance and apology can, in certain circumstances, be considered an act of reparation sufficient to expiate the crime committed. This would be the case if Christ's vicarious penitence were a species of speech-act. According to J. L. Austin, there are two kinds of speech-act, and any one speech-act can include aspects of both. The first kind is usually called an

---

[23] Richard Swinburne, *Responsibility and Atonement* (Oxford: Oxford University Press, 1989), p. 81.

illocutionary act, the classic example of which is the wedding vow which is not only a form of words, but, when uttered in a wedding service by the bride or groom, constitutes the binding of oneself to whomever the 'thee' picks out in the sentence, 'I do thee wed'. Such expressions *are* said to literally constitute an action – the words expressed are the act. In the case of the atonement, the form of words Christ uses in his vicarious penitence would, if illocutionary, constitute an act of atonement, like the wedding vow constitutes an act of wedding oneself to another. Alternatively, it could be that Christ's act of vicarious penitence is a perlocutionary act. In this case, an act is performed by means of uttering of a certain form of words. For instance, exclaiming 'Get out!' enables one to command something. Thus, the words expressed *bring about* the act. It might be that Christ's vicarious penitence is an act that is performed by uttering the words of apology to the Father on behalf of fallen human beings (or some number of those human beings less than the total number, for whom he utters these words of penitence).[24] Or, a third option, Christ's vicarious penitence has both illocutionary and perlocutionary elements.[25] But it is far from clear without some explanation that a perfect apology for human sin is *sufficient* to atone for that sin, or that it might constitute a speech-act of some sort. For, as it stands, it does not appear to account for the fourth aspect of Swinburne's quartet: penance.

It might be thought that a perfect act of vicarious penitence that has a worth sufficient to atone for human sin (because it is uttered by the God-man) itself constitutes an act of penance. In which case, if the vicarious penitence of Christ is a speech-act, it is an act that both expresses penitence, and is, or brings about, an act of penance.

---

[24] For a brief discussion of speech-act theory see A. C. Grayling, *An Introduction to Philosophical Logic*, third edition (Oxford: Blackwell, 1998), pp. 226 ff. The *locus classicus* for speech-act theory is, of course, J. L. Austin's *How To Do Things With Words*, second edition (Oxford: Oxford University Press, 1975).

[25] Might Christ's act of vicarious penitence be something other than a speech-act – perhaps a private belief or set of beliefs? We do not need to express sorrow and repentance to be sorrowful or penitent. Yet one might think that it is important in the case of sin to express that penitence verbally, where this is possible. And although Christ is not a sinner, he is acting vicariously in the place of sinners. Perhaps, for this reason, it is important that he articulate that penitence on behalf of sinners. A speech-act is able to incorporate this public aspect to penitence that a privately held and non-verbalised belief cannot.

If, in a fit of passion, my daughter says something horrid to her brother, she might apologize and it may be that this penitential act constitutes sufficient reparation for her unkind words. Is her apology an act of penance as well as an act of penitence? Not clearly. Perhaps in such cases we do not demand penance as well as penitence on the part of the guilty party because penitence is thought to be sufficient. (We could enforce penance in such cases, but there is what we might call a principle of legal relaxation at work here.[26] That is, we do not *require* that, say, my daughter crawl on her knees across the drawing room to offer her contrition to my son.) But this is not the case with serious crimes like murder, a point we have already had cause to touch upon. If a murderer were to demonstrate real contrition for his or her crimes, repenting and apologizing for them, this, I suggest, would not be sufficient for atonement to take place, even if such an act were one part of reparation. Something more – some act of penance – is also needed. And, if Edwards is right, then all sin committed against God is of such seriousness that we might think it warrants some penance as well as penitence on the part of the sinner, or a vicar, in addition to penitence and contrition.

Well, then, might it be that the act of vicarious penitence offered up by the God-man is one part of a larger act of penance, which provides the missing component sufficient to atone for sin? This might seem rather counterintuitive at first blush. But if, like McLeod Campbell or P. T. Forsyth, we take the Incarnation into consideration as part of the atoning work of Christ (what classical divines called Christ's active obedience, as opposed to his passive obedience on the cross[27]), then the defender of an Edwardsian argument for non-penal substitution could claim that in order to offer up vicarious penitence, the Son of God had to humble himself and become a human being, and live a morally blameless life, of which his vicarious penitence is the culminating act. Forsyth says something similar to this at one point:

---

[26] This notion of 'legal relaxation' can be found in scholastic discussions of penal substitution. For discussion of this, see Oliver D. Crisp, 'Scholastic Theology, Augustinian Realism and Original Guilt' in the *European Journal of Theology* 13 (2004): 17–28.

[27] Compare Louis Berkhof, *Systematic Theology* (Edinburgh: Banner of Truth, 1988 [1939]), pp. 379 ff. For a standard account of this theological distinction.

> The great confession [that is, Christ's confession] was made not alone
> in the precise hour of Christ's death, although it was consummated there.
> It had to be made in life and act, and not in a mere feeling or statement;
> and for this purpose death must be organically one with the whole life.
> You cannot sever the death of Christ from the life of Christ . . . The death
> of Christ must be organic with his whole personal life and action.[28]

In other words, on this way of thinking, the Incarnation and life of
Christ is a necessary condition for his offering up vicarious penitence
that is satisfactory. This is because the Incarnation and morally blameless life of Christ, when taken together with his act of vicarious penitence, constitute *one* act of reparation and penance sufficient to atone
for the sin of fallen human beings. To this we could also add that
Christ's willingness to undergo the humiliation of the Incarnation and
the cross (*vide* Phil. 2) are part of this act of vicarious penitence.[29]
Thus, the advocate of an Edwardsian version of non-penal substitution could help him- or herself to the concept of the vicarious humanity of Christ that is a constituent of the Campbellian version of the
doctrine, in order to make sense of how it is that Christ's vicarious
action is an effective atonement for human sin.

It may be that a version of non-penal substitution could be given
which does show how Christ's vicarious action is a speech-act. In
which case, there would be no need for the Campbellian notion of
Christ's vicarious humanity to shore up the putative gap in the
Edwardsian version of the doctrine, viz. explaining how vicarious
penitence is an atoning act. This might be possible if a condition for
the 'success' of Christ's speech-act of vicarious penitence is that it is
the culmination of a life of perfect moral obedience to the will of the
Father. Then, Christ's vicarious penitence would be a complete action,
but one which requires the fulfillment of a prior condition in order for
it to be brought about. This is the case even with the example of the
wedding vow. I can only 'successfully' utter the speech-act 'I thee
wed' if the person to whom I am addressing myself is a consenting
adult who has previously agreed to become my spouse. In a similar

---

[28] Forsyth, *The Work of Christ*, p. 153. This should not be taken to imply
Forsyth would have concurred with the Edwardsian version of non-penal
substitution, only that he shared with Campbell and others the notion that
Christ's life and death are, for the purposes of the atonement, two phases
of one action.

[29] I am grateful to Paul Helm for pointing this out to me.

way, Christ's speech-act of vicarious penitence is 'successful' because he has already become Incarnate and lived a morally blameless life of obedience to the Father's will.

This, then, is an outline of two ways in which an Edwardsian version of non-penal substitution could be expressed, that we might call the *vicarious humanity version* and the *speech-act version*, respectively. How do they compare with the version of the doctrine favoured by McLeod Campbell and those that have followed his lead?

A Campbellian version of non-penal substitution

First, the *Campbellian* approach (as we might call it) supposes a rather different picture of the divine attributes than that suggested by those who defend a classical penal substitutionary theory of the atonement, such as John Owen or Jonathan Edwards (or, for that matter, defenders of satisfaction theories like Anselm of Canterbury or Thomas Aquinas). Campbell, and a number of those who have found his arguments convincing, like James Torrance, claim that the developed Calvinism of the post-Reformation period occluded the truly gracious nature of the atonement by presenting it in terms of a penal substitution, effective for the elect.[30] They argue that, according to this high Calvinist way of thinking, God's divine justice and wrath take centre-stage, and it is in terms of the penal consequences of sin that penal substitution is set up. Campbell and Torrance think this makes divine benevolence into something arbitrary. The justice of God is such that God must ensure that just deserts are meted out. But the mercy and grace of God manifest in his benevolence towards the elect is entirely capricious. It does not take account of any merit God may foresee these individuals exhibiting at some point in the future. Instead, God simply ordains the election of some, but not all of humanity – it is a sheer act of will. But, so Campbell maintained, in practice this led to a doctrine of conditional grace, whereby only those who lived a blameless life could be sure they were amongst those God had chosen as his elect. Thus, Campbell writes,

---

[30] J. B. Torrance makes this claim with particular force in 'The Incarnation and "Limited Atonement"', *The Evangelical Quarterly* 55 (1983). Paul Helm offers a response to this, 'The Logic of Limited Atonement' in *Scottish Bulletin of Evangelical Theology* 3 (1985): 47–54.

While they [viz. Edwards and Owen] set forth justice as a necessary attribute of the divine nature, so that God must deal with all men according to its requirements, they represent mercy and love as not necessary, but arbitrary, and which, therefore, may find their expression in the history of *only some* men. For according to their system justice alone is expressed in the history of all men, that is to say, in the history of the non-elect, in their endurance of punishment; in the history of the elect, in Christ's enduring of it for them. Mercy and love are expressed in the history of the elect alone. Surely, not to enter into the question of the absolute distinctness of the Divine Attributes, or their central and essential unity, if any one attribute might be expected to shine full-orbed in a revelation which testifies that 'God is love', that attribute is love.[31]

And, as James Torrance explains,

Campbell saw that fundamental to the whole issue was the doctrine of God. Instead of thinking of God as the Father, who loves all men, and who in Christ gives us the gift of sonship and who freely forgives us through Jesus Christ, they [high Calvinists like Owen or Edwards] thought of God as One whose love is conditioned by human repentance and faith, and whose forgiveness had to be purchased by the payment of the sufferings of Christ on behalf of the elect.[32]

Against this view of God, Campbell developed his idea that the incarnation and atonement show God loves human beings and, through the work of Christ, offers reconciliation to human beings.[33] As with the Edwardsian version of non-penal substitution, there are two elements to the Campbellian doctrine. First, the vicarious humanity of Christ, whereby the Son of God assumes human nature in order to live a life of moral blamelessness so that he may offer up vicarious penitence on behalf of sinful human beings. Christ's life of active obedience to the will of the Father is one part of his work that is completed in his act of vicarious penitence. And, of course, this vicarious

---

[31] Campbell, *The Nature of the Atonement, Fourth Edition* (1873), p. 54. Compare Paul Helm, 'The Logic of Limited Atonement', which gives a more thorough treatment of these issues.

[32] See Torrance, 'The Contribution of McLeod Campbell to Scottish Theology', p. 298.

[33] Campbell again: 'The atonement, I say, presupposes that there is forgiveness in God', *The Nature of the Atonement*, p. 17.

penitence is the second part of the Campbellian doctrine. Campbell maintained that the atonement has a *retrospective* as well as *prospective* aspect. The retrospective element involves deliverance by Christ from the evil of sin. The prospective component involves the good bestowed upon the sinner by the work of Christ. It is the retrospective aspect of the cross that we are particularly concerned with here. This also has two parts, according to Campbell. The first has to do with Christ dealing with *fallen human beings on behalf of God*. The second has to do with Christ dealing with *God on behalf of fallen human beings*:

> That oneness of mind with the Father, which towards men took the form of condemnation of sin, would in the Son's dealing with the Father in relation to our sins, take the form of a perfect confession of our sins. This confession, as to its own nature, must have been *a perfect Amen in humanity to the judgement of God on the sin of man*.[34]

He goes on,

> That response [i.e. Christ's] has all the elements of a perfect repentance in humanity for all of the sin of man, – a perfect sorrow – a perfect contrition – all the elements of such a repentance, and that in absolute perfection, all – excepting the personal consciousness of sin; – and by that perfect response in Amen to the mind of God in relation to sin is the wrath of God rightly met, and that is accorded to divine justice which is its due, and could alone satisfy it.[35]

What we have seen with the Edwardsian version of non-penal substitution is that a doctrine of Christ's vicarious humanity and vicarious penitence can be set forth without tinkering with a traditional account of the divine attributes. (On this basis, it would be fairly straightforward to show that a version of non-penal substitution is also consistent with a limited atonement doctrine, although, of course, this is a separate issue from the question of the relationship between non-penal substitution and the traditional account of the divine nature.[36])

---

[34] Ibid., pp. 116–117, italics original.

[35] Ibid., pp. 117–118.

[36] It is a separate issue because it someone could defend an Edwardsian account of non-penal substitution, assuming a traditional account of the divine nature, and also subscribe to some version of universalism, which, for our purposes is the notion that all human beings will finally be reconciled to God.

This is important because it means that, contrary to what Campbell and some of his followers appear to have thought, the logic of non-penal substitution is consistent with a traditional doctrine of the divine attributes and with a traditional understanding of the operation of (strong) retributive divine justice.[37]

Problems with non-penal substitution

We are now in a position to consider objections to non-penal substitution doctrines of the atonement. The first and most common criticism of non-penal substitution is that it does not answer the question of how Christ can offer a perfect vicarious penitence for sins of which he is guiltless.[38] It makes perfect sense to say that, in partial reparation for some misdemeanour I have committed, I offer an apology, because I am the guilty party. Perhaps I have accidentally disembowelled your dog in a freak gardening accident. Although an apology might not be sufficient reparation (perhaps, as Richard Swinburne suggests, penance of some kind is also required to satisfy the demands of justice) it would, nevertheless, be a good start. I have committed this misdeed and I offer my humble apologies for having done so. But Christ is not in a position to do this because he is not the offending party. He cannot confess my guilt. As P. T. Forsyth puts it, 'there is that in guilt which can only be confessed by the guilty. "I did it." That kind of confession Christ could never make.'[39]

However, it is not unheard of for one person to offer an apology on behalf of another: 'I am so very sorry about your dog' my wife might say, 'and do want to apologize on behalf of my husband – he really is quite hopeless with that chainsaw.' But such an apology, while well meaning, cannot expunge my guilt because my wife is not the guilty party (even if it does something to alleviate *my* guilt in the eyes of my neighbour).

---

[37] Of course, this presumes, with Edwards, that divine justice could be satisfied either by a punishment that deals with the penal consequences of sin, or offers up vicarious penitence for sin, a matter that is moot.

[38] This criticism is raised by, amongst others, P. T. Forsyth in *The Work of Christ*, pp. 148–149 and by Tom Smail in 'Can One Man Die for the People?' in *Atonement Today*, ed. John Goldingay (London: SPCK, 1995).

[39] Forsyth, *The Work of Christ*, p. 151. Forsyth did think Christ could confess human sin in some sense (ibid, p. 149). But it is not clear to me what this amounts to.

There are more serious cases than this, where the representative of a group, community, or even a whole country is said to offer an apology for the past misdeeds of the group (or some of the group) of which he or she is a representative. One example would be the regret expressed by the Japanese government for their part in wartime atrocities. But I think we cannot take such actions with metaphysical seriousness. They have to do with the observation of diplomatic convention, or perhaps of international etiquette, or courtesy. Real regret is surely offered in many such cases; I am not denying that. But the representative of any group, or nation cannot literally offer an apology for sinful actions committed by some members of the community he or she represents, if by apology is meant a real act of contrition and repentance for past sin. The reason is simple: the representative is not guilty of that sin. He or she may be able to offer an apology in these terms if he or she is part of one metaphysical entity whose constituents comprise the representative and the members of the community or group that have committed the crime for which the apology is offered. But most people, even most theologians, will baulk at this requirement for vicarious penitence. Yet, unless some such metaphysical argument can be had, such representatives are not the parties guilty for the crimes in question, and the apology he or she offers cannot satisfy the demands of justice that such crimes require. What is more to the point, for such an apology to have purchase, the representative offering the apology would have to be in a position to act as a substitute for the offender. But to offer a real apology on behalf of the guilty party that expunges that guilt, one would have to be the guilty party, or be one part of an entity that also included the guilty party. It seems to me that this has to be the case because guilt is not something that is transferable from one person to another, as Forsyth too seems to believe.

Now, an advocate of non-penal substitution might respond to this criticism in one of several ways. First, she might say that Christ's vicarious penitence does not require the assumption of my guilt. Like penal substitution, in this particular respect, non-penal substitution only requires that God acts *as if* Christ were confessing my sin and guilt in vicarious penitence. In other words, at the heart of non-penal substitution, as with traditional versions of penal substitution, there is a divinely ordained fiction, according to which Christ's vicarious action is treated for the purposes of atonement as if it was my action, thereby atoning for my sin. God imputes Christ's act to me, and my sin to Christ. But this only avoids the problem with guilt at the very considerable cost of admitting that the vicarious act Christ performs on my behalf is not really my act at all. And I suggest this is a very real problem because it means that, strictly speaking, neither my sin, nor my guilt, is actually atoned for. Treating someone as if they were guilty of murder is not the same as finding that the person in question is the murderer. And treating Christ as if he were offering reparation for my sin is not the same as offering reparation for my sin. I suggest that the former would not be just, whereas the latter would be.

Alternatively, the advocate of non-penal substitution could concede the point about guilt and argue that Christ is *really* the guilty party. That is, God somehow brings it about that Christ and all fallen humanity (or all of fallen humanity Christ saves, if this is some number less than the total number of fallen human beings) are constituted by God one metaphysical entity (for the purposes of atoning for sin).[40] Then, Christ is able to act as a vicar because he is really part of the whole entity comprising fallen human beings (or the elect part thereof) that God ordains to save. We might call this a *realist version of non-penal substitution*, since, like the doctrine of Augustinian realism, it assumes God can gerrymander entities for certain purposes, such as the transmission of sin from Adam to his progeny (in the case of Augustinian realism), or the atonement (in the case of this version of non-penal substitution).[41] Although there is not the space to flesh this out here, I suggest that this realist version of Edwardsian non-penal substitution may succeed where the fictionalist account does not (the fictionalist account being one where God acts as if Christ were the guilty party, as he does in the case of traditional accounts of penal substitution).

This brings us to a second objection to non-penal substitution. Even if a realist version of non-penal substitution is able to overcome the

---

[40] This would require a metaphysical argument taking in issues like the identity-across-time of particular objects. But we cannot go into that here. For those that are metaphysically minded, this sort of realist argument would require some version of perdurantism or stage theory about persisting objects. Two recent texts on this are Theodore Sider, *Four Dimensionalism: An Ontology of Persistence and Time* (Oxford: Oxford University Press, 2001), ch. 1 and Katherine Hawley, *How Things Persist* (Oxford: Oxford University Press, 2001), passim.

[41] Interestingly, for our purposes, this sort of argument would fit with some aspects of what Jonathan Edwards says about the imputation of sin and persistence through time. See Jonathan Edwards, *Original Sin, The Works of Jonathan Edwards Volume 3*, ed. Clyde A. Holbrook (New Haven: Yale University Press, 1970).

question of guilt, it is not clear why the cross is necessary for the atonement at all, according to some versions of non-penal substitution. Recall the speech-act version of Edwardsian non-penal substitution. On that version of the doctrine, if Christ's act of vicarious penitence is truly an atoning work, then why does Christ need to die? It is not his death that is the atoning act, on this view, but his vicarious penitence. But then, the cross is otiose: Christ could perform an act of vicarious penitence without needing to die on the cross. In fact, Christ could have performed his act of vicarious penitence without having to die *at all*. Robert Letham thinks that similar things can be said of Campbell's doctrine, which 'leaves us with the overwhelming centre of the Christian faith (the cross) as little more than a frightening charade.'[42] This, I suggest, is a very serious problem for versions of non-penal substitution, including the speech-act version of the Edwardsian view, that do not have a sufficiently strong understanding of the vicarious humanity of Christ. But it may not be a problem for the vicarious humanity version of the Edwardian account, because the vicarious humanity of Edwardsian doctrine does include the idea that Christ's vicarious penitence is of a piece with his vicarious humanity, and this includes not only his morally blameless life (a prerequisite for his being able to atone for sinners), but also the humiliation and death on the cross. On this sort of view the cross is taken up as the culmination of Christ's vicarious penitence. So, at least one version of non-penal substitution is able to overcome this problem.

A third objection is closely related to the previous two. It has to do with whether vicarious penitence can be an act of atonement at all. Earlier, in the context of outlining the Edwardsian argument for non-penal substitution, I argued that, given a certain way of thinking about the relationship between Christ's vicarious humanity and his vicarious penitence, the Edwardsian doctrine might satisfy all four components of atonement outlined by Swinburne (that is, repentance, apology, reparation, and penance). But, it might be argued, what non-penal substitution cannot do is explain *how* the penal consequences pertaining to the sin of fallen human beings is dealt with by the atoning work of Christ.

Perhaps such an objection merely begs the question: of course non-penal substitution does not deal with the penal consequences of sin; it offers an alternative to penal substitution that does not require that the penal consequences of sin be dealt with. But if this is the case, then

---

[42] Robert Letham, *The Work of Christ*, p. 170.

non-penal substitution actually implies a different account of divine justice to that given by defenders of penal substitution. Specifically, it must allow that, under certain conditions, and for certain acts, God may forgive sin without the penal consequences for that sin having been atoned for. God can accept Christ's vicarious humanity and penitence as sufficient without additional satisfaction for the penal consequences of human sin. This means amending the strong version of divine retributive justice with which we began. The defender of non-penal substitution might just opt for the weaker view instead, which stipulates only that divine justice does not require forgiveness. This leaves the door open for the idea that God may forgive fallen human beings their sins if Christ offers an adequate vicarious penitence. But it also suffers from the same debilitating problems affecting this weaker view of divine retribution, to do with the fact that if God could have created a world where he simply forgave all sin – and this is just – such a world would be objectively morally superior to this one (presuming this is a world where that state of affairs does not obtain).

But this is not the only avenue open to the advocate of non-penal substitution. One alternative is to opt for a strong version of divine retribution, but deny that there is only one *manner* in which satisfaction for sin can be offered. This was exactly the direction in which I suggested the Edwardsian argument might go. But this still requires some explanation of how it is that the nature of divine justice requires satisfaction for sin, while the mode of satisfaction may vary. It might seem curious to think that Christ's vicarious humanity and penitence may serve as adequate atonement for human sin that is infinitely heinous (if we follow Edwards on this point), whereas the contrition and apology of a mass murderer does not. But this superficial similarity between the two cases obscures significant differences. The contrition and confession of a mass murderer does not include adequate reparation and penance for that sin. But, on the Edwardsian non-penal substitutionary view, Christ's atonement does. In fact, on the Edwardsian view, Christ's life and death are two parts of one act of vicarious penitence that is a substitution for sin that is penitential, not penal in nature, but which deals with the penal consequences of sin. There is nothing about the logic of non-penal substitution that prevents advocates of the doctrine from claiming this, provided we distinguish between the *nature of the atoning act* of Christ from the *nature of what is atoned for*. The penal consequences of sin are atoned for (on the Edwardsian view, and, perhaps the Campbellian too). But the nature of that atoning work is not penal, though it is substitutionary. So I suggest that this third objection can be met by a defender of the vicarious humanity version of an Edwardsian non-penal substitutionary view of the atonement.

Conclusion

We have seen that McLeod Campbell was right to suggest Edwards' thinking on the atonement lent itself either to a doctrine of penal substitution or a doctrine of vicarious penitence. In fact, an Edwardsian account of non-penal substitution can be set forth which retains a traditional understanding of (a strong version of) divine retributive justice, and maintains that Christ's atoning work incorporates both his vicarious humanity and work of vicarious penitence into one theanthropic work of atonement. This Edwardsian doctrine also enables us to see that not all the components of the Campbellian version of non-penal substitution are essential to the logic of the doctrine. Although, like McLeod Campbell, one could take Edwards' ruminations on the nature of the atonement in the direction of a revised doctrine of the divine nature, the Edwardsian version of non-penal substitution does not require this. So a defender of non-penal substitution need not reject a classical account of the divine attributes, and in particular, a strong version of divine retributive justice.[43] But the success of the Edwardsian version of the doctrine also has another consequence: it may offer a robust account of the atonement that avoids certain problems that beset traditional arguments for penal accounts of substitution (to do with the fact that traditional accounts of penal substitution involve a 'legal fiction'). It may be that a version of the Edwardsian doctrine of non-penal substitution succeeds on this score, where traditional accounts of penal substitution do not.

---

[43] I have not given a defence of the strong version of divine retributive punishment here and a complete account of an Edwardsian version of non-penal substitution would have to do so. Thus, it might be better to say that a defender of non-penal substitution need not reject a classical account of the divine attributes and in particular, a strong version of divine retribution *provided a coherent, plausible account of both of these doctrines can be provided* – as I think they can. For more on this matter, see Crisp, 'Divine Retribution: A Defence'.

CHAPTER SIX

On Karl Barth's Denial of Universalism

> The story is indeed a little difficult to believe.
> Still you might try.
> – E. Nesbit, The Phoenix and The Carpet

It is notorious among theologians that Karl Barth defends doctrines of election and atonement that appear to lead to universalism, but that Barth steadfastly maintained did not lead to universalism. As Jüngel records it, Barth emphatically claimed, 'I do teach it (universalism), but I also do not teach it.'[1] There have been many who are willing to defend Barth in this matter. For instance, John Colwell claims that:

> [I]f some of Barth's critics refuse to take this divine freedom seriously with respect (especially) to Barth's doctrine of election and consequently suspect him of implicit universalism then it is their problem rather than his and probably says more about them than it says about him.[2]

Similar views can be found among other Barthians both present and past. Thus, for example, Joseph Bettis says that 'for Barth, one can

---

[1] Eberhard Jüngel, *Karl Barth: A Theological Legacy*, trans. Garrett E. Paul (Philadelphia: Westminster Press, 1986), pp. 44–45. Compare also *Church Dogmatics* IV/3, eds. Geoffrey W. Bromiley and Thomas F. Torrance (Edinburgh: T&T Clark, 1958), pp. 477–478. Hereinafter, CD, followed by volume, part volume and pagination.

[2] John Colwell, 'The Contemporaneity of the Divine Decision: Reflections on Barth's Denial of Universalism' in Nigel Cameron, ed. *Universalism and the Doctrine of Hell* (Carlisle: Paternoster, 1992), p. 160.

reject both Arminianism and double predestination without having to accept universalism.'[3]

However, there have also been those voices raised in opposition to this view. For instance, Hans Urs von Balthasar says:

> It is clear from Barth's presentation of the doctrine of election that universal salvation is not only possible but inevitable. The only definitive reality is grace, and any condemnatory judgement has to be merely provisional.[4]

Similarly, G. C. Berkouwer observes that:

> In original universalism, the issue is a universal offer because Christ died for all, and election remains in the background for the moment. But with Barth, Christ's death touches precisely upon the election of all, which election has become manifest in Christ's death. The universality of the message is no longer at odds with the fact of election, for it is based on the universality of election.[5]

Even Geoffrey Bromiley, one of the translators of Barth's *Church Dogmatics* into English, and a theologian sympathetic to Barth's account of election, nevertheless closes his own overview of Barth's doctrine of election with these words: 'The ambivalence at this decisive point – will all be saved or not, and if not, why not? – by no means outweighs the solid merits of Barth's presentation.'[6]

So what is the logic of Barth's position? Does his view yield a version of universalism or not? In this chapter, I will attempt to show that Barth's doctrines of election and atonement do indeed yield a version of universalism, despite the protestations of both Barth and his defenders to the contrary.

---

[3] Joseph D. Bettis, 'Is Karl Barth a Universalist?' in *Scottish Journal of Theology* 20 (1967): 423. Compare George Hunsinger, *How to Read Karl Barth* (Oxford: Oxford University Press, 1991), p. 132.

[4] Hans Urs von Balthasar, *The Theology of Karl Barth*, trans. John Drury (New York: Holt Rinehart and Winston, 1971), p. 163.

[5] G. C. Berkouwer, *Divine Election*, trans. Hugo Bekker (Grand Rapids: Eerdmans, 1960), p. 229.

[6] Geoffrey W. Bromiley, *The Theology of Karl Barth* (Grand Rapids: Eerdmans, 1979), p. 97.

Barth's doctrine of atonement and election

The argument depends upon a number of theological terms pertaining to universalism that it might be helpful to explain at the outset. First, I take it that the term 'universalism' refers to a family of similar views which share in common the notion that all humanity will be saved by God. None will be finally damned to hell. In the current literature these different versions of universalism have been categorized into two groups: necessary and contingent universalism. Necessary universalism is the view that it is not just true, but *necessarily* true that all humanity will end up in heaven. By contrast, contingent universalism states that, although a human being *could* be consigned to hell, as a matter of contingent fact no one *will* end up there.[7]

Second, I will use the terms 'elect' and 'reprobate' to refer to two non-overlapping groups of humanity. The former term denotes that group which God decrees to save; the latter that group which God decrees to damn.

With these clarifications in mind, let us turn to Barth himself. I take it that Barth's denial of universalism depends upon his doctrines of election and atonement in particular. In the argument that follows, I will show that Barth's denial of universalism is either disingenuous (he was a universalist) or just plain muddled (his position is not coherent). There is a third option: that Barth did not see the logical implications of his position. However, this seems unlikely, so I will ignore it. Either result means Barth's denial is false.

The argument depends on two assumptions:

A1. There is a domain of moral agents comprising all human agents.

I will not comment on the fate of angelic moral agents, if there are any. Nor is the subject of angelic moral agents one which Barth touches upon in any great detail with respect to his doctrine of election (as opposed to his doctrine of creation, where he has a lot to say on the subject). In common with the Augustinian tradition, Barth appears to believe that the question of the fate of demonic angelic agents is a separate issue from that of human moral agents.

---

[7] See Jonathan L. Kvanvig, *The Problem of Hell* (New York: Oxford University Press, 1993), p. 74 for these distinctions.

A2. By Christ's death atonement is procured for the sin and guilt of those for whom he died.

Barth clearly does believe this. However, I will not discuss the mechanism by which Christ's atonement is achieved according to Barth. All the argument requires is that his death brings about the atonement for sin required for those who are elect-in-Christ.

First, I will set out Barth's argument for atonement. This can be found in passages from the *Church Dogmatics* like the following:

> The rejection which all men incurred, the wrath under which all men lie, the death which all men must die, God in his love for men transfers from all eternity to him in whom he loves and elects them, and whom he elects at their head and in their place.[8]

And:

> For if God Himself became man, this man [i.e. Christ], what else can this mean but that He declared Himself guilty of the contradiction against Himself in which man was involved; that He submitted Himself to the law of creation by which such a contradiction could be accompanied only by loss and destruction; that He made Himself the object of the wrath and judgment to which man had brought himself; that he took upon Himself the rejection which man had deserved; that he tasted Himself the damnation, death and hell which ought to have been the portion of fallen man? . . . If we could know what it was that God elected for Himself when He elected fellowship with man, then we can answer only that He elected our rejection. He made it His own. He bore and suffered it with all its most bitter consequences.[9]

---

[8] CD II/2, p. 123. In commenting on this passage, Colin Gunton observes that 'the cross is a substitutionary bearing by God in Christ of God's rejection of human sin. Barth can speak of the one rejected, because through Jesus' rejection the rejection that the human race has merited is taken away.' Colin Gunton, 'Salvation' in John Webster, ed. *The Cambridge Companion to Karl Barth* (Cambridge: Cambridge University Press, 2000), p. 145. For a more critical account of Barth's doctrine of atonement, see Garry Williams 'Karl Barth and the doctrine of the atonement' in David Gibson and Daniel Strange, eds. *Engaging with Barth: Contemporary Evangelical Critiques* (New York: T&T Clark, 2008), pp. 232–272.

[9] CD II/2, p. 164.

We can express his argument for the atonement of Christ in the following way:

1. Given A1 and A2, Christ's death atones for the sin of all human agents.

By this Barth seems to mean that,

2. Christ's death is sufficient and efficient for all human agents.

That is, Christ's death is not simply potentially universal in scope (it could save all humanity); it is actually universal in scope (all humanity are saved by it). It might be argued that Barth's position is merely that the atonement is universal in scope, not effectiveness. However, that Barth's position does involve a universally efficient atonement can be seen from passages such as the following:

> There is no-one who does not participate in Him [Christ] in His turning to God. There is no-one who is not . . . engaged in this turning. There is no-one who is not raised and exalted with Him to true humanity. 'Jesus Christ lives, and I with Him.'[10]

We shall return to this issue at a later point. For the present, let us assume that Barth does endorse something like (2) above. From here we move to:

3. This work is completed at the cross.
4. This work is appropriated not via the traditional Reformation formula, 'If you repent and believe, you will be saved; if you do not repent and believe, you will not be saved', but by agents coming to realize that 'this is what God in Jesus Christ has done for your sake. Therefore repent and believe.'[11]

This raises a question. It is this: if the atonement is universally effective, according to Barth, then how does this tie into his doctrine of

---

[10] CD II/2, p. 271.

[11] See CD II/2, p. 317 ff. The two citations are from George Hunsinger's *How to Read Karl Barth*, p. 130. Hunsinger points out the unconditional nature of the Barthian formula, observing, 'since, in Barth's understanding, God has already freely included us [in salvation], it falls to us henceforth freely to receive our inclusion as the gift it is proclaimed to be.' Ibid., pp. 130–131.

election? To answer this, let us lay out Barth's doctrine of election in brief. This aspect of Barth's theology can be found in passages such as the following:

> This, then, is the message with which the elect community (as the circumference of the elect man, Jesus of Nazareth) has to approach every man – the promise, that he, too, is an elect man. It is fully aware of his perverted choice. It is fully aware of his godlessness . . . It is fully aware, too, of the eternal condemnation of the man who is isolated over against God, which is unfailingly exhibited by the godlessness of every such man . . . It knows of the wrath and judgment and punishment of God in which the rejection of the man isolated over and against God takes its course . . . It knows that God, by the decree He made in the beginning of all His works and ways, has taken upon Himself the rejection merited by the man isolated in relation to Him; and on the basis of this decree of His the only truly rejected man is His own Son; that God's rejection has taken its course and been fulfilled and reached its goal, with all that that involves, against this One, so that it can no longer fall on other men or be their concern. The concern of other men is still the sin and guilt of their godlessness – and it is serious and severe enough. Their concern is still the suffering of the existence which they have prepared for themselves by their godlessness (in the shadow of that which the One has suffered for them) – and it is bitter enough to have to suffer this existence. Their concern is still to be aware of the threat of their rejection. But it cannot now be their concern to suffer the execution of this threat, to suffer the eternal damnation which their godlessness deserves. Their desire and their undertakings are pointless in so far as their only end can be to make them rejected. And this is the very goal which the godless cannot reach, because it has already been taken away by the eternally decreed offering of the Son of God to suffer in place of the godless, and cannot any longer be their goal.[12]

---

[12] CD II/2, pp. 318–319. Of this view Bruce McCormack has recently commented, '[t]aken on the most superficial level, the revolution which Barth effected in the Reformed understanding of predestination was to replace Calvin's version of double predestination with a universal election . . . Jesus Christ is the Subject of election and its Object, the electing God and the elected human. That is the fundamental thesis which shapes the whole of Barth's doctrine of election.' From 'Grace and Being: The Role of God's Gracious Election in Karl Barth's Theological Ontology' in John Webster, ed. *The Cambridge Companion to Karl Barth*, p. 93.

We can express what Barth says about election thus:

5.   Christ is the Elect One. (That is, the set of the elect comprises one
     member, Christ.)
6.   Christ is the Reprobate One. (That is, the set of the reprobate com-
     prises one member, Christ.)

In this way, Barth's doctrine fuses the so-called 'double decree' of
Calvinism in the person of Christ, who is both the Elect and the
Reprobate One. But the way in which this is applied to the set of
human agents is asymmetrical.

7.   All human agents are elect only in a derivative sense of having a
     saving relation to the set of the elect and it single member, Christ.

And:

8.   The sin of all human agents is atoned for by Christ, the Reprobate
     One, who is the only member of the set of the reprobate.

Rather than (8), it might be tempting to construe Barth as saying
something more like:

8*. All human agents are reprobate only in the derivative sense of
     having a relation to the set of the reprobate and its single member,
     Christ.

But this would entail:

9.   All human agents are simultaneously members of the sets 'elect-
     in-Christ' and 'reprobate-in-Christ'.

And this is incoherent. For then, all humanity would be derivatively
elect and reprobate simultaneously, and, presumably, co-terminously.
This would be absurd, of course. (Compare the idea that someone
could simultaneously be both an associate member and a non-associ-
ate member of a country club.) I suggest that Barth must mean (8)
rather than (8*), in order for his argument to make sense. Let us proceed on this assumption. Then, given (8), we have:

9*. All human agents are members of the set 'elect-in-Christ'.

On this understanding of Barth's doctrine of election, the relation between election and reprobation is asymmetrical. Christ takes on the sin of all humanity, becoming the Reprobate One, whose death atones for that sin, and Christ is also the Elect One whose death brings about the (derivative) election of all humanity.

The problem with this is that it seems to entail some form of universalism. But a universalism of what kind? This depends on Barth's understanding of, among other things, free will. And it is not entirely clear whether Barth wishes to endorse a compatibilist notion of free will, or a libertarian notion of free will. Since much hangs on whether Barth holds one or other of these positions, let us define them as follows:

C1. According to compatibilism, freedom of choice means being able to actualize what one desires. More precisely, a subject S is free with respect to any action A if S desires to perform A.

L1. According to libertarianism, freedom of choice means being able to refrain from an action. More precisely, a subject S is free with respect to an action A if S could have refrained from performing A.[13]

The (C1) definition of compatibilism means that human freedom is compatible with divine determination, whereas, on the libertarian definition of (L1), it is not. Let us apply these two views to Barth. Take, for example, the following passage from his Table Talk:

> The decisive point is whether freedom in the Christian sense is identical with the freedom of Hercules: choice between two ways at a crossroad. This is a heathen notion of freedom. Is it freedom to decide for the devil? The only freedom that means something is the freedom to be myself as I am created by God. God did not create a neutral creature, but his creature. He placed him in a garden that he might build it up; his freedom is to do that. When man began to discern good and evil, this knowledge was the beginning of sin. Man should not have asked this question about good and evil, but should have remained in true created freedom. We are confused by the political idea of freedom. What is the light in the Statue of Liberty? Freedom to choose good and evil? What light that would be! Light is light and

---

[13] I owe these definitions to Myron Penner.

not darkness. If it shines darkness is done away with, not proposed
for choice! Being a slave of Christ means being free.[14]

It is not clear from passages like this what position Barth endorses
with respect to freedom of the will. So, in order to clarify the logic of
Barth's position, we shall set out two models of Barth's view, the first
of which is commensurate with compatibilism, and the second of
which is commensurate with libertarianism. Neither of these options
is consistent with Barth's denial of universalism.

If Barth is a compatibilist then it follows that, given the foregoing:

10. All human agents are necessarily (and derivatively) elect-in-
    Christ, the Elect One, by virtue of his universally efficient atone-
    ment.

This seems the most straightforward way to understand the compat-
ibility of (1)–(4) and (5) – (8) with (9'). Barth claims, however, that his
views are not universalistic. Instead, he seems to believe something
like the following conjunction:

10'. All human agents are elect-in-Christ, the Elect One, by virtue of
    his universally efficient atonement, and:
11. A human agent may reject Christ, and may, ultimately, not be
    saved.

This seems fallacious. For, given (1) – (4) and (5) – (8) and (9'):

12. If a human agent is a member of the set 'elect-in-Christ', then a
    human agent will inevitably be numbered among those who are
    saved.

This, once again, yields a version of universalism. Perhaps another
way of looking at Barth might not result in the same problem. Let us
try a different tack. Barth has already allowed that:

i. Christ's atonement is universal in scope and efficacy (from
   (1)–(4)).

---

[14] Karl Barth, *Table Talk* ed. John D. Godsey, Scottish Journal of Theology
Occasional Papers No. 10 (Edinburgh: Oliver and Boyd, 1963), p. 37.

ii. Christ is the Elect One and therefore the sole member of the set 'elect', in whom all human agents are elected (from (5)–(8) and (9˚)).

iii. Christ is the Elect One whose atonement for the sin of human agents is universal in scope and efficacy, and all human agents are members of the set 'elect-in-Christ'.

The problem is that this appears to mean that all the members of the set 'elect-in-Christ' will be saved, since it is not possible that the Elect One's atonement will not be effective for all members of the set 'elect-in-Christ'.

But why is this so? Because, as previously noted, Christ's death is not merely *potentially* effective, according to Barth (as it is for, say, traditional Arminians). It is actually effective for all human agents. This understanding of Barth is reflected in the fact that he labours the point that (according to (4)), the appropriation by a human agent of the benefits of Christ's death now is a matter of coming to realize that one is already saved, and in the light of that knowledge, turning from sin to salvation. (Recall also, Barth's claim that the attempt to reject God is pointless since, 'this is the very goal which the godless cannot reach, because it has already been taken away by the eternally decreed offering of the Son of God to suffer in the place of the godless, and cannot any longer be their goal.'[15])

Therefore, on Barth's account, Christ's atonement is both universal in scope and efficacy, and potentially and actually universally effective. But if Christ's atonement is like this, and if election is in Christ, the Elect One, then there are no reprobate humans. For on such a view, God has decreed the election and reprobation of Christ; the atonement by Christ's death; and that the atonement be actually, universally effective for all human agents. This seems to require theological determinism as its concomitant. But Barth wants to affirm (11), which appears to reflect libertarianism.

So it seems, logically speaking, that he cannot affirm both (10˚) and (11) without incurring a contradiction. From what we have just seen of Barth's position, either all are (derivatively) elect in Christ, whose atonement is universally effective, and this is decreed by God, or it is only potentially universal in scope and agents are free not to opt into God's saving work in Christ. Barth denies that his own position entails the first conditional here. But even the second

---

[15] CD II/2, p. 319, cited above.

conditional cannot work, because Barth has already conceded that Christ's election as the Elect One means that all human agents are elect in Christ. They are not merely potentially elect, or some such conditional, depending on the free choice of each individual agent. If all are elect in Christ, then no meaning can be given to the affirmation of (11).

That is, on the libertarian reading of Barth's argument, what he says appears incoherent. So Barth is caught on the horns of a dilemma – call it, *the universalism dilemma*. Either his view is a species of necessary universalism, via theological determinism, which is the view that, necessarily, all people will be brought to salvation. In which case, Barth's view is coherent. Or, his position is a species of contingent universalism, via libertarianism – the view according to which, as a matter of contingent fact, all people will be saved – in which case his view is incoherent. Either way, his position does not appear to be consistent with his denial of universalism.

However, there is one other way in which Barth could be understood on this matter. It could be that Barth believes in a universal atonement that is not efficient for all humanity. Then he might be able to pass through the horns of the universalism dilemma like this:

10*. All human agents are elect-in-Christ, the Elect One, by virtue of his universally unconditional atonement, and
11*. A human agent may deny Christ's atonement, and may ultimately not be saved.

Barth seems to suggest at certain points in the *Church Dogmatics* that the atonement may be universal in scope as far as human agents are concerned, and yet be opted out of by those self-same human agents. For instance:

> If he [the believer] believes in Him, he knows and grasps his own righteousness as one which is alien to him, as the righteousness of this other, who is justified man in his place, for him. He will miss his own righteousness, he will fall far from it, if he thinks he can and should know and grasp and realize it in his own acts and achievements, or in his faith and the result of it. He will be jeopardizing, indeed he will already have lost, the forgiveness of his sins, his life as a child of God, his hope of eternal life, if he ever thinks he can and should seek and find these things anywhere but at the place where as the act and work of God they are real as the forgiveness of his sins,

as his divine sonship, as his hope, anywhere but in the one Jesus Christ.[16]

Passages such as this appear to mean that Christ's death applies unconditionally to every human being, such that all human beings are justified (as per (4)). Propositions (10**) and (4) together mean that the atonement is still applied to a particular human agent on the condition that it has not been consciously refrained from by that particular human agent.

This, however, will not work as a solution to the universalism dilemma Barth faces, for two reasons. First, it is not clear what this view means. Barth does not mean simply that the atonement is universal in scope (potentially all human agents could be saved), but not necessarily in its effect (actually, not all human agents are saved, because they have libertarian freedom and some choose not to be saved). This looks like a traditional Arminian view of the atonement. Instead, he means something more like this. The atonement applies unconditionally to all humanity, such that all humanity is justified before God, but, given (4), the atonement is only applied on the condition that it has not been consciously refrained from, or opted out of, by a human agent. The problem here is that this is not a solution to the universalism dilemma that is any more coherent than the alternatives already outlined. For, if this is Barth's position, then a person can be both derivatively elect in Christ, such that their sins are atoned for by Christ, whose death has already justified them before God (as per (4)), and, at the same time, be able to opt out of this justification and election in Christ. But this appears, *prima facie*, to be contradictory. For how can a person be both justified and (derivatively) elect, and yet be able to reject that status?

There are two potential strengths to Barth's position here. He could mean that, (a) a person might be justified and derivatively elect at one moment, and reject that status at the next. Or, he could mean that (b) a person can be in a state where they are both justified and rejected simultaneously. But how could a person be both justified and rejected at one and the same time? This seems to be confused, if not incoherent. To illustrate: it would be a strange state of affairs indeed if a subject was ennobled by her king, and given a place of prominence at court, and *at the same time* turned out of the court, and banished from the realm. But this is what (b) amounts to.

---

[16] *CD* IV/1, p. 631. I am grateful to Myron Penner for drawing my attention to this reference.

Nor does (a) fare any better. The problem with (a) is that it makes for a strange doctrine of election if one can opt out of election, and the status it confers on an individual, at any moment. What is more, this does not seem compatible with Barth's position as laid out in (5)–(8) and (9').

Secondly, this does not seem to be in agreement with what Barth says elsewhere about the pointlessness of persisting in rebelling against God, when one's election is secure (as per CD II/2, p. 319). If a person's election is guaranteed in such a way that any rebellion against that election is a pointless exercise, it is not clear what Barth can mean by saying, in addition to this, that election is conditional. But, from what we have seen, he does appear to make both of these statements in his *Church Dogmatics*.

So, this attempted solution to the universalism dilemma will not work. The dilemma remains intact.

Barth's way out?

Barth himself seems to realize the logic of his own position and retreats from its consequences. Despite his comments on the scope of election and reprobation that we noted earlier, he says, 'Even though theological consistency might seem to lead our thoughts and utterances most clearly in this direction,' that is, in the direction of universalism, 'we must not arrogate to ourselves that which can be given and received only as a free gift.'[17] In commenting on this, Joseph Bettis maintains that this is the reason why those who understand Barth's position to be universalistic have fundamentally misunderstood him. 'They contend', he says,

> that while Barth has allowed for temporary estrangement, he has excluded the possibility of permanent rejection through his insistence on the completeness of the atonement of Jesus Christ. Barth's reply is clear. The threat of eternal rejection remains a real threat.[18]

But far from being an adequate reply to his critics, Barth's response appears to be simply the recognition that his own views would, if he were 'theologically consistent', lead in the direction of universalism.

---

[17] CD IV/3, p. 477.
[18] Bettis, 'Is Karl Barth a Universalist?', p. 433.

Barth, however, is happy to withhold this requirement of theological consistency, because he deems that such a move would compromise divine freedom. (Recall his reference to receiving grace as a 'free gift', above.) Bettis is even willing to go as far as to say, 'Barth does not reject universalism because the future of the pagan is uncertain. He rejects universalism because the future of all men is uncertain.'[19] But if this is true, then Barth's attempted way out, via divine freedom, yields a contradiction. We can express this as follows, using propositions (i)–(iii) given earlier:

i. Christ's atonement is universal in scope and efficacy (from (1)–(4)).
ii. Christ is the Elect One and therefore the sole member of the set 'elect', in whom all human agents are elected (from (5)–(7)).
iii. Christ is the Elect One whose atonement for the sin of human agents is universal in scope and efficacy, and all human agents are members of the set 'elect-in-Christ'.

But what Barth is claiming at this juncture in his argument is something like this:

iv. Because God is free, the eschatological destiny of all humanity is uncertain.

The problem is that (iv) simply does not appear to be consistent with (i)–(iii). In fact, it seems to contradict (i)–(iii). One cannot consistently hold both that all humanity have been (derivatively) elected, so that all their sin has been efficaciously atoned for by Christ, *and* that the soteriological status of all humanity is uncertain. Similarly, one cannot hold both that all Conservative Party candidates fielded have been elected to Parliament, so that they may all return to their offices in the Palace of Westminster, and that the future candidacy of all Conservative Party parliamentary candidates fielded is uncertain. Either their future candidacy is uncertain, or it is not. If they have been returned to Parliament, then their future candidacy simply cannot be uncertain.[20] Similarly, either the question of whether all

---

[19] Ibid.

[20] Of course, a parliamentary candidate who has been returned to Parliament might withdraw from his position, or may withdraw at some later date. But that is beside the point. My claim here is about the

humanity is (derivatively) elect and efficaciously atoned for by Christ is uncertain, or it is not. If all humanity have been (derivatively) elected and efficaciously atoned for by Christ (as per (i)–(iii)), then their soteriological status simply cannot be uncertain, as per (iv). This seems fatal to the consistency of Barth's position.

(cont.) consistency of saying the future candidacy of a particular Conservative MP is *at one and the same time* a settled question (he has been returned to Parliament) and an open question (it is not clear whether this MP has retained his seat or not). Whether that MP, having been re-elected, then withdraws or not, is a separate issue.

PART III

THE CHRISTIAN LIFE

CHAPTER SEVEN

John Calvin and Petitioning God

Prayer is an offering up of our desires unto God, for things
agreeable to his will, in the name of Christ, with
confession of our sins, and thankful acknowledgment
of his mercies.
– Westminster Shorter Catechism, *Answer to Question 98*

John Calvin's discussion of prayer in the final edition of his
Institutes is second only to the chapter on faith in length. It is situat-
ed immediately prior to his discussion of divine election in Book
Three. And in it, he has much to say that is of value in contemporary
discussion of the theology of prayer. Calvin deals with a range of
issues clustered around prayer as petition and prayer as thanksgiving, and ends up with a careful exposition of the Lord's Prayer as a
pattern for the Christian life – an earlier version of which can be
traced right back to the first edition of the *Institutes* in 1536. In this
chapter I will not attempt to expound Calvin's doctrine of prayer as
a whole, or as it developed in the different editions of the *Institutes*.
Instead, I will focus on one besetting problem for petitionary prayer
or impetration (I shall use the two terms interchangeably). This has
to do with whether or not such prayer is pointless or redundant
given the nature and purposes of God. At first glance, such a concern may seem rather more narrowly philosophical than the sort of
issues Calvin is engaged with in the *Institutes*, his biblical commentaries, or even his controversial works. However, this issue raises
important pastoral and practical concerns for a theology of the
Christian life. What is more, the specific form of Calvin's doctrine
makes the concern about the apparent redundancy of impetration
particularly pressing. For these reasons, the resources Calvin's doctrine can bring to bear on this particular problem with what we
might call the metaphysics of impetration actually serve the sort of

practical purpose with which Calvin's theology is deeply concerned.[1]

The argument falls into three parts. In the first, I situate the
Calvinian doctrine within a broader account of the doctrine of God.[2] I
then consider what a Calvinian notion of impetration amounts to. In
the course of this scene-setting section, I introduce the pointlessness
problem. The second section examines the contribution Calvin makes
to the resolution of this problem, as part of his doctrine of prayer. The
third section offers a defence of a Calvinian doctrine of impetration
against the pointlessness problem.

Three problems for impetration

a. Situating the Calvinian doctrine

If God is essentially omniscient, he knows all that will come to pass.
(*How* he knows all that will come to pass was not a problem Calvin
seems particularly concerned with.) To co-opt the language of
scholastic theology for a moment, via his natural knowledge God
knows all that is necessary and possible at all possible worlds.
And via his free knowledge, he knows all that will happen in this
world, the world that obtains as a consequence of God's creative

---

[1] Charles Partee observes that Calvin treats prayer as a given rather than a
problematic. 'Nevertheless, if Calvin is not regarded as developing a *complete* doctrine of prayer, his teaching on the subject seems to constitute a
distinctive view which may be called, not improperly, a doctrine.' 'Prayer
as the Practice of Predestination' in Wilhelm H. Neusner ed., *Calvinus
Servus Christi* (Budapest: Presseabteilung des Raday Kollegiums, 1988), p.
246. I will be treating impetration as a problem, using Calvin's doctrine to
see whether it has the resources to overcome the apparent pointlessness of
petitioning God. This is not improper because, as I shall argue, Calvin
presents a distinctive doctrinal contribution to a theology of prayer that
has an important bearing on the question of the pointlessness of impetration.

[2] In this paper I use the term 'Calvinian' to designate any view that takes
up the particular concerns of Calvin himself. This seems preferable to
'Calvinist' which is a broader term, associated with the theological tradition that looks to Calvin as its fountainhead. I am not primarily concerned
with that tradition in this essay, but with the ideas of Calvin himself and
how they might be put to use in a theology of prayer.

fiat.[3] Through similar conceptual distinctions, scholastic theologians of the medieval and post-Reformation period sought to express the exhaustive nature of divine knowledge. Thus, an omniscient God will know what we desire before we pray, and will know what is best for us in every possible circumstance, all things considered. In which case, and from the point of view of a theology of impetration, God knows the content of a given petition directed to God in prayer in advance of its being uttered by the petitioner (Ps. 139: 4[4]). What is more, whether or not granting that petition is a good idea all things considered, is known prior to any petition we make (Prov. 16:33; Is. 46:10; Jer. 29:11; Jas. 1:17). God knows what we want and what we need and his knowledge of these things is not affected one whit by our petition.

Still, knowing what a person desires and what is best for that person, all things considered, is not the same as having the power to bring about what is best for that person all things considered. So, we need to add essential divine omnipotence to essential divine omniscience.[5] Calvin does not really offer a philosophical definition of

---

[3] For a very clear exposition of the distinction between divine natural and free knowledge, as well as the concept of 'middle knowledge' first articulated by the sixteenth century Spanish Jesuit divine, Louis de Molina, see Thomas P. Flint, *Divine Providence* (Ithaca: Cornell University Press, 1991), ch. 1. I shall not delve into divine middle knowledge here, since it is a development that postdates Calvin.

[4] In his commentary on Psalm 139:4 Calvin allows two possible meanings of the verse. God knows what we are about to say before we say it, or God knows our secret intentions even if we try to keep them from him. 'Either rendering amounts to the same thing', says Calvin; 'it is of no consequence which we adopt.' For, says Calvin, on both renderings of the verse the net result is the same: God knows the thoughts of our hearts as intimately as we do. But this is not strictly true. If God knows our secret intentions logically or temporally *prior* to our knowing them, then he knows my thoughts before I know them. But if he knows our secret intentions despite our trying to hide them from him, this does not imply that God knows such intentions in advance of, or prior to, our knowing them. So the first rendering of the verse has an important consequence for divine knowledge that the latter rendering does not. See Calvin, *Commentary on The Book of Psalms*, Vol. V trans. James Anderson (Edinburgh: Calvin Translation Society, 1850), p. 209.

[5] In fact, as we shall see, in light of his doctrine of divine providence, it seems that Calvin, like a number of other Augustinian theologians,

divine power, preferring instead to refer to God's 'ceaseless activity' whereby he brings about all he ordains (*Inst.* 1.16.3). But he does speak of divine omnipotence as being that 'power ample enough to do good' that exists 'in him in whose possession are heaven and earth' (*Inst.* 1.16.3).[6] Interestingly, this is commensurate with a much weaker account of divine power than is found in some contemporary analytic philosophical discussions of omnipotence.[7] But it is consistent with the idea that God has the power to bring about what we desire and what is best for us all things considered, as well as knowledge of what we desire and what is best for us all things considered, which is sufficient for present purposes.

Now, petitioning a being who has the knowledge and power requisite to bring about what is best for us all things considered may not be pointless. Such a being may or may not have the motivation to do

---

(cont.) maintains that God's knowledge is causal. It brings about what is the case according to his divine power. This is one way in which a traditional doctrine of divine simplicity bears upon this particular aspect of the divine nature. Each of God's attributes implies all the others, on the classical, traditional account of divine simplicity. See *Institutes of the Christian Religion* 1.13.2, ed. John T. McNeill, trans. Ford Lewis Battles (Philadelphia: Westminster Press, 1960). (All references to the Institutes are from this edition, and referenced in the text as Inst.) There Calvin says 'the essence of God is simple and undivided'.

[6] A related issue here has to do with the medieval distinction between the absolute and ordained power of God, which Calvin makes reference to in a number of places in the *Institutes* and his commentaries. Some Calvin commentators, like David Steinmetz, think Calvin denies this distinction – see, e.g., Steinmetz, 'Calvin and the Absolute Power of God' in *Calvin in Context* (Oxford: Oxford University Press, 1995). But recently Paul Helm has persuasively argued that Calvin endorses this distinction. See Helm, *John Calvin's Ideas* (Oxford: Oxford University Press, 2004), ch. 11.

[7] What Calvin actually says on the matter in the *Institutes* seems, on the face of it, to be consistent with something like Peter Geach's account of divine power in terms of God being 'almighty' rather than 'omnipotent'. See *Providence and Evil* (Cambridge: Cambridge University Press, 1977), pp. 3–28. There has been considerable dispute about the definition of omnipotence in recent analytic philosophy. But usually the discussion turns on how to construe the idea that God can do, bring about, or otherwise actualize all that is logically possible – whether states of affairs, actions, events, or whatever. Calvin is not interested in this sort of definition of omnipotence. His is the concrete language of piety rather than the abstract problems faced by philosophical reflection on this topic.

what is best for us all things considered. So we need to add essential benevolence to the list of divine attributes under consideration. If God is essentially benevolent as well as omniscient and omnipotent, then he desires the best for us, and will only bring about what is best for us, all things considered.[8] (Bringing about the best for us all things considered is not inconsistent with permitting certain evils to obtain, such that we suffer. Some measure of suffering might be for the best, all things considered – compare Lk. 22:42.) Indeed, if we do petition God then doubtless he will only bring about our petition if it is in accord with what he already knows is best for us, all things considered. However, presumably God will bring about what is best for us regardless of our petition – he is not free to act contrary to his essentially benevolent nature in this regard. But then it looks like God will bring about what he wills to bring about regardless of my prayer (Job 1:21; Jon. 4).[9] And what he wills to bring about is, given the foregoing, the best for his creatures, all things considered.[10]

---

[8] At one point as he discusses the necessity of prayer, Calvin remarks that by praying 'we invoke the presence both of his providence, through which he watches over and guards our affairs, and of his power, through which he sustains us . . . and of his goodness, through which he receives us . . . in short, it is by prayer that we call him to reveal himself as wholly present to us . . . We . . . rest fully in the thought that none of our ills is hid from him who, we are convinced, has both the will and the power to take the best care of us.' *Institutes* 3.20.2. Note in this passage the appeal to divine providence – which, for Calvin, includes divine knowledge of all that comes to pass – divine power, and divine benevolence.

[9] It might be argued that this is a good reason for preferring non-essential divine benevolence. If God is not essentially benevolent but must be impetrated to act in a benevolent way, this might be a motivation for prayer. But I presume that only an essentially benevolent deity is trustworthy and perfect. A non-essentially benevolent God hardly comports with Calvin's doctrine. See, for example, *Inst.* 2.16.3.

[10] 'The best for his creatures all things considered' does not entail that this is the best of all possible worlds (which is a term that becomes important after Calvin, with the theodicy of Leibniz). I am using this phrase as shorthand for 'the best that God has in mind for us consistent with divine benevolence'. It may be that there are other logically possible maximal states of affairs which have a different distribution of good and evil and which have a total objective moral value equal to, or commensurate with, the world that does obtain (i.e. with this world). And it may be that there are numerous possible worlds that have an objective moral value beyond some particular threshold, which makes such worlds one of a set of 'best

But is that quite right? Provided God is essentially omniscient, omnipotent, and benevolent – three essentials of Christian theism endorsed by Calvin – impetrating God may seem problematic in circumstances where what the petitioner asks for is not actually what is the best for her all things considered.[11] But commitment to these three components of traditional, classical theism does not *entail* the pointlessness of impetration. For it seems conceivable that there are situations in which God could bring about one of two or more circumstances each of which have an equal objective moral value. He knows what will obtain in each circumstance. He has the power to bring about each circumstance. And the bringing about of each circumstance would be consistent with his essential benevolence. But perhaps God has ordained that a believer impetrates him to bring about one, and only one, of the possible outcomes in question. And perhaps God desires that his creatures express their desires to him in prayer and that, other things being equal, where there is a circumstance in which a human creature impetrates God for one amongst several possible outcomes all of which have an equal objective moral value, God will grant the petition of his creature. Then, given such a state of affairs, it may be that the fact that a human creature impetrates God for one, and only one, of the situations in question gives God reason to bring about that state of affairs over the other, equally objectively moral states of affairs he could have brought about.

Yet this is itself not unproblematic. God ordains and brings about this world. He decides which of the myriad possible worlds will obtain. Where there are two possible states of affairs that could obtain, both of which have the same objective moral value, where there are no other overriding moral or metaphysical reasons for bringing about one or other of these states of affairs, why would God choose one over

---

(cont.) possible' or 'most valuable'. It may also be that there are worlds whose objective moral value is incommensurable with one another, such that we cannot assess which world, if any, is a best possible world. There may be other metaphysically possible options in the neighbourhood. All we need here is the notion that God's best for his creatures in this world, all things considered, has the right objective moral value to be consistent with his essential benevolence whether or not he could have brought about other worlds with an equal or commensurate objective moral value.

[11] An example: St Paul prays three times that God will remove his 'thorn in the flesh'. But God does not. Eventually, Paul realizes God refrains from granting this petition because it is for the best, all things considered (see II Cor. 12:7–10).

the other? The idea here is that God has no good reason to strongly actualize one over the other state of affairs. Both would suit his purposes such that there is a sort of axiological stand off: the value of either state of affairs is equivalent in the divine economy, all things considered. And God has no overriding reason to strongly actualize one or other of the two states of affairs before his mind's eye, as it were. Might human impetration provide a reason for God to bring about one, rather than the state of affairs, provided the human petitions God for only one of the two otherwise axiologically equivalent states of affairs? The problem here is that this will only have metaphysical purchase if the act of human impetration is free in a libertarian sense. God may have reason to bring about one rather than the other state of affairs in our imagined scenario if the human act of impetration is not ordained by God – is not determined by his divine decree. But Calvin would not allow this. He thinks God determines all that comes to pass. According to Calvin's way of thinking, it is unhelpful to speak of human 'free will' because this presumes that the one willing has some innate power to choose between a good and a bad option (or between any set of options) without divine ordination. The 'illusion' is thereby generated, that the human will 'has both good and evil within its power, so that it can by its own strength choose either one of them.'[12] But Calvin maintains this is not the biblical way of thinking about human free will. Instead, in his treatise on free will directed against his opponent Pighius, he offers the following by way of explaining what he means by 'free will':

> We say that it [i.e. the human will] is self-determined when of itself it directs itself in the direction in which it is led, when it is not taken by force or dragged unwillingly . . . We allow that man has choice and that it is self-determined, so that if he does anything evil, it should be imputed to him and his own voluntary choosing . . . We deny that choice is free, because through man's innate wickedness it is of necessity driven to what is evil and cannot seek anything but evil. And from this it is possible to deduce what a great difference there is between necessity and coercion. For we do not say that man is dragged unwillingly into sinning, but that because his will is corrupt he is held captive under the yoke of sin and therefore of necessity wills in an evil way.[13]

---

[12] Calvin, *On the Bondage and Liberation of the Will*, ed. A. N. S. Lane, trans. G. I. Davies (Grand Rapids: Baker Books, 1996), 2.279–280, 68.

[13] Ibid., 69. Compare *Inst.* 2.2.2–11.

The problem is this: if God determines all that comes to pass, including acts of human free will, then it is difficult to see how impetrating God – an act that is itself ordained by God – should in-and-of-itself give God reason to actualize one state of affairs over another state of affairs, other things being equal. Or, to put it another way, the reason God has for actualizing one over the other state of affairs is not to do with the fact that a particular human creature impetrates God to do so. For this act is itself ordained by God as part of the unfolding of his divine plan in the created order. The reason God brings about one state of affairs rather than another must be sought elsewhere.

With this in mind, we turn to consider two complications to the account of the divine nature outlined thus far that do in fact yield the pointlessness problem that Calvin faces. These are that God is essentially immutable and that he is the determiner of all that comes to pass. Most traditional, classical Christian theologians have thought God was both immutable and the one who ordains all that comes to pass. So adding these two complicating factors into the mix is really only a matter of including as aspects of the problem of pointlessness two divine attributes that are very much part of much historic Christian theology, including, as we shall see, the theology of Calvin.

Now, if God is immutable, then he cannot change. There are different ways in which one can parse this claim.[14] Here I assume a traditional, classical notion of divine immutability, according to which God is immutable if, and only if, he is essentially unchanging. That is, he cannot change in any substantive way whatsoever.[15] Calvin seems to agree with this view. For instance, in his commentary on Malachi 3:6, he says that

> God continues in his purpose, and is not turned here and there like men who repent of a purpose they have formed, because what they had

---

[14] For discussion see for example Richard Creel, *Divine Impassibility: An Essay in Philosophical Theology* (Cambridge: Cambridge University Press, 1986); Katherin A. Rogers, *Perfect Being Theology* (Edinburgh: Edinburgh University Press, 2000), ch. 4; and Richard Swinburne, *The Coherence of Theism*, revised edition (Oxford: Oxford University Press, 1993), ch. 12.

[15] I take it that this is consistent with Scripture, although it may not be the only way one could read Scripture. So, for instance, when God says 'I am the LORD I do not change, therefore you are not consumed O House of Jacob' in Mal. 3:6, this is consistent with the notion that God is immutable in the strong sense intended here. But it is also consistent with something metaphysically weaker, such as that God's character remains the same.

not thought of comes to their mind, or because they wish undone what they have performed, and see new ways by which they may retrace their steps. God denies that anything of this kind can take place in him, for he is *Jehovah*, and *changes not*, or is not changed.[16]

One sort of change that *can* be ascribed to God on this sort of view is what philosophers these days call a 'merely Cambridge change'. These are relational changes that involve no alteration to the subject in question. An example of such change occurs when at a particular moment in time I begin to be shorter than my son, having previously been taller than him at some earlier time. I have not changed at all; my son has grown such that the relation of his height to mine has altered over time. Such 'mere Cambridge change' may obtain with respect to God. But the change needed for God to respond to my petition, altering his plans accordingly, is ruled out on this understanding of divine immutability, because this would constitute a substantive change to what God has ordained will obtain.

Add to this divine determinism, roughly the thesis according to which God ordains all that comes to pass, and nothing comes to pass without God's determining it (Deut. 29:29; Prov. 16:33, 21:1; Is. 45:7; Amos 3:6; Mal. 1:2–3; Matt. 10:29–31; Rom. 8:28–30; Eph. 1–2). If God determines all that comes to pass, then, coupled with his omniscience and omnipotence, nothing can frustrate the divine will. Necessarily all things that take place occur according to divine ordination. But if this is so, then not only is it the case that impetration is redundant because God will bring about what he wills to bring about regardless of my prayer, in accordance with his benevolence, omniscience, and omnipotence. It transpires on this expanded view that *necessarily* impetration is redundant because God will bring about what he wills to bring about regardless of my prayer and my petition can have no effect upon what God wills because he is immutable.[17]

---

[16] Calvin, *Commentary on the Minor Prophets, Vol. V, Zechariah and Malachi*, trans. John Owen (Edinburgh: Calvin Translation Society, 1850), p. 579.

[17] Further to the earlier citation from Calvin's *The Bondage and Liberation of the Will*, it is interesting to consult *Inst.* 2.3.5, where Calvin distinguishes between the sin of human beings, which occurs of necessity, but without compulsion. The idea is that through the fall humans are morally depraved, sinning from necessity of nature – the noetic effects of sin having fundamentally warped the moral nature of fallen humans. Nevertheless, that sin is voluntary, not compelled. This is one indication of Calvin's adherence to a doctrine of theological compatibilism, according to which

The first, more theologically modest account of the divine nature which we examined requires only that God is essentially omniscient, omnipotent, and benevolent. This, as we have seen, is commensurate with the idea that God may factor human impetration into the bringing about of certain states of affairs that are for the good, all things considered. But such an account also implies that God is mutable and does not determine all that takes place. But if God is mutable, then, presumably, he can change his mind. And if he does not determine all that comes to pass, then at least some things that come to pass may be the result of the significantly free actions of created moral agents. For this reason, and for want of better terms, I shall refer to the former, more modest view as the *nondeterminist account of the divine nature*, and the latter, expanded view as the *determinist account of the divine nature*. As is well known, Calvin's understanding of the divine nature is a version of the determinist account:

> To sum up, since God's will is said to be the cause of all things, I have made his providence the determinative principle for all human plans and works, not only in order to display its force in the elect, who are ruled by the Holy Spirit, but also to compel the reprobate to obedience (*Inst*. 1.18.2).

Although Calvin is set against what he calls 'bare permission' – as if God merely permits certain events or actions to occur, rather than bringing them about – he is willing to concede that there are different 'levels' of causal activity in particular acts. God is the one who brings about a particular action, but he may use mediate causes to achieve his ends, such as his use of Satan to test Job's faith. Only in this sense can we speak of divine permission, according to Calvin:

(cont.) which divine determinism is consistent with human freedom provided this means a liberty of spontaneity (very roughly, freedom to act as I desire, choosing on that basis; not freedom to choose between alternative possibilities open before me, any one of which is a live option as far as my choice if concerned, prior to actual volition.) It is worth noting that Francis Turretin, one of Calvin's successors in the Academy in Geneva, who regarded his own theology as an extrapolation of a basically Calvinian position, explicitly aligns himself with theological compatibilism, in his *Institutes of Elenctic Theology Vol. I* trans. G.M.Giger, ed. James T. Dennison Jr. (Philipsburg, NJ: Presbyterian and Reformed Publishing Co., 1992–1997), pp. 665–683.

The Lord permits Satan to afflict His servant; He hands the Chaldeans over to be impelled by Satan, having chosen them as His ministers for this task . . . Satan is properly said, therefore, to act in the reprobate over whom he exercises his reign, that is, the reign of wickedness. God is also said to act in His own manner, in that Satan himself, since he is the instrument of God's wrath, bends himself hither and thither at His beck and command to execute His just judgments. I pass over here the universal activity of God whereby all creatures, as they are sustained, thus derive the energy to do anything at all. I am speaking only of that special action which appears in every particular deed. Therefore we see no inconsistency in assigning the same deed to God, Satan and man; but the distinction in purpose and manner cause God's righteousness to shine forth blameless there, while the wickedness of Satan and of man betrays itself by its own disgrace (*Inst.* 2.4.2).[18]

'In a word', as Calvin puts it elsewhere in his treatise on predestination, 'when inferior causes, like veils, withdraw God from our sight, as they usually do, we must penetrate higher by the eye of faith, so as to discern God's hand working in these instruments.'[19] Although his view is not equivalent to Stoic fatalism, as has sometimes been asserted, it is clear that Calvin does believe that God ordains all that comes to pass, saying things like 'For he is deemed omnipotent . . . because, governing heaven and earth by his providence, he so regulates all things that nothing takes place without his deliberation.'[20] This is consistent with his approval of the notion that God is timeless, ordaining all that comes to pass eternally. He observes,

When we attribute foreknowledge to God, we mean that all things always were, and perpetually remain, under his eyes, so that to his

---

[18] Compare *Inst.* 1.16.2, where Calvin denies that there are fortuitous events, claiming of animate and inanimate objects that 'These are, thus, nothing but instruments to which God continuously imparts as much effectiveness as he wills, and according to his own purpose bends and turns them to either one action or another.'

[19] Calvin, *Concerning the Eternal Predestination of God*, trans. J. K. S. Reid (London: James Clarke and Co., 1961), 10.6, 168.

[20] *Inst.* 1.16.3. See also Calvin's definition of predestination in *Inst.* 3.21.5. On the relationship between Calvin's determinism and Stoic fatalism, see Charles Partee, 'Calvin and Determinism', *Christian Scholars Review* 5 (1975): 123–128, which refutes the charge that Calvin's position is indistinguishable from Stoicism.

knowledge there is nothing future or past, but all things are present. And they are present in such a way that he not only conceives them through ideas . . . but he truly looks upon them and discerns them as things placed before him.'[21]

Moreover, as we have already had cause to note, it is clear that Calvin believes God is essentially immutable. In this way, Calvin's doctrine of impetration, being a species of the determinist account of the divine nature, does yield the pointlessness problem.

b. A Calvinian understanding of impetration

We are now in a position to turn to the concept of impetration itself. I take it that impetration is that aspect of prayer which has to do with petitioning God. Plausibly, when one petitions God in prayer, one aims to ask God to do something that *would not otherwise obtain*. That is, it looks like a prayer only counts as a petition (and thus, as impetration) if the one praying asks God for something that, as far as she is aware, will not come about without such petition.[22] Impetration, then, is not merely expressive of a desire one might have; it is prescriptive of what one wants to happen.[23] One does not ask God to grant things that one thinks of as inevitable, or impossible. Thus, I would not ask God to change the date of the Battle of Hastings to AD 1106 or make $1 + 1 = 5$. Or, if I did, these would be pretty peculiar requests. And at least part of the reason we would think them pecu-

---

[21] *Inst.* 3.21.5. Cf. Inst. 1.10.2. See also similar comments with respect to the Trinity in *Inst.* 1.13.18.

[22] The caveat 'as far as she is aware' has to do with the epistemic limitations placed upon any act of impetration. As far as I am aware, my friend will not recover from terminal cancer without divine intervention. So I pray God heals her in the hope that my petition is answered. It may be that in certain circumstances, the limited epistemic vantage of the one praying renders the prayer ineffective or beside the point, e.g. praying that my friend will be healed of the condition he suffers from when he has been prescribed a course of drugs that will cure him regardless of my prayer, as the drugs take effect. Hence, epistemic limitations are an important consideration when assessing the effectiveness of a particular instance of impetration.

[23] Compare Peter Geach, *God and the Soul* (London: Routledge, 1969), p. 87 and Vincent Brümmer, *What Are We Doing When We Pray?* (London: SCM Press, 1984), pp. 29–30.

liar is because we have the intuition that one cannot change events that are wholly in the past and one cannot change the modal status of necessary truths. Nor would it make much sense to ask God to grant something that is inconsistent with the divine character, such as the instantaneous and entirely gratuitous death of a rather irritating, but otherwise harmless relative. Some requests may be within the bounds of metaphysical possibility, not inevitable, and not inconsistent with the divine nature, and yet theologically dubious. For instance, magical or superstitious requests that are forbidden by divine fiat (Deut. 18:10–12). I suppose God would not normally grant this class of requests either, though for rather different reasons.[24]

Closely related to this understanding of petitioning God (in the recent analytic philosophical literature at least) is what several contemporary philosophers have called a *two-way contingency*. Take, for instance, the Roman Catholic logician, Peter Geach. He maintains that 'if we are to be justified in saying that a state of affairs S came about from somebody's impetratory prayer, then at the time of the prayer S must have had two-way contingency: it could have come about, it also could not come about.'[25] That is, God may or may not grant the request made in impetration. My request does not compel God to act one way or another. It is not a sufficient condition for God's action or apparent inaction. But might a given act of impetration be a necessary condition for God acting one way rather than another? Consider the following homely example. My son asks me to play a game of chess with him when I am reading a book. His request is, we might think, a necessary condition for my deciding to put down the book and pick up the chessboard, though it does not compel me to act in one way rather than another. I might have refused my son's request. Perhaps I am a selfish parent, or the book is too interesting to put down, or my son is supposed to be doing his homework rather than playing board games. I might ignore his request, which, though distinct from refusing his request, has the same effect. But if I comply with his request, I do it because he has asked me to do so.[26] In which case, his request is

---

[24] And yet, God does appear to permit the successful prosecution of at least some magical acts. See, for example, the story of the Witch of Endor, whose necromancy summons up the shade of Samuel for a disobedient King Saul in I Sam. 28:3–25.

[25] Peter Geach, *God and the Soul*, p. 89.

[26] Or, at least, I may comply with my son's request largely because he has asked me to do so. I may have other reasons for complying with his

an insufficient but necessary condition of my putting down the book and beginning to play chess with him. Complying with his request or refusing it constitutes a two-way contingency of the sort philosophers like Peter Geach seem to have in mind.

There are numerous biblical examples of petitions made by human agents that fall within the bounds of what is metaphysically and theologically permissible, given the foregoing, and which appear to depend on something like a two-way contingency. To take just one example, King Hezekiah is told via the prophet Isaiah that he is going to die from an illness. He petitions God. 'Remember, O LORD, how I have walked before you faithfully and with wholehearted devotion and have done what is good in your eyes' (2 Kings 20:3, NIV). God hears and sends Isaiah back to Hezekiah to tell him he will recover and have another fifteen years of life. But this raises the following question. Did God change his mind in response to the impetration of Hezekiah? On the face of it, this seems like a plausible explanation of the data. The advocate of the indeterminist account of the divine nature may find this conducive. For on that account, God can change his mind. Still, even if God can change his mind it seems odd to think he requires the petition of some created agent in order to bring about a particular action. God does not need prompting to do the right thing. Unlike the example of the chess game, he knows every thought before it is on our lips (Ps. 139). He does not need to be asked to know what we need. And he has the power and motivation to ensure that we are provided with what he thinks we need, all things considered. If God is immutable and determines all that comes to pass, it is even harder to see how to make sense of Hezekiah's request. For then God has determined all that takes place according to his immutable will, and Hezekiah is either asking for what will inevitably take place, or asking for what cannot obtain, given what God has determined upon. So, whichever of the indeterminist or determinist accounts one opts for (if one opts for either of them), the example of Hezekiah shows that there is a serious problem with the apparent pointlessness of impetration as I have just characterized it.

One means by which the pointlessness problem can be ameliorated is to deny one or more of the aspects of the divine nature with which

---

(cont.) request in addition to this one, of course. For instance, wanting to spend time with my son, wanting to be a good parent, wanting to impress my spouse, wanting to encourage my son's burgeoning chess skills in the hope that one day he will become a Grandmaster, and so on.

we began. This is a popular manoeuvre in the recent philosophical literature on impetration. Few Christian philosophers today are willing to stand by the claim that God determines all that takes place, though it has been the majority view in the tradition. Alongside this concern, a number of recent philosophers and theologians have argued that the doctrine of divine immutability must be circumscribed or redefined – perhaps even rejected – in order to avoid problems raised by the fact that an essentially unchanging God cannot *respond* to the actions of his creatures. For such a response would constitute a change in God that the traditional doctrine of divine immutability could not countenance.[27] Such revisions to the doctrine of God do have the consequence that at least some human petitions may not be pointless after all. But this is not a cost Calvin would have tolerated. He thought his own position had the theological resources to avoid having to make such a concession.

John Calvin on impetration

Thus far, we have seen that the task of making sense of impetration in Calvinian terms is that much harder than it would be for a defender of a doctrine of God without commitment to immutability and determinism. What does Calvin have to say by way of addressing this pointlessness problem for impetration?

Interestingly, Calvin raises this matter early on in his discussion of prayer in Book III of the *Institutes*. He puts it like this:

> But, someone will say, does God not know, even without being reminded, both in what respect we are troubled and what is expedient for us,

---

[27] There are all sorts of reasons for these revisions to the divine nature and I am not suggesting that theologians and philosophers have opted to make these revisions simply because of the problems they raise for petitioning God. But the idea that God is responsive is an important consideration for many who have made such changes. To give just two examples, see Jürgen Moltmann, *The Crucified God* (London: SCM Press, 1970), and Nicholas Wolterstorff, 'Suffering Love' in Thomas V. Morris ed., *Philosophy and the Christian Faith* (Notre Dame: University of Notre Dame Press, 1988). For a response to this sort of objection from a Calvinist point of view, see Paul Helm, 'Prayer and Providence' in Marcel Sarot, Gijsbert van den Brink and Luco van den Brom, eds. *Christian Faith and Philosophical Theology: Essays in Honour of Vincent Brümmer* (Kampen: Kok Pharos, 1992), pp. 103–115.

so that it may seem in a sense superfluous that he should be stirred up by our prayers – as if he were drowsily blinking or even sleeping until he is aroused by our voice?

To which he responds, that 'they who thus reason do not observe to what end the Lord instructed his people to pray, for he ordained it not so much for his own sake as for ours' (*Inst.* 3.20.3). He then goes on in the same section of the Institutes to adduce six reasons for petitionary prayer. These are,

1. That our hearts may be 'fired with a zealous and burning desire ever to seek, love and serve him' and to flee to him in time of need.
2. That our hearts become trained so as to refuse to entertain wishes that we should be ashamed to make of God a witness. In this way we will learn to lay all our desires before the plain sight of God.
3. That we be prepared to receive his benefits 'with true gratitude of heart and thanksgiving' – all of which come 'from his hand.'
4. That having been granted that for which we petitioned God, we should be drawn to meditate upon his goodness in granting our desires.
5. That we 'embrace with greater delight those things which we acknowledge to have been obtained by prayers.'
6. That our experience may confirm divine providence, whereby God 'promises never to fail us' as well as that 'he ever extends his hand to help his own, not wet-nursing them with words but defending them with present help.'

God may appear not to respond to our petitions, but, says Calvin, this is simply a means by which he intends to train us 'to seek, ask, and entreat him for our great good' (*Inst.* 3.20.3). Calvin castigates those who 'with excessive foolishness' 'prate' that petitioning God for what he will gladly bestow upon us anyway, renders such prayer otiose. For according to Calvin, prayer is an opportunity for the exercise of faith.

This, I suggest, offers us a rather different perspective on the nature of impetration than that favoured by philosophers like Geach. Calvin says that what is important in petitioning God is that our faith is exercised and that the desires of our hearts are brought into conformity with the desires of God. Paramount among his concerns here is the divine will, not what we may desire. For, as a consequence of our fallen state, what we desire may not necessarily be for our good all things considered. It is also worth noting that God's desire to encourage the believer in prayer is, in fact, part-and-parcel of this concern with what we might call a theocentric account of impetration. At root what is important is that petitioning God be seen primarily in terms of God's aims and objectives, rather than mine.[28] This is reinforced by Calvin's exposition of the third petition of the Lord's Prayer later in the same section of the *Institutes* There he says things like the following:

> We are therefore bidden to desire that, just as in heaven nothing is done apart from God's good pleasure . . . the earth be in like manner subject to such a rule, with all arrogance and wickedness brought to an end. And in asking this we renounce the desires of our flesh for whoever does not resign and submit his feelings to God opposes as much as he can God's will, since only what is corrupt comes forth from us. And again by this prayer we are formed to self-denial so God may rule us according to his decision . . . In consequence, our wish is that he may render futile and of no account whatever feelings are incompatible with his will (*Inst.* 3.20.43).

The first three petitions of the Lord's Prayer are concerned with God's glory, says Calvin, not with our own advantage which 'though it amply accrues from such a prayer, must not be sought by us here.' Yet, 'even though all these things must nonetheless come to pass in their time, without any thought or desire or petition of ours, still we ought to desire and request them.' The reason being that we should desire God's greater glory in all we do because 'this is what we owe our Lord and Father' (*Inst.* 3.20.43). So our petitions are both ordained by God, and yet also an obligation that is enjoined upon all believers, as an exercise of faith.

Even when approaching the last three petitions of the Lord's Prayer that are specifically to do with our human needs, Calvin warns that we should 'seek nothing for ourselves without the intention that whatever benefits he confers upon us may show forth his glory' (*Inst.*

---

[28] It also looks like this Calvinian account of impetration means that the impetrator has to have a belief that God would not, or might not, perform what he is praying for without his prayer for it. In other words, it may be that the impetrator has to have a different reason for offering his prayer than God does for ordaining it.

3.20.44). We are 'bidden to ask [sic] our daily bread that we may be content with the measure that our Heavenly Father has deigned to distribute to us, and no get gain by unlawful devices' (*Inst.* 3.20 44).

In effect, throughout his discussion of the Lord's Prayer, impetration functions as a corollary of his doctrine of divine Providence. God will provide what he knows we need; we are enjoined to pray earnestly for what God wills for us in accordance with his grace, not what we desire from the sinfulness of our hearts; to which God will respond in his own good time. When faced with the prospect of answers to prayer deferred or apparently withheld after prolonged impetration, Calvin responds by saying that the Christian should take heart because God will not forsake his people, even if circumstances suggest, on the face of it, that he has. God may well test the faith of the one praying, often driving his people 'to extremity' and allowing them, so driven, 'to lie a long time in the mire before he gives them any taste of his sweetness.' (*Inst.* 3.20.52). Hope and patience in prayer are, it seems, as important for Calvin as the fact that prayer is the outworking of faith.

There is no appeal to a two-way contingency here. But that should come as no surprise, since Calvin endorses divine determinism. Every event that comes to pass has been ordained by God for his own glory, but also for the good of his people, all things considered. In which case, my impetration is part of the plan of God. He has ordained that I pray as I do for the things that I do, although I do this of my own volition, not of compulsion, but (in some sense) of necessity, as a consequence of divine ordination. This raises a further, subsidiary, problem for Calvin's doctrine of petitioning God, related to the matter of its apparent pointlessness. This is, whether impetration boils down to something merely therapeutic – whether, in fact, it helps me to accept God's will, but really changes nothing.

In defence of a Calvinian account of impetration

In the philosophical literature on impetration, Paul Helm has come to the defence of a determinist account of the divine nature, arguing that acceptance of this picture of God does not render impetration redundant. He offers the following response to this sort of objection:

> In the case of the prayer for rain one would have to say that God did not only ordain 'from the beginning' the meteorological sequence that

included rain on Thursday, but that he also ordained that at least one phase of the sequence (the 'rain on Thursday' phase) was to follow prayer for rain on Thursday, and also that he ordained the rain because of the prayers.[29]

On this way of thinking, talk of God ordaining all that comes to pass, impetration included, need not render such prayer pointless. If God ordains every event, then he ordains the petition uttered on Wednesday for rain on Thursday. And he ordains that the rain occurs on Thursday. But importantly, according to Helm, it makes sense on this view to say that God ordains the rain on Thursday at least in part because of the petition for rain on Thursday. Although both the petition and the fulfillment of that petition are ordained by God, this does not mean that the one does not happen because of the other; quite the contrary.

To illustrate this point, suppose an author conceives of an entire novel one day sitting on the train from London to Manchester. Over some period of time she writes the whole thing down. In the narrative, as one would expect, one event follows another, and some events in the beginning of the narrative have important causal implications for later events in the narrative. Helm's view seems to be that God's determining all that comes to pass is rather like an author conceiving of, and executing, a work of imagination. Just because the author decides all that comes to pass in the novel does not mean (from the point of view of the reader, at least) that a later event in the novel does not happen because of an earlier event, to which it is intimately connected in the broad sweep of the narrative. If the author conceives of the novel all at once, and commits it to paper without any changes to the narrative, plot and characterization (let us say), then this does sound rather like the sort of deterministic account that Calvin enunciates in his writings. In which case, the divine author of the created order may have ordained my prayer and its fulfillment as two related parts of the one overall 'plotline' of history. He does not just ordain the whole plot. He ordains all the parts thereof, and the sequence in which they occur in the narrative that makes up the whole. In this sense, and on a Calvinian account of impetration, certain events may well obtain *because* I have prayed for them to happen.

But this raises a very real additional problem, having to do with conflicting petitions. These come in many guises, but they need not be

---

[29] Paul Helm 'Asking God', *Themelios* 12.1 (1986): 24.

instances where one petition is clearly morally inappropriate or otherwise suspect, and therefore unlikely to be answered by God. If I
pray that my friend recovers from cancer while, unbeknown to me, a
second party is praying that my friend dies a horrible death, there are
good theological reasons for doubting that God would grant the petition of the second party. However, even in this instance what is interesting is that on a Calvinian view, the prayer of the second party is
also part of the divine design. God has ordained that this second
party pray as she does and that her prayer is ineffective because
immoral. This also gives us an inkling of how the Calvinian may
respond to those situations in which two or more people are impetrating God for different, mutually conflicting outcomes, where none
of the petitioners is asking God for things which are immoral or
unreasonable. Consider a scenario where I pray that it will be a fine
day all day long so that I can enjoy a trip to the exquisite Dyrham Park
in Gloucestershire, while a local farmer prays that it will rain in the
same area, on the same day, during the same period, in order that her
crops flourish. God ordains both prayers, on the Calvinian account.
But at most only one of the prayers can be answered. Which will it be?
Whichever one it is (if either) God will bring about what he does
according to his good purposes, all things considered. In this case, it
may be for the best that it does rain on the day I asked for sunshine,
because God deems the crop flourishing to be the outcome that best
comports with his purposes, all things considered. My prayer is not
unanswered. It is denied because my request was not in line with
what God ordained. So the rain is granted because of the prayer of the
farmer. But my prayer is refused. It plays no part in the subsequent
meteorological events God has ordained – though it may play a part
in subsequent events in other ways. Perhaps God ordains my prayer
and its frustration as part of a larger project which involves my coming to see that my prayer life is shallow and selfish, and needs to be
more focused on seeking God's will, rather than my own.

Let us take stock. According to Calvin, God ordains all that comes
to pass. As such my petitioning God is part of what God has determined will obtain. There is nothing 'open-ended' on Calvin's account
of impetration, as if my petitioning God will bring about a change of
heart on the part of the Deity, who may, as a consequence of my
prayer, change his mind and bring about some state of affairs that
would not have obtained without my prayer (e.g. the healing of my
friend's cancer). So my prayer is consequentially necessary. That is, it
is necessary as a consequence of what God has ordained will come to

pass. It is a part of the whole matrix of events that God has ordained that, given Calvin's adherence to a determinist account of the divine nature, cannot include any notion of a two-way contingency. For the sort of two-way contingency philosophers like Geach and Brümmer presume requires a libertarian account of human freedom that Calvin will not countenance. We have seen that, on Calvin's way of thinking, doing something of necessity does not entail compulsion. I may act of necessity without being forced or coerced into so acting. Which is to say his is a version of theological compatibilism: my being determined by divine decree to offer the prayer I do is consistent with my doing so freely. After all, I choose to offer the prayer I do. So my impetration is part of the nexus of events that make up the unfolding of history as God has ordained it. Just as God is not surprised by any other mundane event that takes place, he is not caught off-guard by my request. He does not have to deliberate, making changes to his plans in light of my petition. All things, my prayer included, are part of what he has ordained will occur. And this means that the Calvinian must give up the notion of a two-way contingency as an integral component of impetration.

This is a very different understanding of the metaphysics of impetration than that offered by a number of philosophers in the recent literature, including Geach and Brümmer. It is also an account which, I venture to say, will seem counterintuitive to many non-philosophers. But does it render impetration pointless? Not unless one thinks that any given human act that obtains on a determinist account such as that offered by Calvin entails that such action is pointless. The determinist is committed to the idea that every act I perform, from praying for my friend who has cancer to expressing my preference for a tuna sandwich over a chicken sandwich, is determined by God. But this does not necessarily render all such action pointless. Consider a situation in which my child comes to me crying after having fallen from her bicycle. Assume that it is in my nature to be caring and loving towards my offspring, such that I am, in some sense, *bound* to offer comfort to my injured daughter. Would we think this a pointless act if I cannot help but offer comfort in such a circumstance because it is in my nature so to act? That seems like a very odd thing to say. In fact, the opposite seems to be the case: we typically think that such an act, borne out of my natural desire to comfort my child is very worthwhile, one which will promote the flourishing of my children.

Transpose this reasoning onto a situation of impetration. God brings it about that I impetrate him for my friend with cancer. In one sense, this is determined. But in another sense, it is my voluntary action. Is it pointless because it is determined that I act in this way, pouring out my concern to God? Of course God could bring about the healing of my friend without my prayer. But then, God could bring about numerous logically possible states of affairs without intermediaries. So this is not necessarily an objection to impetration on the determinist account, since almost all parties who have a stake in a doctrine of impetration think God is able to bring about all sorts of events directly and immediately – though, in the normal course of things, he does not. What the Calvinian wants to say is that God has ordained that I pray as part of the nexus of events that obtain in this world, including the outcome of my prayer. My friend will recover or will die according to divine ordination, just as I will pray, or refrain from praying, according to divine ordination. All these things are in the hand of God. But this does not mean I have no reason to pray. And it does not mean my prayer is not a voluntary action.

But does such a Calvinian account of impetration reduce prayer to something merely therapeutic? It makes me feel better, we might think. But does it make any difference beyond that, all things considered? Granted, it is part of the divine plan. This does not necessarily mean it has any efficacy apart from its therapeutic value.

There are several things to say in response to this. First, the therapeutic value of prayer is not to be underestimated. This is a good in and of itself. The issue is whether this is the only good outcome of petitioning God. But what we have seen from Calvin is that this is clearly not the only good outcome. Prayer is a means by which the believer exercises her faith. It is also an expression of Christian patience and hope. So, according to Calvin, petitioning God develops certain virtues which are not merely therapeutic in nature. For one thing, they help the believer to rely upon divine grace and trust to God's providential care, even when events seem to run contrary to what we might expect if God does oversee all that takes place. This may have a therapeutic dimension. But it is no more *merely* therapeutic than the trust one places in a lifeguard who throws a drowning man a buoyancy aid.

But also, if impetration is part of the very fabric of the divine plan, then it has a purpose beyond the therapeutic, being something that is ordained in order (ultimately) to bring glory to God. We are assured that God does all things for a good purpose (Rom. 8:28). And we are enjoined to pray that God's will is done 'on earth as it is in heaven', a matter Calvin takes very seriously. Bringing our desires into line with what God desires is no small matter. It may well be a very hard thing to do, as, no doubt, St Paul found when he asked for his 'thorn in the flesh' to be removed, though it was not.

We might put it like this: the Calvinian perspective on impetration means petitioning God is more about bringing my will into line with God's will, than it is seeking to change God's mind. It is about praying that God's will is done, and that we are given the grace to accept that, in the understanding that all things work to the good for those who trust God. But if this isn't reducible to a therapeutic account of impetration, is it a quiescent account of prayer – impetration as resignation, as it were? Not exactly; it is more like impetration as conforming to the divine will, rather than impetration as giving up, 'letting go, and letting God', so to speak. I pray; I bring my desires before God. But I endeavour to ensure that my impetration is framed by values and concerns that are fitting for a Christian seeking to honour God, who, we trust, provides for and sustains his people according to his good plan for them. In this way, Calvin's account of prayer is of a piece with what he says about providence. It is also, I suggest, a reminder that impetration is an aspect of the Christian life that involves self-discipline and the development of Christian virtues. Perhaps it is not too much to characterize Calvin's position on impetration as one concrete way in which the Christian is enjoined to pursue the glory of God in the exercise of patient submission to his will and in the hope of salvation, come what may.

CHAPTER EIGHT

John Williamson Nevin on the Church

> The Church, the sacraments, and the scriptures became for
> him the very embodiment of Christ's glorified humanity in
> the life of the world. The ideal and spiritual, thus, are
> externalized in history.
> – *William DiPuccio, 'Nevin's Idealistic Philosophy'*[1]

If history is written by the victors, then the American theologian
John Williamson Nevin was not on the winning side. Alongside his
younger colleague, Philip Schaf (or Schaff, as he styled himself in
America), Nevin put the small German Reformed denomination on
the theological map in the first half of the nineteenth century. It is
their work that gave rise to what is now called the Mercersberg
Theology, centred on the denominational seminary at which both
taught, in Mercersberg, Pennsylvania. Between them, Schaff and
Nevin made a strong case for high church Calvinism, including a
robust and theologically interesting doctrine of the Church. But
Nevin has been largely forgotten by theologians today. Schaff is
still remembered for his work on historical theology and Christian
symbols. But, arguably, his place in the history of American
Reformed theology was secured after his removal from
Mercersberg to Union Seminary in New York. By that stage the
Mercersberg Theology was on the wane, gradually receding from
the public gaze in the years after the American Civil War. Today,
the popular understanding of nineteenth-century American
Reformed theology is (almost) synonymous with the Old Princeton
theology of Archibald Alexander, Charles Hodge and Benjamin

---

[1] In Sam Hamstra and Arie J. Griffioen, eds. *Reformed Confessionalism in
Nineteenth-Century America*, ATLA Monograph Series, No. 38 (Lanham,
MD: The Scarcrow Press, 1995), p. 55.

Warfield. And Hodge, for one, was no friend to the high church Calvinism of Nevin.[2]

When Nevin is remembered, it is for being the author of two works, *The Anxious Bench* and *The Mystical Presence*.[3] The first of these is a trenchant defence of confessional Calvinism against the 'new measures' of revivalism instituted in America by Charles Finney. Finney and his epigone thought that the churches needed to be revived through the introduction of theologically entrepreneurial innovations like the 'anxious seat', to which the penitent were encouraged to come at the end of divine service for prayer and counsel. However, Nevin was convinced that this was 'quackery'. What the churches needed was a return to confessional standards, catechesis, and appropriately orderly liturgical services. There decorum and a deep spiritual understanding of the organic nature of the Church could be fostered.[4]

---

[2] Hodge was Nevin's teacher at Princeton Seminary. But as Nevin's career developed and his thinking took on a 'high church' hue, academic relations between the two became strained. Hodge's review essay on Nevin's book, *The Mystical Presence*, shows just how unhappy Hodge had become with the direction taken by his erstwhile student. See Hodge, 'The Doctrine of The Reformed Church on The Lord's Supper', reprinted from *The Princeton Review* in *Essays and Reviews* (New York: Robert Carter and Brothers, 1852), pp. 341–392.

[3] *The Anxious Bench* (Chambersburg, PA: Offices of the 'Weekly Messenger', 1843; second edition, Chambersburg, PA: Publication Office of the German Reformed Church, 1844). The second edition of this work included some expansion of the text and an additional chapter, which takes up Nevin's understanding of the incarnational and organic nature of the Church, developed in his later publications. *The Mystical Presence: A Vindication of the Reformed or Calvinistic Doctrine of the Holy Eucharist* (Philadelphia: J. B. Lippincott and Co., 1846) is Nevin's most substantial work. Although there is large volume entitled *Dr Nevin's Theology* (Reading, PA: I. M. Beaver Publishers, 1913), this is based on student notes of Nevin's classroom course on systematic theology, compiled and edited by William H. Erb, one of Nevin's students. It is a useful resource that supplements his other works, but was not prepared for publication by Nevin himself.

[4] Thus, for example, Nevin's acerbic comment: 'The Bench is against the Catechism, and the Catechism is against the Bench.' Later in the same passage he goes on to say, 'It is the living Catechism, the Catechism awakened and active, that is intended in this opposition [to the Anxious Bench]. As such it stands as the representative and symbol of a system, embracing its own theory of religion, and including a wide circle of agencies peculiar

The Mystical Presence is Nevin's major theological contribution. In it, he offers a thorough account of the Calvinistic doctrine of Christ's real, though non-corporeal, presence in the celebration of the Eucharist. There is much to be said for this work, which is a substantial contribution to Reformed theology.[5] However, in this chapter, I want to focus on Nevin's understanding of the nature of the Church – something he says a great deal about in *The Mystical Presence*.

In fact, Nevin wrote several important essays on ecclesiology in the early part of his career, while at the seminary in Mercersberg.[6] His ruminations were never merely academic. He worried about 'the Church question', as he called it, throughout much of his working life, even resigning his position at Mercersberg in large part because of qualms over the nature of the Protestant form of the church with which he was associated. Although Nevin flirted with Roman Catholicism, seriously contemplating conversion, in the end he decided to remain within the Reformed tradition, to which he returned in his later years to serve in the capacity of President of Franklin and Marshall College, in Lancaster, Pennsylvania.[7]

Nevin's struggle to make sense of the nature of the Church was born from a deep engagement with German philosophy and theology, which

---

(cont.) [to] itself for carrying this theory into effect . . . Between such a Christianity and that which is the produce of the Bench, there can be no comparison . . .' Nevin, *The Axious Bench*, pp. 102–103.

[5] This has not gone unnoticed in the contemporary literature. See, for example, George Hunsinger, *The Eucharist and Ecumenism* (Cambridge: Cambridge University Press, 2008). Although Nevin does not feature very much in the body of the text, Hunsinger notes in the acknowledgements the importance the 'catholic' doctrine of the Mercersberg Theology was for the development of his own work.

[6] These include 'Catholic Unity' (1844); 'The Church' (1847); 'Wilberforce on the Incarnation' (1850); and *Antichrist, or the Spirit of Sect and Schism* (1848). These works (in whole or part) are reproduced in James Hastings Nichols, ed. *The Mercersberg Theology* (New York: Oxford University Press, 1966). All references are to this edition of these works.

[7] For useful biographical resources on Nevin's 'dizziness', as his ecclesiological uncertainty was called, see for example Theodore Appel, *The Life and Work of John Williamson Nevin* (Philadelphia: Reformed Church Publications House, 1889); D. G. Hart, *John Williamson Nevin: High Church Calvinist* (Phillipsberg, NJ: Presbyterian and Reformed, 2005); and James Hastings Nichols, *Romanticism in American Theology: Nevin and Schaf at Mercersberg* (Chicago: University of Chicago Press, 1961).

began early in his career at Western Seminary (now Pittsburgh Theological Seminary), and continued into his time at Mercersberg. He claimed that his 'sense of the church' had not been 'borrowed in any direct or immediate way from German theology.'[8] Yet quite clearly the ideas he had imbibed from the Germans shaped his whole religious outlook.[9] The most important influence upon Nevin in this regard was the work of Augustus Neander, one of the so-called 'mediating theologians' in Germany, who had taught Schaff and left a lasting impression upon both men. In Nevin's own words, 'As Kant says somewhere of the influence the philosophical writings of David Hume had upon him, so I may say in all truth of the new ides of history set before me by Neander – "they broke up my dogmatic slumbers." They were for me an actual awakening of the soul'. What is more, this theological awakening at the hands of Neander 'made itself profoundly felt also in the end on my whole theological and religious life.'[10]

After being awakened from his 'dogmatic slumbers' and removing to Mercersberg, where he was joined by the younger Schaff, fresh from his studies and a stint as a *privatdozent* in Berlin, Nevin began to develop an American high church Calvinism that was deeply indebted to German mediating theology and the idealism upon which it drew. His ecclesiology is not unproblematic. But the core ideas that motivated much of what Nevin wrote concerning the Church are worthy of serious consideration. We shall focus on these ideas in the next section of the chapter. Then, in a third section, I shall draw on Nevin's doctrine in order to sketch out an account of the organic union of Adam and his progeny, and Christ and his Church.

---

[8] Cited in Nichols, *Romanticism in American Theology*, p. 159.

[9] It is ironic that Nevin, who never travelled very far beyond the borders of New Jersey and Pennsylvania, imbibed the German theology his mentor Charles Hodge had travelled all the way to Europe to study first-hand, but had repudiated on returning home to Princeton.

[10] Cited in Appel, *The Life and Work of John Williamson Nevin*, p. 83. See also Luther J. Binkley, *The Mercersberg Theology* (n. p.: Franklin and Marshall College, 1953), p. 13; Stephen Graham, 'Nevin and Schaff at Mercersberg' in *Reformed Confessionalism in Nineteenth-Century America*, pp. 69–96; and, more recently, D. G. Hart, *John Williamson Nevin*, pp. 71–77. On the Mediating Theologians, see, for example, Hans Schwarz, *Theology in a Global Context: The Last Two Hundred Years* (Grand Rapids: Eerdmans, 2005), ch. 2 and Claude Welch, *Protestant Thought in The Nineteenth Century, Vol. I, 1799–1870* (New Haven: Yale University Press, 1972), ch. 12.

Nevin's doctrine of the Church

There are a number of themes in Nevin's ecclesiology and several useful accounts of his work in the secondary literature.[11] Since I am concerned to get at Nevin's *ideas*, I shall not rehearse the development of his
ecclesiology in detail – that has been done elsewhere.[12] Instead, the focus
will be on his conception of the Church as explicated in *The Anxious
Bench* and *The Mystical Presence*, alongside several of his shorter works
written in the 1840s, including his essays *The Church* and *Catholic Unity*,
supplemented where necessary with William Erb's compendium of
Nevin's theology. The Mercersberg theologian's writings are dispersed
over a range of media, with many of his polemical and apologetic pieces
preserved in the pages of the organ of the German Reformed Seminary
begun by Nevin with Schaff, namely, the *Mercersberg Review* (now
defunct). But the works considered here are certainly the chief places in
which he sets out his understanding of the Church.

 Nevin was concerned to argue for a Reformed construal of the catholic-
ity of the Church despite its failure to adequately express the ideal that it
sought to reflect. His understanding of ecclesiology proper, as we might
call it, involves several interrelated ideas that I want to focus on in what
follows. (These are not the only ideas he is concerned with in his writings
on the Church. But I think it is true to say that these motifs are of fundamental importance for what he does say.) These ideas are: the relationship
between the Incarnation and the Church, and the notion of the Church as
an organism. Both of these notions are aspects of Nevin's understanding
of the mystical union between the Church and Christ, as we shall see.

Incarnation and the Church

We begin with the Incarnation and the Church. Nevin conceived of
the actual, historic Church in all its various branches as the imperfect,

---

[11] See in particular Binkley, *The Mercersberg Theology*, ch. IV; Walter Conser,
Jnr. 'Nevin on the Church' in *Reformed Confessionalism in Nineteenth-
Century America*, pp. 97–111; William B. Evans' excellent study *Imputation
and Impartation: Union with Christ in American Reformed Theology* (Milton
Keynes: Paternoster Press, 2008), ch. 5; Brian Gerrish, *Tradition and The
Modern World: Reformed Theology in the Nineteenth Century* (Chicago:
University of Chicago Press, 1978), ch. 2; and James Hastings Nichols,
Romanticism in American Theology, chs. 4–6.

[12] See, for example, Appel, *The Life and Work of John Williamson Nevin*, and
Nichols, *Romanticism in American Theology*.

partial instantiation of an ideal Church. Rather than appealing to the distinction between the visible and the invisible Church common in much Reformed thought, Nevin adopted the language of German idealism to express the distinction between the Church that exists and develops through time, and the ideal Church to which it only partially, and imperfectly corresponds, as (in Nevin's phrase) the 'externalization' of the ideal. Nevin gives some indication of what he means by the ideal Church in the following passage from his essay, 'The Church':

> We take *Idea* here in its true sense, by which it expresses the very inmost substance of that which exists, as distinguished from its simply phenomenal character in time and space. As such it is not opposed to what is actual, but constitutes rather its truth and soul. All life is Ideal, that is, exists truly in the form of possibility, before it can become actual; and it is only in the presence and power of this potential life, this invisible, mysterious living nature which lies behind and beyond all outward manifestations, that these last can ever be said to carry with them any reality whatever. In this sense only do we speak of an Ideal Church.[13]

So the actual, concrete Church – that is, the Church as it is manifest at a particular time, as Nevin understands it – is something that is gradually manifested in history as it develops through time. It remains dependent upon its ideal counterpart, from which it draws its life, which is actualized in concrete ways as the Church more closely approximates to the ideal in history.[14] At times what Nevin says suggests that the ideal Church is something like a substratum with the actual, concrete Church at a particular time its currently manifest empirical aspect. In this respect the actual Church is rather like the copy of an Old Master painting made by a skilled craftsman, which gradually comes to resemble the original as the painter puts more paint on the canvas. But unlike the copy of the Old Master painting, the actual, historical Church remains dependent upon the ideal Church for the whole of its existence. The Church will only have realized the potentiality of the ideal Church in *toto* at the end of time, with

---

[13] Nevin, 'The Church' reprinted in James Hastings Nichols, ed. *The Mercersberg Theology*, p. 58.

[14] Nevin says at one point that the Ideal and actual Church 'can never fall asunder, nor is their conjunction accidental simply and external. The relation that joins them is inward and vital, like that which holds between soul and body.' 'The Church', pp. 64–65.

the dawning of the eschaton. The reason for this, according to Nevin, is that the potentiality of the ideal is only gradually made manifest in the life of the actual Church as its history unfolds.[15]

Nevin emphasizes that this ideal Church is not some 'fantastic figment of any man's brain', including, one presumes, his own, but is 'the most real of all realities that God has established in this world'.[16] It is, in fact, 'the power of a new supernatural creation' which has been 'introduced into the actual history of the world by the Incarnation of Jesus Christ'.[17] What is more, Christ himself is the principle of this new, supernatural creation. His Incarnation included within itself 'all the resources of life and salvation that were needed for the full redemption of humanity' to the great fulfillment of this destiny in the world to come. 'The Church', Nevin declares triumphantly, 'is the depository of these resources.'[18] The life and powers of the Church were 'all comprehended originally in the person of Jesus Christ', which they continue to reveal in history. Christ is the 'beginning and the end' of the Church 'which is denominated on this account his body, the fullness of him that filleth all in all.'[19]

Not only is the actual Church the partial, gradual realization of the ideal Church, which is rooted in Christ. It is also one organic whole, 'a living system, organically bound together in alls its parts, springing from a common ground, and pervaded throughout with the force of a common nature.'[20] The common ground referred to here is Christ himself. Nevin maintains that in his view the Church 'cannot be less single or less comprehensive than the Idea of the human race as a whole.' Its ideal is always one and catholic, despite

---

[15] Compare William DiPuccio, who says 'The actual Church is the historical Church which extends from the incarnation to the present. It is the "externalization" of the ideal in space and time. In its ideal aspect it remains unchanged throughout the vicissitudes of history because it is grounded in the power of a single fact, vis., the life of Christ. But as a truly historical constitution, it is in the process of moving towards what it is ideally. Historical development, therefore, is the ongoing actualization of the Church's ideal potential.' DiPuccio 'Nevin's Idealistic Philosophy', p. 55.

[16] 'The Church', p. 58.

[17] Ibid.

[18] Ibid., p. 59. Later Nevin goes as far as to say 'The Church is the historical continuation of the life of Jesus Christ in the world.' 'The Church', p. 65.

[19] Ibid, p. 59.

[20] Ibid. We shall have more to say about the organic nature of the Church in the following section.

the actual fissures in the historic Church. The ideal Church, unlike the actual Church, is also 'absolutely holy and infallible, free from error and free from sin.'[21]

Nevin also makes clear that the ideal Church is identical to Christianity *per se*; one cannot exist independently of the other. Both Christianity and the ideal Church are inherently social entities. In its very conception, Christianity has to do with 'the power of a common or general life' which can never be reduced to 'something isolated and single simply' but 'always includes the idea of society and commun- ion, under all its manifestations.'[22]

Finally, on the question of the nature of the ideal Church, Nevin maintains that it 'includes within itself the necessity of a visible exter- nalization in the world'[23] – namely, the actual Church. The very idea of an 'invisible Church' is, as far as Nevin is concerned, a 'great absurdity'. 'The Idea of the Church includes visibility, just as the idea of a man supposes a body.'[24] A Church that is said to be one, holy, catholic and apostolic cannot be a mere intellectual abstraction, as far as Nevin is concerned. It must be visible.[25]

What then of the nature of the actual Church? Although we can speak in one sense of the Church at particular moments of its history – say, the Patristic, the Medieval or the Reformation – Nevin thinks that this is to refer to only one part of the whole Church as it extends through time. It 'includes always the past along with the present, as well as a reference also to the future.' He goes on, 'The actual Church is a process not only covering a large field in space, but reaching over a long tract in time; and to be understood at all, it must be appre- hended and viewed in this way.'[26] The historic Church is never perfect this side of the grave. But it is, Nevin says, like leaven that grows until it leavens out the whole.[27] In the end, this process will be completed,

---

[21] Ibid. Cf. Erb, *Dr Nevin's Theology*, pp. 427–431.

[22] 'The Church', p. 60.

[23] Ibid.

[24] Ibid., p. 61.

[25] Ibid. The objection seems to be that the Church cannot be invisible; it must always be visible in history. But this is no real criticism of the distinction between the visible and invisible Church, since those who defend this dis- tinction can claim that there is always a visible Church, just as Nevin thinks there is always an actual Church, which corresponds to the ideal. We shall return to this matter presently.

[26] Ibid., pp. 61–62.

[27] Ibid., p. 62.

and only then 'the actual will be found commensurate in all respects with the Ideal.'[28]

In addition to this notion that the actual Church is one whole that extends across time, gradually instantiating the life of the ideal Church on the way towards the eschaton, Nevin makes a strong connection between the actual, presently manifest Church and Christ. As we have seen, on Nevin's reckoning the ideal Church is identical to Christianity. In speaking of the actual, empirical Church, he emphasizes its connection to faith in Christ, saying that 'Without faith in the Church, there can be no proper faith in Christ'. Furthermore 'If there be no such supernatural constitution in the world as the Idea of the Church implies, the whole fact of the Incarnation is turned into an unreal theophany, and the gospel is subverted to its very foundations.'[29]

So, far from being merely a witness to the truth of Christ, the actual Church is, in Nevin's estimation, the entity that comprehends that truth, despite the faults and failings that can be found in the historic Church at a given moment in time.[30] Quite how the actual, concrete Church is able to 'comprehend that truth' is another matter. It certainly seems problematic to say both that the actual Church only ever partially 'externalizes' the ideal Church in history and that the actual Church always comprehends, or encompasses the entire truth of the Incarnation, or of Christianity. Given the other things he says about the relation between the ideal and the actual Church, it would appear that the most Nevin can claim in this regard is that the actual Church reflects the truth of the Incarnation and of Christian doctrine, albeit partially and falteringly, given its particular, incomplete instantiation of the ideal to which it corresponds at any given moment in history.

Nevin is keen to distance his own idealist understanding of the nature of the Church from the distinction between the visible and invisible Church. Yet it is not entirely clear how he can do that. Presumably the actual Church includes those who have died in the faith. They are no longer 'visible' in any obvious sense of the word, yet, one presumes, Nevin does not want to exclude them from the life of the Church. But the saints who are dead are not part of an ideal Church either – at least, not in Nevin's sense of that term. They are very much part of the Church that is 'externalized', but are no longer

---

[28] Ibid., p. 64.
[29] Ibid., p. 67.
[30] Ibid.

subject to the moral and theological shortfalls of the actual Church in history, and are, in addition, no longer present in space or time.[31]

Perhaps the charitable thing to do here would be to grant that Nevin's understanding of the actual Church could be extended to include the great cloud of witnesses that comprise what many theologians have traditionally referred to as the Church Triumphant – that is, the complete number of the saints in glory. Then, the organic whole that is the actual Church across time somehow includes within its life those who are removed from it in time and space, and who presently enjoy the company of the heavenly host. But this does not really address the problem that those saints who are glorified are not subject to the moral and theological shortfallings of the actual Church in time. Perhaps one could say that the actual Church has a part which is spatio-temporally disjunct from the rest of its life, which comprises the glorified saints, and which is not subject to the vicissitudes of the life endured by the actual Church this side of the eschaton (in particular, its moral and theological failings). But this is a rather artificial way of 'correcting' Nevin's doctrine at this point, and one that requires a great deal of metaphysical explanation. (For instance, how can one entity, the actual Church, have parts that are spatio-temporally disjunct and that do not share the moral and theological failings of the rest of this entity?)[32]

---

[31] I presume the traditional theological idea that the dead continue to exist in some immaterial state beyond the grave. Nevin does speak in these terms, e.g. *The Mystical Presence*, p. 177, affirming that 'man is one, soul and body.' (See also, *The Mystical Presence*, pp. 170, 197–198.) And in speaking of the hypostatic union as reported in Erb's *Dr Nevin's Theology*, pp. 241–242, he says 'By the human nature of Christ is meant that he had a human body and a human soul. We cannot speak of humanity without a soul . . . The doctrine of the Church has required that the humanity of Christ should be possessed of a "true body and a reasonable soul."' A number of Nevin interpreters have noted his tendency to integrate the immaterial and the material in his work, eschewing 'dualism'. Glen A. Hewitt even states quite bluntly that 'Nevin rejected body-soul dualism.' But this is clearly a mistake. See Hewitt, *Regeneration and Morality: A Study of Charles Finney, Charles Hodge, John W. Nevin, and Horace Bushnell* (New York: Carlson Publishing, Inc. 1991), p. 100. See also David Wayne Layman 'Nevin's Holistic Supernaturalism' in *Reformed Confessionalism in Nineteenth Century America*, pp. 193–208.

[32] The fact that Nevin is attempting to give an account of the Church as such, rather than just the Church Militant, is the reason this problem arises. If he

This is not to say that Nevin's emphases upon the gradual development of the actual Church, its unity across time, or its being truly the Church of Christ despite its moral and theological failings, are not helpful. Indeed, one could affirm his strong understanding of the relationship between Christ and the Church, and (in some sense, at least) the practical necessity of the Church in the divine scheme for salvation. But quite how Nevin's doctrine can account for that portion of the actual Church now glorified (i.e. dead saints) is more difficult to fathom.

A second problem drives this point home. Nevin's conception of the relationship between Christ and the Church includes his idea that the Incarnation brings about a fundamental moral reordering of creation from that moment onwards. What is achieved in God becoming human changes history, inaugurating the 'new creation' exemplified by the Church, which is (somehow) organically united to Christ as its head. What is more, prior to this event, God's relations with human beings were significantly different. Although God revealed himself to human beings in the Old Testament, 'holding out the promise of a real union of the divine nature with the human' to such a real union 'it is true, the dispensation itself never came.'[33] God did increasingly condescend to this ancient people during the Old Testament period. Yet the 'wall of partition that separated the divine from the human, was never fully broken down . . . The revelation to the end, was a revelation of God *to* man, and not a revelation of God *in* man.'[34] The Old Testament is, on this way of thinking, wholly preparatory for the change brought about in the event of the Incarnation.

But, as Charles Hodge pointed out in criticism of Nevin, this appears to mean that those believers who lived temporally prior to Jesus of Nazareth bear a very different relation to Christ than those who live after his Incarnation. 'The union between the divine and human began with Christ, and from him this theanthropic life passes over to the church. There neither was nor could be any such thing before.'[35] Hodge maintains that in separating out the life of the Old

---

(cont.) were simply giving an account of the Church Militant, then his views could be understood in terms of a rather abstract understanding of the actual Church and how it comes to be in history, and is no mere aggregation of individuals.

[33] Nevin, *The Mystical Presence*, p. 203. Cf. pp. 195–196.

[34] Ibid.

[35] Hodge, 'The Doctrine of the Reformed Church on the Lord's Supper', p. 381.

Testament believers from those of the New Testament, Nevin has departed from Reformed doctrine. This is made clear, he thinks, in Nevin's understanding of the relationship between the sacramental life of Old Testament Israel, and that of the New Testament Church. What Nevin says about the differences between the sacramental expression of life in the Old and New Testaments reflects his understanding of the dramatic change brought about by the Incarnation, a change which does not appear to have any proleptic or retroactive efficacy.

Nevin does distinguish the sacramental expression of the two Testaments, speaking of the Passover as a 'shadow' prefiguring the work of Christ, to which the Eucharist looks back. He does not deny that there is something approximating sacramental life in the Old Testament – indeed, at times he affirms there was sacramental life in the Old Testament.[36] But he does qualify its nature, saying things like 'The sacraments of the Old Testament are no proper measure, by which to graduate directly the force that belongs to the sacraments of the New.' This is because the Old Testament 'ordinances and ministrations were all more or less shadowy and incomplete. The substance of their sense is revealed only in Christ.'[37] But what really incensed Hodge was Nevin's claim that the Passover 'was a picture or a sign only of what it was intended to represent; not a sacrament at all indeed in the full New Testament sense, but a sacrament simply in prefiguration and type.'[38]

It is difficult not to sympathize with Hodge's objection to this aspect of Nevin's doctrine. Nevin does seem to conceive of the life of the Old Testament saints as being different in nature to that of the New Testament saints. The work of Christ does not include the robustly proleptic element of traditional Reformed theology, where the Old Testament saints participate through the sacraments of Passover and circumcision in the life of the Church and are truly and really members of Christ's body. So in addition to the problem of how

---

[36] See Erb, *Dr Nevin's Theology*, pp. 214–215 where he speaks of the tree of the knowledge of good and evil in sacramental terms. At one point later in Erb's volume, Nevin reportedly waxes lyrical about the sacramental nature of the whole created order, saying 'The whole constitution of the world is sacramental, as being not simply the sign of, but the actual form and presence of invisible things.' Ibid., p. 373.

[37] Nevin, *The Mystical Presence*, p. 251.

[38] Ibid.

Nevin's distinction between the ideal and actual Church can incorporate the saints now glorified, he has a problem with how to include the Old Testament believers in the life of the Church, and in union with Christ.

Resolving the second of these problems may be easier than retaining Nevin's idealist understanding of the life of the Church. But these are matters to which we shall return in the final, constructive section of the essay.

The organic nature of the Church

We come now to the question of Nevin's understanding of the organic nature of the Church. This component of his ecclesiology is already present in *The Anxious Bench*. There, in a final chapter added to the 1844 edition, he remarks:

> Thus humanity fallen in Adam, is made to undergo a resurrection in Christ, and so restored, flows over organically as in the other case to all in whom its life appears. The sinner is saved then by an inward living union with Christ as real as the bond by which he has been joined in the first instance to Adam. This union is reached and maintained through the medium of the Church by the power of the Holy Ghost. It constitutes a new life, the ground of which is not in the particular subject of it at all, but in Christ, the organic root of the Church.[39]

As is clear from what he says here, Nevin's use of this analogy of organic union had a particular, Incarnational twist. Christ's Incarnation is the first-fruits of a particular sort of 'life' in which the members of his Church became incorporated through union with him, a union that was not merely spiritual, but which included mystical participation in his flesh.[40]

---

[39] Nevin, *The Anxious Bench*, p. 107.

[40] In this last respect Nevin's defence of a robust account of Christ's real but non-corporeal presence in the elements of the Eucharist is the place at which his doctrine of the Church meets his doctrine of the Incarnation, with some very interesting results. See *The Mystical Presence*, ch. III section 2 and ch. IV section 5. His position can be summarized thus: 'Christ's body is not in or under the bread, locally considered. Still, the power of his life in this form is actually exhibited at the same time in the mystery of the sacramental. The one is as truly and really present as the other. The elements are not simply significant of that which they represent, as

These views are given fuller expression in *The Mystical Presence*. There he attempts, amongst other things, to unpack the idea that the development of the Church in Scripture and tradition involves a generic and organic unity between the disparate elements that make up the Church (the individual believers) that are scattered across time.

This in turn led to his rather remarkable way of conceiving the relationship between Adam and his progeny and Christ and his elect along the line of the 'two Adams' Christology of Romans 5:12–19. Nevin was willing to speak in terms of two organic wholes: the 'organism' that is composed of Adam and his progeny; and Christ and his people, the Church. According to Nevin's way of thinking, the Church derives its life from that of Christ, just as Adam's progeny derive their sinfulness from the fall of Adam. In this way, Nevin's doctrine echoed that of the Augustinian realist,[41] which he seemed

---

(cont.) serving to bring it to mind by the help of previous knowledge. They are a pledge of its actual presence and power. They are bound to it in mystical, sacramental union, more intimately, we may say, than they would be if they were made to include it in the way of actual local comprehension. There is far more than then than the mere commemoration of Christ's death. Worthy receivers partake also of his body and blood, with all his benefits, through the power of the Holy Ghost, to their spiritual nourishment and growth in grace.' Ibid., p. 179. Though Christ's presence in the Eucharist is real and non-corporeal, yet somehow the believer participates in Christ's flesh via the work of the Spirit. This is the hard-core of Nevin's mystical approach to the Lord's Supper, the full consideration of which is beyond the scope of this chapter. But, as Brian Gerrish has shown, the sort of Eucharistic theology Nevin espouses, including the mystical participation in Christ's flesh, is in all essential respects Calvinian. See Gerrish, *Grace and Gratitude: The Eucharistic Theology of John Calvin* (Minneapolis: Fortress Press, 1993), p. 136.

---

[41] Augustinian realism is the doctrine according to which Adam's sin is really my sin because Adam and his progeny are somehow one metaphysical entity. This is often combined with traducianism, which states that human beings are united to Adam via their souls which are passed down from parents to children in a way analogous to the passing on of genetic material. On one construal of this doctrine souls are fissiparous, such that Adam possessed an original, 'whole' soul, from which all subsequent souls arise. In which case, my soul is literally a chip of the old (Adamic) block! However, in Nevin's case it is not clear that he held to traducianism, although he sometimes uses language that sounds like it. See, e.g. his comment that 'When Christ died and rose, humanity died and

willing to extend in some ways, so as to conceive not just of Adam and his offspring as somehow one organic, metaphysical whole, but of Christ and his Church as well.[42] Just as Adam and his posterity are somehow organically united so that Adam's sin is passed mediately to his progeny, and from them down through the line of his race,[43] so Christ may be thought of as the one from whom the Church springs in all its various permutations. Thus, at one point in *The Mystical Presence*, Nevin comments,

> Strange, that any who hold to the Augustinian view of Adam's organic union with his posterity, as the only basis that can properly support the doctrine of original sin, should not feel the necessity of a like organic union with Christ, as the indispensible condition of an interest in his salvation.[44]

The human race is not merely an aggregate of particular individuals, like a colossal heap of sand. 'Men have been one before they became many; and as many, they are still one.' The transfer of Adam's sin to his progeny is not merely a matter of a legal or moral fiction, God imputing Adam's sin to me, though it is not my sin, strictly speaking. Rather, Adam's sin is counted mine because it is mine in fact. We are 'born into Adam's nature, and for this reason only, as forming with him the same general life' we are 'born also into his guilt.'[45] The union

---

(cont.) rose at the same time in his person; not figuratively, but truly; just as it had fallen before in the person of Adam.' *The Mystical Presence*, p. 166. (But compare p. 165 – to which we shall return.)

[42] This interest in Augustinian realism, which owes something to the philosophical influence of organic analogies of Christ and the Church borrowed from nineteenth-century German idealism, can be seen in other American theologians of the second half of the nineteenth century. The two most prominent examples of this are the Presbyterian theologian William Shedd and the Baptist Augustus Strong. I have considered Shedd's contribution in *An American Augustinian: Sin and Salvation in the Dogmatic Theology of William G. T. Shedd* (Milton Keynes: Paternoster, 2007), and of Shedd, Strong and Hodge in 'Federalism vs. Realism: Charles Hodge, Augustus Strong and William Shedd on The Imputation of Sin' in *International Journal of Systematic Theology* 8 (2006), pp. 1–17.

[43] See Nevin, *The Mystical Presence*, p. 164 and Erb, *Dr Nevin's Theology*, p. 218.

[44] Nevin, *The Mystical Presence*, p. 212.

[45] Ibid., p. 164.

we have with Adam 'resolves itself at last into an invisible law; and it is not one law for the body, and another law for the soul; but one and the same law involves the presence of both, as the power of a common life.'[46] Similar language applies to Christ and the Church: 'when Christ died and rose, humanity died and rose at the same time in his person; not figuratively, but truly; just as it had fallen before in the person of Adam.'[47]

The language Nevin uses here is suggestive. But it is not entirely clear how Adam's life is my life, or how Christ's life is my life. Am I somehow 'part' of Adam? Stranger still: am I 'part' of Christ? If yes, some explanation of how it is that I am distinct from each of these 'two Adams' is required. Nevin does not want to say that Adam and his progeny or Christ and his Church are so united that they are *numerically* identical. (At least, what he does say strongly suggests this.) For then Adam would be identical to me, and I would be identical to Christ, so that – by application of the principle of transitivity that applies in cases of numerical identity – Adam is identical to Christ. Even aside from considerations of transitivity, my being numerically identical to Adam or to Christ seems obviously mistaken. For instance, Adam is guilty of original sin, Christ is not; Adam is merely human, Christ is not, and so on.[48] Yet Nevin uses language that is very robust. We are 'really', 'truly' united to Adam on the one hand, and to Christ (as members of the Church) on the other. Such language suggests something approaching identity – perhaps a *qualitative* relation that unites us into one organic whole. Then, Adam and I share a great number of qualities – perhaps all the properties necessary to being human, belonging to the human race, and being related to Adam through genes and sin, as it is passed down the generations from parents to children. But we are not numerically the same thing. The same would be true of Christ and his Church, the relevant changes having been made. Christ and his Church share a great many qualities that unite them in one common life, including the righteousness of Christ, which is transferred from Christ to his people by divine fiat, yet in such a way that Christ's righteousness really becomes the righteousness of his people, rather than something that is simply imputed to them.

---

[46] Ibid., p. 165.

[47] Ibid., p. 166.

[48] Nevin does think Christ has a fallen human nature. But he does not think Christ is guilty of original sin. See *The Mystical Presence*, pp. 165–166 and Evans, *Imputation and Impartation*, pp. 161, 166.

This seems to be closer to what Nevin has in mind. But it is not the whole picture, and, in any case, much more would be needed in order to make this a plausible account of the relation between Adam and his progeny and Christ and the Church.[49] We shall return to these matters in the final section of the paper.

Let us take stock. From what we have seen, Nevin seems committed to the following statements about the nature of the Church:

1. The Church is mystically united to Christ.
2. There is an intimate connection between the life of the Church and the Incarnation; indeed, the Church is somehow the continuation of the new creation inaugurated by the Incarnation.
3. The Old Testament has a largely, perhaps almost exclusively preparatory role to play in the history of salvation. Old Testament 'sacraments' are not truly sacraments in the same sense as New Testament sacraments are, though they prefigure the New Testament sacraments in important respects.
4. The Old Testament saints are in a benighted state in comparison to New Testament saints after the Incarnation.
5. The Church has both an ideal aspect, and an actual, concrete aspect. The concrete aspect is the externalization, or realization of the ideal, perfect Church, in time.
6. Whereas the ideal Church is perfect in all respects, the actual, concrete Church in time is imperfect, gradually realizing the ideal as it develops through history towards the final goal of the consummation of all things at the eschaton.
7. The actual, concrete Church is adequate to the task of instantiating the truth of Christianity, despite its manifest failings.
8. Adam and his progeny are an organic whole. Adam and his progeny are (in some sense) a single entity; Adam's life continues in the life of his offspring, and Adam's sin is mediately passed onto his offspring.
9. Christ and the Church are another organic whole. Somehow the members of Christ's Church really participate in his life and

---

[49] For one thing, this does not take account of the idealism in which Nevin couches his argument. For another, it does not give more than the barest hint of how Adam and his progeny as one organic whole is related to Christ and his progeny as the second organic whole such that there are members shared between to two entities (there is some overlap of membership between the two), and yet they are distinct entities.

death, in which they are (mystically) united so that the benefits accruing to the life and work of Christ are the benefits of the Church.[50]

With these tenets of Nevin's doctrine in mind, we turn to consider a constructive argument about the nature of the Church which picks up some of the key theological themes of Nevin's doctrine, and addresses some of its shortcomings.

Towards a Nevin-esque doctrine of the Church

The organic analogy Nevin uses so liberally in order to make sense of the relationship between Christ and his people was common currency amongst those nineteenth-century thinkers influenced in various ways by the regnant idealism of the German intellectual tradition.[51] But there are theologians prior to the nineteenth century for whom an organic analogy between Christ and his Church is important. Take, for example, St Thomas Aquinas, who says:

> As the whole Church is termed one mystic body from its likeness to the natural body of a man, which in divers members has divers acts, as the Apostle teaches (Rom. Xii and 1 Cor. Xii), so likewise Christ is called the Head of the Church from a likeness with the human head[.][52]

---

[50] I shall not consider the related matters of justification and sanctification, as Nevin understands them. This is largely because I do not think I have much more to say on the matter that has not already been said in Evans' study, *Imputation and Impartation*. And, in any case, I am interested in the metaphysics of the Church, rather than the metaphysics of union with Christ.

[51] In fact, Nevin was not only influenced in an idealist direction by his reading of Neander, Schleiermacher and other German theologians. On arrival at Mercersberg in 1840 he had a brief but influential association with Friedrich Rauch, who was at the time of Nevin's appointment the only other member of faculty at the Seminary, and the President of Marshall College, a position Nevin filled when Rauch died in 1841. Rauch's Hegelian idealism, which he had introduced to the American churches through his book *Psychology*, went through a second edition just after his death, with a preface by Nevin. See Nichols, *Romanticism in American Theology*, pp. 46–48 and Richard E. Wentz, *John Williamson Nevin, American Theologian* (New York: Oxford University Press, 1997), pp. 4–5.

[52] St Thomas Aquinas, *Summa Theologica* IIIa. 8. 1, trans. Fathers of the English Dominican Province (New York: Benzinger Brothers, 1948).

Similarly, Calvin:

> First, we must understand that as long as Christ remains outside of us, and we are separated from him, all the he has suffered and done for the salvation of the human race remains useless and of no value for us . . . For, as I have said, all that he possesses is nothing to us until we grow into one body with him.

And,

> The same purpose [viz. union with Christ] is served by that sacred wedlock through which we are made flesh of his flesh and bone of his bone [Eph. 5: 30], and thus one with him. But he unites himself to us by the Spirit alone. By the grace and power of the same Spirit we are made his members, to keep us under himself and in turn to possess him.[53]

Other, strikingly realist-sounding use of the organic analogy can be found elsewhere in the tradition, from the Patristic period onwards, dependent upon the Pauline image of the body in places like Romans 12 and 1 Corinthians 12.[54]

---

[53] John Calvin, *Institutes of the Christian Religion*, trans. Ford Lewis Battles, ed. John T. McNeill (Philadelphia: Westminster Press, 1960), 3.1.1 and 3.1.3, respectively. Concerning the union between Adam and his progeny, Calvin has this to say: 'There is nothing absurd, then, in supposing that, when Adam was despoiled, human nature was left naked and destitute, or that when he was infected with sin, contagion crept into human nature. Hence, rotten branches came forth from a rotten root, which transmitted their rottenness to the other twigs sprouting from them. For thus were the children corrupted in the parent, so that they brought disease upon their children's children. That is, the beginning of corruption in Adam was such that it was conveyed in a perpetual stream from the ancestors into their descendants.' Calvin, *Inst.* 2.1.7, p. 250.

[54] Compare the language of Eusebius of Caesarea: 'And how can He make our sins His own, and be said to bear our iniquities, except by our being regarded as His body, according to the apostle, who says: "Now ye are the body of Christ, and severally members?"' in *Demonstratio Evangelica X. 1*, in *The Proof of The Gospel*, ed. and trans. W. J. Ferrar, Vol. 2 (Eugene, OR.: Wipf & Stock, 2001), p. 195. Similar imagery is used in St Cyril of Alexandria in *De adoratione et culta in spiritu et veritate*, III. 100–102, PG 68: p. 293 and p. 296. The Puritan divine John Owen (whom Nevin cites with approbation in his early work), says of the individual members of the

I labour this point in order to show that the concept of organic union with Adam and with Christ, found in Nevin's writings about the Church, is not merely the preserve of nineteenth-century idealists and those influenced by their philosophy. A number of influential theologians from various periods in the history of the Church have used such language to good effect. Some, like Calvin or Edwards, have made great play of the organic union between Adam and his progeny and Christ and those united with him by the Spirit, not merely as a rhetorical or heuristic device, but as a way of expressing a fundamental metaphysical truth about the union between Adam and his race, or Christ and his people.

What is noteworthy about Nevin's deployment of this notion of an organic union, and the philosophical ideas that underpin it in his writings, is that he extends this way of thinking to include both Adam and his posterity and Christ and the elect. Adam is both a particular and a generic person, with whom the human race is somehow identified, not merely as a representative human being whose sin is imputed to his posterity, but as the first man from whom all humanity is descended, and to whom all humanity is united. It is as if Adam is the prototype from which all subsequent humans are molded; whose fallen human nature becomes the blueprint after which all human

---

(cont.) Church that 'although they are not one in respect of personal unity, they are, however, one, – that is, one body in mystical union, yea, *one mystical Christ* – namely, the surety is the head, those represented by him the members; and when the head is punished, the members also are punished.' In John Owen, *A Dissertation on Divine Justice*, in *The Works of John Owen, Vol. X*, ed. William H. Goold (Edinburgh: Banner of Truth, 1967 [1850–1853]), p. 598. Jonathan Edwards offers a striking example of an organic analogy in his treatise on *Original Sin*, where, in discussing the union of Adam and his progeny he says: 'It appears, particularly, from what has been said, that all oneness by virtue whereof pollution and guilt from past wickedness are derived, depends entirely on a divine establishment . . . And I am persuaded, no solid reason can be given, why God, who constitutes all other created union or oneness, according to his pleasure, and for what purposes, communications, and effects he pleases, may not establish a constitution whereby the natural posterity of Adam, proceeding from him, much as the buds and branches from the stock or root of a tree, should be treated as one with him, for the derivation, either of righteousness and communion in rewards, or of the loss of righteousness and consequent corruption and guilt.' *Original Sin, The Works of Jonathan Edwards, Vol. 3* ed. Clyde A. Holbrook (New Haven: Yale University Press, 1970), pp. 404–405.

beings after Adam are patterned. At times Nevin even speaks as if we are somehow united in Adam and his sin, after the fashion of traducianism. In a similar way, Christ is the one after whom the members of the Church are patterned, the theanthropic person who is not just the blueprint for the elect, but who is the one to whom the believer is united via the Holy Spirit. The mystical union with Christ is a real union, in some ways more intimate than the union between Adam and his progeny.

Perhaps the major shortcoming of Nevin's doctrine is that it does not really offer an adequate understanding of what the union between Adam and his progeny, or Christ and his elect, consists in. (Of course, this is a difficulty he shares with other theologians who utilize a strong doctrine of union with Christ, such as Calvin or Edwards.) In what way does Adam have a 'generic humanity'? In what way can the elect be said to be united to Christ? I do not presume to have a complete answer to these questions – union with Christ, as both Calvin and Nevin saw so clearly, is a divine mystery that cannot be penetrated by human ratiocination. But perhaps something may be said that makes the sort of view Nevin seemed to be struggling to articulate a little clearer.

To that end, consider the following argument. Let *Fallen Humanity* refer to the organic whole that comprises Adam and his progeny (the rest of the human race except Christ). And let *Redeemed Humanity* refer to the organic whole comprising Christ and his elect. These two entities overlap, having some members in common, though not all. (Nevin does not seem to think that Redeemed Humanity has all and only the same constituent members as Fallen Humanity does – that is, some members of Fallen Humanity are not members of Redeemed Humanity; they are not elect.)

Adam and Christ are at the 'head' of their respective organic wholes. That is, Fallen Humanity begins with Adam, who, like an acorn is the first phase of the life of the oak from which it grows. Just so, Adam is the first member of the organism that is Fallen Humanity. Because the 'disease' of sin is introduced to Adam at the beginning of the life of the whole organism, his sin is passed on to later stages or phases of the life of the whole. In a similar way, an acorn that has been infected with some chronic arboreal disease will pass it on to later phases of the life of the tree, from sapling to mature oak. What is the mechanism by which this sin is transmitted from Adam to his progeny? Since we are attempting a Nevin-esque account here, we might, with Nevin, opt for the mediate view, according to which Adam's sin is not imputed to his posterity, strictly speaking. You and I are not merely treated as if we had Adam's sin and are punished accordingly. Rather, Adam's sin is passed down the generations like the disease the acorn passes onto the sapling and the sapling to the mature oak. As a consequence of this, we are guilty because we are sinners; we are not sinners because we are guilty. This applies to human nature, as such. My human nature is corrupted by sin from the first moment of conception, on this way of thinking, because I inherit the disease of sin that is passed down to me from Adam via many intermediate generations to my parents, and from my parents to me. As a consequence of inheriting this sinful condition, I commit actual sins. I am in a sinful condition from the first moment of my existence onwards – the condition passed down from Adam. And I am guilty for committing actual sins. It is not that God immediately imputes Adam's sin to me (as we saw earlier in the chapter on Edwards' doctrine of the imputation of Adam's sin).

But such ideas raise a range of important moral and legal issues for a Nevin-esque account of the Church. For instance, is this a just arrangement? Am I culpable for the sin of another – the sin of Adam? And is this not unjust, given that I had nothing to do with his sin, and that he is separated from my by a great distance in time and space? In answer to these questions we may ask another. Is the mature oak worthy of being cut down simply because it inherits the disease bequeathed to it by the acorn from which it grew? Is this just? We cut down the tree because it is diseased. In one sense it is not the history of the life of the tree that is important. It is the fact that the tree is diseased at the moment it is felled that matters. For that reason it is destroyed. It is not destroyed now because it was diseased at some earlier moment in its history. Similarly, my possessing original sin is what makes me culpable. It might be thought that this does not address the question. What is at stake is the justice of my being created sinful as a consequence of sharing the same human nature as Adam when I am not culpable for committing his sin. But what is interesting about Nevin's position is his claim that Adam's humanity is, as he puts it, generic as well as individual. Or, to state it slightly differently, Adam is not merely an individual human being that sins. He somehow comprehends in himself the whole race, so that when Adam sins, the whole human race sins:

> [t]he human world all slept originally in the common root of the race. Adam was not simply a man, like others since born, but he was the

man, who comprehended in himself all that has since appeared in other men. Humanity as a whole resided in his person. He was strictly and truly the world. Through all ages, man is organically one and the same. And parallel with this precisely is the constitution of the Church. The second Adam corresponds in all respects with the first. He is not a man merely, an individual belonging to the race, but he is *the* man, emphatically the *Son of Man*, comprising in his person the new creation, or humanity recovered and redeemed as a whole.[55]

To transpose this into the context of our present argument, Nevin seems to think that, just as the acorn could be said to 'contain' within it the seed for the life of the whole oak, so also Adam somehow 'contains' within himself the life of the whole of humanity. Nevin thinks that there is an organic law or principle of existence that determines the identity and character of those related to the 'head' of the whole (in this case, Adam).[56] So not only does Adam somehow 'contain' the whole of humanity, there is in place a mechanism (his 'law') whereby the various parts of Fallen Humanity, scattered across space and time, are united as one metaphysical whole such that Adam's sin is 'strictly and truly' their sin.

Something similar obtains with respect to Christ, in Nevin's estimation. Christ is 'the principle or root of the Church' which is one throughout all ages, 'simply because it stands in the presence and power of this root, universally and forever.'[57] Nevin even says that the Church is not an aggregate or collection of individuals, but a strictly organic whole, where that whole 'is older and deeper than the parts' because the parts 'in the end, are only the revelation of what was previously included in the whole.'[58]

From this we can ascertain that, for Nevin the whole of what I am calling Redeemed Humanity (that is, on Nevin's estimation, the Church) is somehow metaphysically united with Christ. Not virtually or, as it were, in abstraction, but 'strictly and truly'. What is more, the whole entity that is Redeemed Humanity is metaphysically prior to its parts, which are added to it through time, as the Church

---

[55] Nevin, 'Catholic Unity', p. 40.
[56] Compare Evans, *Imputation and Impartation*, pp. 161–162 which offers a clear summary of this aspect of Nevin's doctrine.
[57] Nevin, 'Cathlolic Unity', p. 37.
[58] Ibid., p. 40. He goes on to utilize the analogy of the acorn and the oak to illustrate this point.

increases.[59] The individual members of Redeemed Humanity exist at different times and are incorporated into the Church at various moments in their lives. But their incorporation into the whole is rather like adding more clay to a lump; the new parts are absorbed into the whole which precedes it. In this way both Fallen Humanity and Redeemed Humanity look, on a Nevin-esque way of thinking, like growing blocks, or lumps, to which more members are added as humanity and as the Church increase in number through time.

The difficulty Nevin's view encounters when trying to make room for the saints of the Old Testament can be easily accommodated on this view. One need not think, with Nevin, that the Old Testament is merely a sort of shadowy prefiguring of the new creation inaugurated by the Incarnation. For the whole 'lump' or 'block' that comprises Redeemed Humanity may have parts that exist prior to the Incarnation. As new members of the Church are added to the whole after the Incarnation, so, in a similar fashion, new parts may be added prior to the Incarnation. In fact, the resources to make (at least some) sense of this are to be found in Nevin's reasoning. Christ is the 'root' of this Redeemed Humanity; the whole being metaphysically prior to the parts. Christ is prior to his Church. His Incarnation is the outworking in time of God's eternal purposes for his Church. Presumably, these eternal purposes include God's deciding who the members of the Church will be, and how they will be incorporated

---

[59] Question: If the whole is prior to it parts, and Christ is a part of the whole, does this raise potential problems for Nevin? It would seem to mean that Christ's identity is somehow 'conditioned' by the whole entity that is Redeemed Humanity, which is somehow 'prior' to the Incarnation as the metaphysically (though not temporally) first part of the whole. But perhaps one can say this: God ordains Redeemed Humanity, and ordains that, as God the Son, he will assume a human nature and redeem the human beings who comprise the other parts of Redeemed Humanity. In this way, the whole exists prior to the parts (Christ's human nature included), but not in a way that is necessarily theologically damaging to Christ. For, prior to the actualization of any of its parts, the 'whole' exists as a divine idea. In this way, the sort of arrangement I have in mind is quite different from other sorts of corporate entities, such as firms, clubs or governments, which are not usually thought to be directly ordained by God in this fashion. For an interesting discussion of such entities as putative legal and moral 'persons', see Roger Scruton 'Corporate Persons' and the reply by John Finnis, both in *Proceedings of the Aristotelian Society, Supplementary Volume 63* (1989), pp. 239–274.

into Christ – that is, how they will be united with him. Although his work occurs at a particular moment in time, it may well be that the effects of that work are not merely proactive, from the first moment of Incarnation onwards, but also retroactive, incorporating those saints who trusted in Christ prior to his Incarnation. This is indeed mysterious. But since Nevin is perfectly happy with a robust understanding of divine mystery (especially when speaking of the union of the Church with Christ!) this is no more problematic than other things Nevin says. Indeed, this 'correction' to Nevin's doctrine actually makes more sense of his understanding of union with Christ as something that has universal significance. And it also means his understanding of the life of the Church is more in keeping with the Reformed tradition in which he stood.

Could one also adopt Nevin's idealism as the metaphysics by which to underpin the theological claims about the Church he wants to make? Perhaps, although few philosophically-minded theologians today would feel inclined to follow Nevin in this regard. But even if we are not in sympathy with German idealism, all is not lost for someone sympathetic to Nevin's doctrine. Although it would require rather more by way of adjustment to his thought, one could opt for a rather different metaphysical means by which to make good on the sort of organic analogy Nevin utilizes in his version of what I am calling *Fallen* and *Redeemed Humanity*. In other words, we could retain the theological substance of much of what Nevin says while substituting a rather different metaphysics to underpin it.

Here is not the place to offer a detailed explanation of this. But a sketch may suffice: If one thinks of the life of the acorn that becomes the oak as a whole that exists across time, one may also conceive of Adam and his progeny, and Christ and the Church, along similar lines. Each of these wholes comprises one 'life', one 'thing' that has members scattered across space and time. It might be more difficult to see how these members could be one with their respective 'heads' (i.e. Adam and Christ) 'strictly and truly', as Nevin puts it. But here too, one could appropriate some notions culled from contemporary analytic metaphysics in order to come up with results that might be useful to the theologian wanting to redeploy Nevin's insights in a contemporary idiom. Perhaps Fallen Humanity and Redeemed Humanity are two four-dimensional wholes that perdure across time on analogy with the physical parts I have. Just as my body has hands and feet which are different parts of one whole (me), so, on this way of thinking, Fallen and Redeemed Humanity have different parts scattered across space and time which, when taken together and diachronically, form one four-dimensional whole. One satisfying aspect of this metaphysical appeal to four-dimensional entities is that it makes sense of Nevin's claim that the whole object (viz. Fallen Humanity and Redeemed Humanity) is metaphysically prior to its parts. It also has the resources to make sense of the idea that the parts of these wholes (you and I) are really and truly parts of the whole – this is no metaphysical fiction.

Here endeth the metaphysical sketch. Much more would need to be said in order to motivate this Nevin-esque way of thinking about the Church and its relationship to both Adam and Christ. I have begun to do this elsewhere.[60] And more would need to be done by way of working through other, related aspects of Nevin's doctrine that remain problematic. For example, what is the relationship between forensic justification by grace through faith, on this way of thinking, and the organic conception of union with Christ that Nevin conceives of? And what of original sin – is a doctrine of the mediate imputation of Adam's sin sufficient? These are matters all theologians struggle with. Few have managed to bequeath to their theological heirs as interesting and integrated a picture of the Christian life in the Church and union with Christ as Nevin did. The challenge to contemporary divines is to take up where our intellectual forebears left off by changing what is needed, making those adjustments deemed necessary in order to make better sense of the gospel once delivered to the saints. Nevin's theological legacy on the doctrine of the Church is a fruitful one. He may not have all the answers, but he is asking many of the right questions.

---

[60] See my 'Original Sin and Atonement' in Thomas P. Flint and Michael C. Rea, eds. *The Oxford Handbook of Philosophical Theology* (Oxford: Oxford University Press, 2009), ch. 19.

CHAPTER NINE

Jonathan Edwards on the Qualifications for Communion

> In a word, Edwards's ecclesiology reflected his belief that
> the effects of true grace were tangible, visible, and reliably
> discernible.
> – *Mark Noll*[1]

Jonathan Edwards' thinking on the sacraments, and in particular his ruminations on the scope and efficacy of the Eucharist has been recounted in numerous places in the literature. But there has been little by way of theological reflection upon his work in this area of ecclesiology that has a particular focus on what Edwards' views might contribute to contemporary discussion of the matter.[2] It is my

---

[1] Mark A. Noll, *America's God: From Jonathan Edwards to Abraham Lincoln* (New York: Oxford University Press, 2002), p. 45.

[2] Much work has been done on the development of Puritan sacramental theology. Perhaps the most important treatment is E. Brooks Holifield's monograph, *The Covenant Sealed: The Development of Puritan Sacramental Theology in Old and New England 1570–1720* (New Haven: Yale University Press, 1974), although David Hall's editorial introduction to Edwards' *Ecclesiastical Writings* also offers an important assessment. An older work is Edmund S. Morgan's *Visible Saints: The History of a Puritan Idea* (Ithaca: Cornell University Press, 1963). There are numerous biographical essays and monographs that treat the Communion Controversy at Northampton in detail, and the reasons for it. For an early account, see Sereno E. Dwight's memoir of Edwards, prefacing the nineteenth century two-volume edition of Edwards' works, *The Works of Jonathan Edwards, 2 Vols.*, ed. Edward Hickman (Edinburgh: Banner of Truth, 1974 [1834]), especially pp. cxiv–cxxvii. I shall cite this edition of Edwards works in what follows as BOT followed by volume number, colon and page reference, e. g. BOT 1,

contention that what Edwards has to say about the place of the Eucharist in the life of the Church, its affective component, and to whom it should be administered, are important matters relevant to contemporary theology. In this chapter I shall argue that a right understanding of the relationship between Edwards' conception of the Church and his views on admission to the Lord's Table offer a challenge to contemporary theologians to think about these matters more organically, and with an eye to the eschatological importance of our communal life together.

The chapter proceeds in three stages. The first section is a brief recapitulation of the events that contributed to his change of mind in this matter. I shall focus on several issues: the views of Edwards' maternal grandfather, Solomon Stoddard, whose theology of the sacraments was the catalyst for Edwards' change of mind; the writing of his *Humble Inquiry* into the qualification for communion, and his response to objections given in *Misrepresentations Corrected and Truth Vindicated*; the theological reasons that gave rise to Edwards' change of views; and what the nature of those changes were. I will argue, in keeping with the work of other scholars like Thomas Schafer and Douglas Sweeney that Edwards' conception of the Church depends upon a particular metaphysical understanding of what the Church is, and what it is destined for, in the divine economy. Only when Edwards' revised views on communion are seen in light of his doctrine of the Church can we make sense of the reasons why he was unwilling to compromise on his views about qualifications for communion.

(cont.) I, p. 528. For more recent treatments, see especially Patricia Tracy *Jonathan Edwards, Pastor: Religion and Society in Eighteenth-Century Northampton* (New York: Hill & Wang, 1980), George Marsden, *Jonathan Edwards: A Life* (New Haven: Yale University Press, 2003), and Alan D. Strange, 'Jonathan Edwards and the Communion Controversy in Northampton' in *Mid-America Journal of Theology* 14 (2003), pp. 57–97. Gerald R. McDermott's treatment of Edwards' public theology, while not specifically concerned with the Communion Controversy, is nevertheless an interesting and illuminating study of how Edwards conceived of the society in which he lived and the role of the church and its minister. See McDermott, *One Holy and Happy Society: The Public Theology of Jonathan Edwards* (University Park, PA: Pennsylvania State University Press, 1992). For sheer breadth of scope, Mark Noll's *America's God* is difficult to beat, especially chs. 2–3. However, there are very few attempts to assess the ongoing theological relevance of Edwards' contribution to ecclesiology in his writings concerning the Communion Controversy.

Secondly, I shall consider several potential problems with Edwards' revised account of the qualifications for communion. To begin with, there is a concern about the apparent tension between Edwards' requirements for a profession of faith in order to be admitted to communion alongside his admission that he has no infallible means of ascertaining whether anyone professing Christian faith is a true believer. Another potential problem has to do with whether Edwards' position is really any improvement on Stoddard's, when Edwards' view cannot preclude the possibility that those admitted to the communion table are unbelievers. A third objection, related to the previous two, is that a Stoddardean position seems more practical and hospitable than Edwards' view, and therefore preferable.

The third section of the chapter offers some brief reflections on whether contemporary ecclesiology has a richer theological account of the connection between the nature of the Church and its sacramental life than that offered by Edwards.

Historical and theological context

I begin with some historical and theological scene setting. It is well known that Edwards changed his views about how the sacraments ought to be administered, and that this was one important factor, though not the only one, that led to his eventual dismissal from Northampton, where he was minister in succession to his maternal grandfather, Solomon Stoddard.[3] But what was it that precipitated Edwards' change of mind? There are two interrelated issues usually mentioned in the literature: the so-called 'Half Way Covenant'; and the views of Stoddard himself, usually called 'Stoddardeanism' in his honour.

The Half Way Covenant was a scheme brought into operation by the Church of the Massachusetts Bay Colony in 1662 in order to ensure the offspring of the devout who were unable or unwilling to volunteer some account of their own profession of faith, remained within the walls of the church, when numbers in the churches began to decline.[4] The ecclesiastical problem to which the Half-Way

---

[3] See Tracy, *Jonathan Edwards, Pastor, 186–187* and Marsden, *Jonathan Edwards*, pp. 369–374.

[4] 'The Half-Way Covenant . . . sought to check the decline in church membership by allowing the baptism of the children of those second-generation

Covenant was supposed to be a solution was the question that bedevilled New England Puritanism from its inception, namely, what constitutes a visible saint. The Half-Way Covenant meant that many could remain within the Church who did not have a personal profession of faith, but whose lives were sufficiently moral, being children of professing believers and church members, that they could be baptized. The hope was that these 'adult children' as they were dubbed might in time become professing, visible saints and be admitted to the Lord's Supper.

In a long and influential pastorate, Solomon Stoddard came to the view that this arrangement was not sufficiently generous. It is often argued that Stoddard taught the Lord's Supper ought to be open to all whose lives were sufficiently upright and who displayed a true moral sincerity of heart along with assent to the correct congregational doctrine. A public profession of personal faith in Christ was not necessary. Interestingly, the form of words used in Northampton during Stoddard's ministry to admit new members are more rigorous than some historical commentary would suggest. Those wishing to be admitted to membership had to publicly 'take hold of the covenant of the Lord', giving themselves 'to him, to be one of his', subjecting themselves to the 'teachings and government of Jesus Christ in this Church', the welfare of which they were bound to promote.[5] For many mainline Protestant churches today, even this Stoddardean requirement for

---

(cont.) Puritans who were themselves baptized members of the Church but who would not make a public profession of faith. These parents were "halfway" members of the Church in that they could have their children baptized and keep themselves and their children within the Church fold but could not partake of the Lord's Supper.' Conrad Cherry, *The Theology of Jonathan Edwards: A Reappraisal* (Bloomington: Indiana University Press, 1966), p. 204. This 'decline of New England' view is disputed by David Hall 'The New England Background' in *The Cambridge Companion to Jonathan Edwards*.

[5] What is more, Stoddard himself sought evidence of 'true religion' amongst his congregation. After all, he was a revivalist who worked hard to promote true, rather than nominal Christianity, in keeping with his views that the Lord's Table could be a place where people could be converted and assured of their salvation, as was his own experience. The fact that Stoddard thought the Lord's Table might be a converting ordinance does not mean he thought there was no distinction between nominal and true Christianity; far from it. I am grateful to Doug Sweeney for pointing this out to me.

church membership would seem draconian, let alone what Edwards had in mind![6] Nevertheless, Stoddardeanism went beyond the dictates of the Half-Way Covenant scheme to admit more into full Church membership than had previously been thought desirable or theologically acceptable.

But this debate about the scope and nature of sacramental theology in Puritan New England must be set against a wider background of the New England Way, particularly, the manner in which covenantal theology had migrated from Old Europe to the New World, and been transformed by the Massachusetts Fathers and those that succeeded them into a theological scheme by which to cement civil society into one holy commonwealth. Mark Noll speaks of this in terms of the 'Puritan canopy'. He argues that Stoddard 'held that a national covenant existed whenever any people subscribed in the aggregate to the Christian religion. Stoddard's ecclesiology and his reinterpretation of the covenant were based on the assumption that New England was a Christian nation'. On this basis Stoddard regarded the Lord's Table as 'a seal, not of personal regeneration, but of the truth of God's revelation in Christ and of God's willingness to covenant with Christian nations, [such] . . . that all in such a national covenant take part in it for their own good.'[7] The language of 'publicly taking hold of the covenant of the Lord' used for admittance to the table in Stoddard's pastorate certainly suggests this. It was this assimilation of sacramental theology to civic religion, expressed in terms of a national covenant, fused with the Stoddardean notion that the sacrament might be treated as a 'converting ordinance', that Edwards eventually repudiated.

In his preface to his *An Humble Inquiry* of 1749 (hereinafter, HI[8]), the treatise that marked the beginning of his published work on the Communion Controversy that presaged the end of his Northampton

---

[6] The precise form of words used to admit people to full church membership during Stoddard's pastorate at Northampton are given by Douglas Sweeney in his insightful essay, 'The Church' in Sang Hyun Lee, ed., *The Princeton Companion to Jonathan Edwards* (Princeton: Princeton University Press, 2005), p. 187, n. 22.

[7] Noll offers a trenchant overview of how the 'Puritan canopy' of covenant theology was changed and inadvertently destroyed by Edwards in response to Stoddard's innovations. See Noll, *America's God*, pp. 4–50.

[8] See Jonathan Edwards, *Ecclesiastical Writings, The Works of Jonathan Edwards Vol. 12*, ed. David D. Hall (New Haven: Yale University Press, 1994), hereinafter cited as YE12, followed by colon and pagination, e.g. YE12: 250.

ministry,[9] Edwards made it clear that he only moved away from his grandfather's position after much soul-searching, and as a result of changes to the theological convictions he had begun his ministry with. 'I have formerly been of his opinion' he remarks, 'which I imbibed from his books, even from my childhood, and have in my proceedings conformed to his practice; though never without some difficulties in my view, which I could not solve.' He goes on to say that this uneasiness increased as he progressed in his ministry and as he became 'more studied in divinity' and acquired more pastoral experience. It was only after much careful reflection that he reached his mature views, which resolved his own inner theological unrest only at the cost of departing from the views of his grandfather. Publishing these views was, he says, a task he took up 'with the greatest reluctance that ever I undertook any public service in my life.'[10]

As subsequent events unfolded, this reluctance proved prescient. Edwards lost the confidence of his congregation and was dismissed in 1750, ending up as a missionary in the (then) frontier town of Stockbridge, Massachusetts, some forty miles to the west of his old pastoral charge. Sticking to his revised theological principles about matters concerning qualifications for admission to the sacrament had cost Edwards dearly. To make matters worse his cousin, Solomon Williams, who was himself a fellow New England minister at Lebanon, Connecticut, subjected Edwards' views to a very public scrutiny and minute rebuttal, in defence of grandfather Stoddard's doctrine.[11]

---

[9] I shall use the proper noun 'Communion Controversy' to refer to the protracted events that led to Edwards' dismissal from Northampton, and those events subsequent to his dismissal germane to this question, e.g. his response to Solomon Williams' attack on his published views in 1752, entitled *Misconceptions Corrected and Truth Vindicated*. Of course, the Communion Controversy in New England was older than Edwards' part in it. But the role Edwards played was, arguably, an important phase in this larger conflict within New England Congregationalism. For detailed historical discussion of this, see Edmund S. Morgan, *Visible Saints*; Holifield, *The Covenant Sealed*; and David Hall's essay, 'The New England Background' in *The Cambridge Companion to Jonathan Edwards*, pp. 61–79.

[10] YE12: 169–170.

[11] Solomon Williams, *The True State of the Question Concerning the Qualifications Necessary to Lawful Communion in the Christian Sacraments, Being and Answer to the Reverend Jonathan Edwards* (Boston, 1751). The argument of Williams' treatise is summarised by Hall in his editorial introduction to YE12: 69–73.

Ironically, the congregation at Northampton sponsored Williams' reply to Edwards.[12] In responding to Williams in *Misrepresentations Corrected and Truth Vindicated* (hereinafter MCTV), Edwards was at pains to point out that his reason for publishing his own views on the matter were not to rubbish the teaching of Stoddard, but to set out his case in order that his own congregation and those drawn into the controversy, might ascertain what his position amounted to (MCTV II.I).

The controversy was certainly the occasion of his writing; but it might seem insincere of Edwards not to admit that stepping out of his grandfather's shadow played an important theological (and, arguably, psychological) part in the endgame that his controversy with the Northampton congregation, and the publication of HI, precipitated.[13]

Still, as George Marsden points out, in writing MCTV in 1752, when he was settled as a missionary in Stockbridge, Edwards 'truly had some misrepresentations to correct'.[14] Williams distorted crucial components of Edwards' position (as well as that of Stoddard!), claiming Edwards revised view was that an adherent of the church wishing to become a full communicant had to display the highest evidence of godliness (i.e. had to demonstrate they were an authentic Christian beyond any shadow of doubt). Edwards' response in MCTV was a devastating point-by-point rebuttal of the objections raised against him: he demanded only some outward, plausible evidence of godliness – some confession of real faith. He certainly did not think that the highest evidence of godliness was practical let alone possible. As he says, '[t]he point of difference' between himself and his congregation, as reported to the council that severed the connection binding his congregation to him, 'was entirely the matter of profession [of faith], and the thing to be made visible [in a life of manifest godliness]: not the degree of evidence or visibility.'[15] But nor did he think that Stoddard's weaker requirement of mere moral sincerity of heart was sufficient to warrant admission to communion. After all,

---

[12] In the Appendix to *Misrepresentations Corrected and Truth Vindicated* Edwards writes a short letter to his erstwhile parishioners in Northampton, warning them against abandoning what they had been taught by Stoddard and himself, in favour of the doctrinal innovations advocated by Williams, whose work, he notes, 'has been written and published very much by your procurement and at your expense'. *YE12*: 498.

[13] Tracy's *Jonathan Edwards, Pastor*, is particularly helpful in this regard.

[14] Marsden, *Jonathan Edwards*, p. 368.

[15] MCTV in *YE12*: 357.

sincerity, even moral sincerity, was hardly sufficient to demonstrate a person was in the right moral condition for their participation in full communion. A person could be morally sincere in the relevant sense but unregenerate. Of course, a person could live an apparently moral life and make a credible public confession of faith and still be unregenerate. Edwards did not think he was in possession of an infallible means by which to test whether communicants were regenerate or not – this was precisely what Williams had falsely asserted Edwards did teach. But Edwards did think that a profession of faith and evidence of a godly life were good indicators that the person concerned was regenerate, in common with many in the Reformed tradition. And this attempt to isolate reliable, if not foolproof, indicators of regeneration was something Edwards had spent considerable time explicating in his earlier work on the theology of the Great Awakening, culminating in his treatise on *Religious Affections* of 1746 (hereinafter, RA).[16] One might put it like this: Edwards promoted a different ethics of belief regarding prospective communicants than did his grandfather. For Edwards the church ought to recognize a prospective communicant as a visible saint, and therefore worthy of being admitted to the Lord's Table, only if that person was able to make a credible profession of faith in Christ. Stoddard's ethics of belief were less stringent, allowing that a prospective communicant might be admitted to the Lord's Table without such a confession, but with a moral sincerity of heart and adherence to the outward forms and doctrines of congregationalism, including adherence to the covenantal scheme Stoddard, following his Puritan forebears, preferred.

So, according to Edwards, Stoddard's requirement for full communion was simply not sufficient to the purpose; something more was needed, and Edwards' thought he had ascertained what that missing component was: a confession of faith. He was not advocating the establishment of a 'pure' church populated only by the elect. He was no Separatist. For there was no infallible way to establish beyond doubt who was elect and who was not. But he did think, in common with the Apostle in 1 Corinthians 11, that only those who could give

---

[16] In his preface to HI Edwards indicates that he had come to his mature views about the qualifications for communion prior to writing *Religious Affections* in 1746. See YE12: 171. For RA, see Edwards, *Religious Affections, The Works of Jonathan Edwards Vol. 2*, ed. John E. Smith (New Haven: Yale University Press, 1959).

credible evidence of faith in public confession of conversion should be admitted to the Lord's Table. The sacrament was decidedly not established to be a 'converting ordinance' – although it might serve that purpose in an indirect fashion.

If MCTV was a victory against Williams and his supporters, it was very much a pyrrhic one, in two respects. First, by the time of writing MCTV Edwards had been ejected from his charge in Northampton without his revised qualifications for communion being lastingly implemented. His parishioners simply did not believe he had acted sincerely. They were suspicious of the fact that the imposition of his revised regulations for admission to communion had coincided with the death of Colonel John Stoddard.[17] Colonel Stoddard was grandfather Solomon's son, and a powerful political figure in the region that might have championed his father's teaching in the parish. Second, and perhaps partly as a consequence of these circumstances, in the immediate aftermath of the Communion Controversy his views did not have wide currency amongst clergy or congregations, even if his dismissal, and the events surrounding it, did generate a considerable amount of interest. To Edwards in 1752 at the close of the Controversy, exiled in the frontier settlement of Stockbridge with apparently little influence on wider ecclesiastical politics, his argument for tighter theological principles governing admission to the communion table appeared to have fallen on deaf ears.[18]

---

[17] Marsden points out that the reasons for Edwards reticence to make his changed views on the sacraments public was due to a number of different factors, including political in-fighting amongst New England clergy and the ongoing War of Austrian Succession (1744–1745) in which New England had a stake. See *Jonathan Edwards*, ch. 19. But sorting out all the different contributing historical factors is, as Conrad Cherry observes, a matter that is 'staggeringly complex'. Conrad Cherry, *Theology of Jonathan Edwards*, p. 203.

[18] Edwards' views on qualifications for communion were taken up, and adapted, by his immediate disciples who espoused the so-called New Divinity. These included Joseph Bellamy, Samuel Hopkins and his own son, Jonathan Edwards Jr. In the case of Edwards Jr., adherence to his father's principles was a significant factor in his own dismissal from the White Haven Congregational Church in New Haven. See Robert L. Ferm, *Jonathan Edwards the Younger 1745–1801: A Colonial Pastor* (Grand Rapids: Eerdmans, 1976), p. 105 and ch. 9. Compare Holifield, *The Covenant Sealed*, p. 229. Dwight maintains, in suitably admiring tones, that HI 'has been the standard work with evangelical divines from that time [i.e. from the time

This historical vignette has been drawn a number of times in the secondary literature on Edwards.[19] Two issues that this historiographical work touches upon are particularly relevant for our concern. The first has to do with the theological reasons that gave rise to Edwards' change of heart. The second has to do with the nature of that change: why did Edwards come to the view that Stoddardeanism was ecclesiologically poisonous? And what drove Edwards to formulate the position he ended up owning?

As to the theological reasons that gave rise to his change of heart, Edwards says several things that are of interest in the preface to HI, as we have already had cause to note. The first is that he came to his revised views honestly, through theological reflection upon Holy Scripture. Whereas Stoddard's position had been what he was brought up to believe (by his own account), he was uneasy with aspects of Stoddard's position that he was unable to resolve until further reflection over some period of time. If Edwards' report is to be believed, this gradual change of mind occurred at some point during his ministry at Northampton, but after his grandfather's death, by which time Stoddard's views had become the view imbibed by two generations of the congregation.[20] Whether or not he deliberately delayed the implementation of his new position on qualifications for communion until the opportune moment of Colonel Stoddard's death is another matter and one that it is now impossible to adjudicate.

On the question of the nature of Edwards' revised views on qualifications for communion, Edwards' position in HI is clear. First, he thinks the biblical position is that the 'people of Christ' should make heartfelt profession of their faith; should have an understanding of what this means; and should express this in right theological and moral judgments, living consistently with such judgments. Not all within the bounds of the church are capable of fulfilling all these conditions. But infants and children are excluded from the requirement to make public profession, since they are not regular communicants

---

(cont.) of composition] to the present [early nineteenth century].' Dwight, Memoir, in BOT 1, p. cxvi.

[19] Most recently in Philip Gura's biography, *Jonathan Edwards: America's Evangelical* (New York: Hill and Wang, 2005) and Marsden's biographical sketch of Edwards life in the *Cambridge Companion to Jonathan Edwards*, especially pp. 33–34.

[20] Compare Dwight, Memoir, BOT 1, p. cxiv.

(though they are part of the covenant community if baptized[21]). And there are those who by reason of mental incapacity will fall outside of the requirements as well, including some who are baptized adults. (It is not clear whether such persons would be capable of being full communicants on Edwards' reasoning.) But for those who are capable adults, these requirements are obligatory for those who wish to become full communicants in the church. Edwards is clear that the biblical testimony yields only one plausible conclusion: that those admitted to the Lord's Supper must accept Christ (i.e. make public profession of such faith and live lives of evident godliness) because participation in the Lord's Supper is a solemn profession of such faith. But clearly, such sentiments are incompatible with the teaching of Stoddard. Or at least, being willing to publicly 'take hold of the covenant of the Lord giving oneself to him to be one of his', as the Stoddardean form of words stated, was simply not sufficient as far as Edwards was concerned.

There are several reasons for this. The first is easily identified, lying as it does on the surface of the issues Edwards was engaged in: he was adamantly opposed to anything like what E. Brooks Holifield calls 'sacramental evangelism'.[22] But the reasons for Edwards' disquiet over this matter were far more fundamental to his whole theological outlook. For, secondly, he maintained that the only true saint was a visible saint, and the only true church a visibly true church.[23] He would have no truck with the practical division, long associated with New England Puritanism, between these two things. Indeed, he confessed that he could think of 'no other sensible meaning of the phrase "true Church" or "truly God's Church," than either those that are truly and really God's people and Christ's people, or those that truly have the outward appearances of being Gods people'. This did not mean that he identified the visible with the invisible church. But it did mean he thought much greater care had to be taken to ensure only those who are appear to be Christ's people 'in the eye of a Christian

---

[21] *YE12*: 174. Edwards distinguishes between *ordinary members* of the Church and *members in complete standing*. Infants are 'in some respect in the Church of God', but are not members in complete standing.

[22] See Holifield, *The Covenant Sealed*, p. 229.

[23] This is evident in some of his early miscellany entries, e.g. Nos. 335 and 339. Thomas Schafer has a very interesting discussion of this matter in 'Jonathan Edwards' Conception of the Church' in *Church History* 24 (1955), pp. 51–66.

judgment and, according to gospel rules, are to be looked upon, respected, and behaved towards as such.'[24] His conception was of a gathered communicant membership within a mixed state church – New England's Congregationalist standing order – not a separated church, that is, a company of professing believers, some of whom (like Judas) might turn out to be wolves clothed as sheep.

This brings me to the third and most fundamental issue for Edwards' conception of the Church. Axiomatic to Edwards' conception of the nature of the Church was the notion that the elect comprising the true Church are united with Christ as his bride, his mystical body, in some way that involves a *metaphysically real union* between the two. The members of the Church are conjointly Christ's body, are elected to the end of composing this body, in order that the Second Person of the Trinity may have some fitting created thing upon which to lavish his love. Not only is the Church really united to Christ but the creation of the Church is, on Edwards' way of thinking, one of the ends of creation. Thus Thomas Schafer comments,

> Edwards' conception of the Church is rooted in his ontology and cosmology. The Church of the elect is mankind as aimed at in the creation, is the completion of the Trinity's primal urge to love and communicate good. Edwards has a high doctrine of the transcendent oneness of the Church in Christ, a unity buttressed by his theological and philosophical realism.[25]

Edwards speaks in diverse places and times with the same voice, stating plainly, particularly in the treatises and notebook entries of his last decade, that the Church is destined to be united with Christ 'in an infinite strictness'[26] in a union brought about through the assumption of human nature by the *Logos*, who acts as the head of the body of the Church, 'even so as to be one person (i.e. the theanthropic person of Christ) and the rest (i.e. elect humans) to be strictly united to him.'[27]

---

[24] Misc. 339 in Schafer, 'Jonathan Edwards' Conception of the Church', p. 58.

[25] Schafer, 'Jonathan Edwards' Conception of the Church', p. 62

[26] Edwards, *End of Creation II. VII* in *Ethical Writings, The Works of Jonathan Edwards Vol. 8*, ed. Paul Ramsey (New Haven: Yale University Press, 1989), 534. Hereinafter, YE8.

[27] Misc. 1245 in Edwards, *The "Miscellanies" (Entry Nos. 1153–1360), The Works of Jonathan Edwards Vol. 23* ed. Douglas A. Sweeney (New Haven: Yale University Press, 2004), p. 180. Hereinafter, cited as *YE23*.

Moreover, God aims in creation to bring about 'an infinitely perfect union of the creature with himself'.[28] This union is eternal in character, being a process by which the believer becomes ever more closely united with the divine nature, though never absorbed by, or fused with, the divine nature: such is the prospect of the glorified body of Christ.[29] Viewed from this perspective, Edwards' change of views in the Communion Controversy were not so much a tactic for outmanoeuvring his dead grandfather as what he thought of as the natural ecclesiological corollary of a metaphysical vision concerning the relation between creation and redemption, which turns on the person and work of Christ to whom the elect are somehow really united. The wonder is not that Edwards had a change of 'public' views but that he managed to keep private the consequences of this dramatic and realist Christological understanding of the nature of the Church.[30] Indeed,

---

[28] *YE23*: 180.

[29] ''Tis no solid objection against God's aiming at an infinitely perfect union of the creature with himself, that the particular time will never come when it can be said, the union is now infinitely perfect . . . I suppose it will not be denied by any that God, in glorifying the saints in heaven with eternal felicity, aims to satisfy his infinite grace or benevolence, but the bestowment of a good infinitely valuable, because eternal: and yet there never will come the moment, when it can be said, that now this infinitely valuable good has been actually bestowed.' Edwards in *End of Creation II. VII*, *YE8: 536*.

[30] In his recent treatment of the concept of union with Christ via the Holy Spirit in Edwards' thought, Robert Caldwell III offers a much more qualified account of Edwards' apparent endorsement of a doctrine of divinization. He says 'Edwards always places limits on this pushing-of-the-boundaries, especially with regard to the greatest theological and ontological distinction of all: the distinction between Creator and creature. He never crosses this line.' Robert W. Caldwell III, *Communion in the Spirit: The Holy Spirit as the Bond of Union in the Theology of Jonathan Edwards* (Milton Keynes: Paternoster, 2006), p. 192. But this is mistaken. First, Edwards' language about union with Christ is very strong indeed – despite his use of qualifying caveats like 'as it were' and 'in some sense', noted by Caldwell. Second, Edwards never concedes that the Bride of Christ will become Christ. But a doctrine of *theosis* need not grant this; the idea is that one may be united to the divine, not that one may become identical with the divine. (Discussions of theosis often involve distinguishing between becoming partakers of the divine nature (i.e., divinization), and become part of the divine essence, which would mean becoming somehow absorbed into God). Third, although Edwards does

Douglas Sweeney remarks, 'Edwards' late decision to restrict the sacraments in Northampton to those who made a "true" profession proved novel only in its consistency with his doctrine of the church, and not as a deviation in his sacramental theology.'[31]

Potential problems with Edwards' views

Having spent some time outlining the historical background to Edwards' views and the theological reasons he had for his change of mind about the qualifications for communion, we are now in a position to consider some potential problems for Edwards' way of thinking.

In the recent theological literature, Stephen Holmes has drawn attention to what he thinks is a tension between the qualifications for communion contained in HI and Edwards' account of the change brought about by conversion, and the signs that indicate conversion has taken place, enunciated in his earlier treatise, RA.[32] What is interesting in this regard is that by Edwards' own confession he had come to his revised views about qualifications for communion around the same time as he was writing RA. So this is not a case of discovering some tension between the thought of the earlier and later Edwards. Rather, what we have is a tension between two strands of his thinking developed at the same period of his ministry. Holmes is careful to note that there is no absolute incoherence about this, although there is an 'incongruity' and that this 'is surely a question that should be pressed'.[33] As we have already noted in the previous section, the main issue between Edwards' views in HI and Stoddardeanism centres on the distinction between the visible and invisible church. Stoddardeans distinguished between an outward, intellectual assent to

---

have a robust distinction between God and his creatures, there is a tension in his thought on this matter. For Edwards also endorsed a version of panentheism, according to which the world is somehow God's body, the consequence of God's desire to 'expand himself' in some qualified sense, to include the created order. But these are deep waters that cannot be plumbed here. Interested readers might begin by consulting Edwards, *End of Creation* ch. 1, § 4, objection 4, in YE8: 458–463.

[31] Sweeney, 'The Church', p. 184.

[32] Stephen R. Holmes, *God of Grace and God of Glory: An Account of The Theology of Jonathan Edwards* (Edinburgh: T & T Clark, 2000), pp. 184–191.

[33] Holmes, *God of Grace*, p. 186.

doctrine coupled with a moral life, from inward true belief and holiness. The former they required; the latter they believed to be inaccessible to reliable pastoral analysis. The problem with this, as Holmes reports it, was that for the Stoddardean there was no particular connection between these two things. Or at least, 'the interior reality of faith can exist only where the exterior practice also exists, but that such exterior practice does not depend in any way on the interior reality.' Whereas for Edwards 'true interior holiness will necessarily be visible – not so visible as to be unmistakable, but visible nonetheless.'[34]

Holmes focuses on several important issues here that I intend to press a little harder, as he suggests. I shall begin with a few words on the matter of the consistency of Edwards' account of religious affections. In RA, as in HI, Edwards nowhere states that he has devised an infallible means by which to ascertain whether a person is truly a Christian or not. It is true that the main argument of RA concerns twelve signs of true conversion. But Edwards nowhere claims that these are more than good indicators of true conversion, just as we might think whistling the tune of the Fighting Irish, sporting blue and gold clothing on match days, and spending money on getting tickets to particular football games are good indicators that a person supports one well-known college football team. Similar reasoning applies to HI and Edwards' amplification of his own position in MCTV. He is not interested in asking that those applying for communion be able to show infallible signs of true godliness, nor even sure signs – if this means signs which are unquestionably or indisputably true or real. But he does think more than an intellectual assent to doctrine, morally upright life and 'sincerity' are required to warrant admission to the Lord's Table. For the sacrament is a sign for the church, not the whole community. In short, there must be some evidence that the prospective communicant thinks of him- or herself as a member of the invisible, nor merely visible, church, and can offer credible testimony of this in the form of a godly life and public profession of Christian faith. And this is what Stoddardeanism was unwilling to insist upon. In fact, it would appear that someone could fulfill all the requirements of Stoddardeanism with a merely pragmatic view of faith, where the person claiming faith merely acts as if it were true that they were Christians. In the recent philosophical literature Richard Swinburne has set forth something like this idea:

---

[34] Holmes, *God of Grace*, p. 188.

He [the person with merely pragmatic faith] lives the good life, not necessarily because he believes that God will reward him, but because only if there is a God who will reward him can he find the deep long-term well-being for which he seeks. He worships, not necessarily because he believes that there is a God who deserves worship, but because it is very important to express gratitude for existence if there is a God to whom to be grateful and there is some chance that there is.[35]

According to Swinburne, the virtue of this view is that it forecloses the possibility that the person with faith is a scoundrel. For no one whose faith is pragmatic in this sense will live wickedly. It should be clear from the foregoing that the Stoddardean requirements for admission to communion could not exclude someone whose faith was merely pragmatic, in the Swinburnian sense. That is, Stoddardeanism could not exclude from participation in communion those acting *as if* there was a God, assenting to certain doctrines on that basis, and living a life of moral sincerity – but without necessarily having the belief that there is a God, that Christ is the saviour of fallen human beings, and so forth. Or, one could hold that there is a God and trust that *there is a God* and act accordingly. But trusting that there is a God and acting on this basis is hardly the same as trusting God.

Naturally, if one holds that administration of the Lord's Supper is a 'converting ordinance', then, like Stoddard, this reasoning will not necessarily hold any terror – although it is one thing to allow those who have no profession of personal faith into full church membership and quite another to allow those with no propositional belief in God. It is persons of the former sort that Stoddardeans seemed to be interested in. Still, it would be difficult on Stoddardean principles to withhold full church membership and communion from the person with merely pragmatic faith. What grounds could the Stoddardean give for refusing such a person? Presumably not the stated requirements of Stoddardeanism, since such an individual could assent to all these in good faith (literally). The fact that someone with merely pragmatic faith – indeed, with no belief that there is a God at all – could be admitted to the Lord's Table is simply a consequence of embracing 'sacramental evangelism' of the Stoddardean variety. But it is just this sort of consequence that gave Edwards grave ecclesiological concern.

It is not difficult to see the source of Edwards' concern. Not only

---

[35] Richard Swinburne, *Faith and Reason* (Oxford: Oxford University Press, 1981), p. 117.

does Stoddardeanism entail that persons with no faith, perhaps even no formal belief in God, can be admitted to the Table provided they are willing to assent to the right doctrine and live a morally sincere life. It also means that there may be those admitted to communion for whom faith in God is a meritorious act. This is Swinburne's point about pragmatic faith. The pragmatist about faith is a virtuous person just in case his faith is meritorious. But in order to grant this one would have to be willing to concede that faith is a meritorious act, and no one in the Reformed tradition – least of all Edwards – would be willing to do so. As Paul Helm has recently put it, 'the basic religious stance of trustfulness, at least in Christianity, [is] that of one who trusts he will receive, rather than trusting as the basis of doing something and so gaining merit thereby'.[36] The Stoddardean attempt at sacramental evangelism should be a warning to contemporary ecclesiologists: opening the Table to all who will come, or all who will come and have sincerity of heart and a morally upright life not only opens the sacrament to many for whom belief in God is merely notional. It also opens up the possibility that some will come to the Table under the impression that fulfillment of the requirements for admission is meritorious, or an expression of a meritorious act of faith. And this, it hardly needs to be said, is quite contrary to Christian faith (cf. Eph. 2:8–9).

Edwards' view seems to be that religious belief is usually based on evidence, but only those who possess the proper moral and spiritual qualifications can accurately assess the evidence provided.[37] This excludes the possibility of admitting to the Lord's Table those with merely pragmatic faith. It is also, in Stephen Holmes' phrase, a means by which Edwards could hold the visible and invisible church together. Only those with a credible profession of faith and moral life could be admitted to the Table. And at least some of those people would be true believers, that is, amongst God's elect. Of course, a corollary of this is that those admitted to the Lord's Table may be mistaken in their belief that they are Christians. One might think one has good reason to believe one is a Christian, and yet be deceived about this, just as I might think that I have good reason to believe I am perceiving a tree,

---

[36] Paul Helm, *Faith with Reason* (Oxford: Oxford University Press, 2000), p. 151. This point is made in response to Swinburne.

[37] This is certainly the way one recent philosopher has understood Edwards. See William Wainwright, *Reason and the Heart: A Prolegomenon to a Critique of Passional Reason* (Ithaca: Cornell University Press, 1995), especially ch. 1.

when in fact I am not: the 'tree' in question being merely a cardboard cut-out. But what more could one ask for? As Edwards pointed out repeatedly in RA,

> I am far from undertaking to give such signs of gracious affections, as shall be sufficient to enable any certainly to distinguish true affection from false in others; or to determine positively which of their neighbours are true professors, and which are hypocrites. In so doing, I should be guilty of that arrogance I have been condemning.

He goes on,

> It be plain that Christ has given rules to all Christians, to enable 'em to judge of professors of religion, whom they are concerned with, so far as is necessary for their own safety, and to prevent their being led into a snare by false teachers, and *false pretenders of religion* . . . yet, 'tis also evident, that it was never God's design to give us any rules, by which we may certainly know, who of our fellow professors are his, and to make a full and clear separation between sheep and goats.[38]

And, as we have already noted in response to Williams in MCTV, Edwards makes it perfectly clear there was never any suggestion that the dispute between himself and the Stoddardeans 'was only about the degree of evidence [of godliness]; but what was the thing to be made evident; whether real godliness or moral sincerity'. He is not concerned to set out which degree of certainty a person's profession of faith must meet in order to be credible. That was not the point at issue in the Communion Controversy. The problem was that followers of Stoddard were willing to engage in sacramental evangelism, which is quite another matter. It is the difference between saying 'you do not have to trust your spouse is faithful to enjoy the benefits of marriage, but it helps' and 'you *do* have to trust your spouse is faithful to enjoy the benefits of marriage'. For the Stoddardeans, no trust in Christ on the part of the prospective communicant needed to be established or presumed in advance of admission to the sacrament. For Edwards, admission to the Lord's Table depended on evidence of such trust between the prospective communicant and Christ. Surely that is what Edwards' requirement amounts to: 'none should be admitted to full communion in the church of Christ, but such as in

---

[38] RA, in YE2: 193. Emphasis added.

profession, and in the eye of a reasonable judgment, are truly saints, or godly persons.'[39] In light of this, and *pace* Holmes, I suggest that Edwards' position in RA and his views laid out in HI and MCTV are entirely consistent, and that there is no discernible tension between them.

But there is another problem for Edwards' revised view in HI that Swinburne's recent discussion of faith raises. Swinburne objects to several accounts of religious faith that include knowledge and/or assent, and a fiducial component because, he thinks, they cannot exclude the possibility that the man of faith is a scoundrel.[40] Might Edwards' account be open to a similar objection? That is, might it be the case that a person could fulfill Edwards' criteria for full communion and yet be a scoundrel? If so, in what way is Edwards' position an advance on that of the Stoddardeans whose position entails this?

There are several things to say by way of response to this objection. First, it is true that the logic of Edwards' position means that a person might be so depraved that, though they claim to profess faith and live a life that appears to be godly, they are in fact wicked. Edwards is quite clear that this is possible and that all the Christian can do is apply those tests of faith one finds in Holy Scripture to persons applying for communion, in the full knowledge that no human judgment based on these scriptures this side of the grave is infallible. This is not materially equivalent to the Stoddardean position. But it might be thought to have practical consequences that are almost indiscernible from the Stoddardean position, and this seems to be theologically troubling. For it means that the Edwardsian cannot ensure that no scoundrels are admitted to the Lord's Table, any more than the Stoddardean can. However, not being able to exclude a possible consequence of one's position is not the same as holding to a position that entails that consequence. Consider the difference between putting security safeguards in place at an airport in the knowledge that no security safeguard is foolproof, and putting no safeguards in place at the airport. The official who says 'we need the highest specification security protocols in place in our airport' would also have to say 'of course, we cannot ever have protocols in place that will screen out all troublemakers, but we hope that having the protocols in place will significantly reduce the numbers of terrorists who get through our

---

[39] *YE12*: 356.
[40] Swinburne, *Faith and Reason*, ch. 4. For instance, one might be an antinomian, 'sinning that grace may abound'.

airports'. But this is hardly the same as the incompetent official who says 'we will not have any security protocols in place in our airport because one cannot infallibly ascertain whether someone passing through the airport is a terrorist or not.' Edwards' position is like the view expressed by the first official, the Stoddardean position is like the second. Clearly, the two views do not necessarily yield the same results, although they might. Still, the fact that they might yield the same practical outcome should give the defender of Edwards pause for thought. For the Edwardsian cannot say that necessarily the practical upshot of her view will not be the same as that of the Stoddardean.

But thirdly, even if we grant the foregoing, is Edwards' position preferable to Stoddardeanism? It might be thought that Stoddard's position has a number of attractions that Edwards' views do not. For one thing, Stoddard's conception of the Lord's Table as an ordinance open to all who will 'publicly take hold of the covenant of the Lord', who have a moral sincerity of purpose and a blameless life, and accede to Congregational doctrine appears more 'hospitable' (in the sense of that term used by some contemporary Christian ethicists) than that offered by Edwards'. In eighteenth century New England, where Congregationalism was effectively the state Church, and where local taxes were levied in support of the Meeting House and minister, it is strange to think that the conception of the nature of the Church was still that of a gathered congregation of believers. Stoddardeanism was a way of maintaining the ecclesial *status quo* when it seemed to be in danger of being compromised by an increasing number of nominal believers. One might even think of it as a creative way of keeping people in the Church in the hope that, given time, they might also come to a personal profession of the faith preached each Sabbath. The Stoddardean conception of the sacrament would then be a sort of forerunner to the rather crass postmodern notion of 'belonging, before believing'.

But things look rather different if Edwards' vision of the Church as the body of Christ metaphysically united to him, is taken into account. If the Church really is the elect body of Christ, then, on Edwards' way of thinking, access to the sacramental expression of the life of the Church must be carefully guarded so as to preserve the sanctity of the Bride of Christ. It is not just that those partaking of the ordinances are partaking in the central mystery of Christian worship. It is that to participate in that mystery, one must be somehow metaphysically united to Christ – or at least, show good evidence that you think of yourself in this way. Of course, one need not hold to Edwards' metaphysical vision of union with Christ in order to find his arguments about the qualifications for communion appealing. And one could approve of his metaphysical conception of the Church and have another idea about the way the sacraments ought to be administered. The same could be said for Stoddardeanism. One might find the idea of sacramental evangelism attractive even if one has never heard of the Half Way Covenant. But when Edwards' conception of the Church is understood, his sacramental change of mind becomes much easier to comprehend. Stoddard's way of thinking involved a much less extravagant notion of the nature of the Church, and much more concern with maintaining the Puritan Way in a community life bound by national and local covenant. Edwards, by contrast had in mind an essentially eschatological vision of what the Church is and what it is destined for, in *theosis*.[41] What is more, his vision of the Church as the Body of Christ, united with her head, has a strongly realized component. This is not simply something that will happen in the eschaton. For Edwards, there is a sense in which this act is brought about now, as the Church is formed.[42] Participation in the Lord's Table was participation in that communion between the Lover and Beloved that could only be undertaken by those who already belonged to Christ, and who would spend eternity becoming ever more like him in a union that would grow ever more intimate, and yet never result in the coalescing of the creature and Creator.

Coda

I end with a challenge. At the close of the second volume of his *Systematic Theology*, Robert Jenson, inspired by Edwards' vision of heaven as a world of love, says

---

[41] Whether or not Edwards' endorsed a full-blown doctrine of *theosis* is a moot point in contemporary Edwardsian scholarship. For a clear argument in favour of this view, see Michael J. McClymond, 'Salvation as Divinization: Jonathan Edwards, Gregory Palamas and the Theological Uses of Neoplatonism' in *Jonathan Edwards: Philosophical Theologian*, eds. Paul Helm and Oliver D. Crisp (Aldershot: Ashgate, 2003), pp. 139–160.

[42] Compare Caldwell's more nuanced analysis of the stages of 'heavenly development' in *Communion in the Spirit*, pp. 170–193.

God will deify the redeemed: their life will be carried and shaped by the life of Father, Son, and Spirit, and they will know themselves as personal agents in the life so shaped. God will let the redeemed see him: the Father by the Spirit will make Christ's eyes their eyes. Under all rubrics, the redeemed will be appropriated to God's own being . . . The end is music.[43]

Such an eschatological vision of the Church is simply Edwardsian. We (post)moderns may find the way in which Edwards expressed this vision in his sacramental theology, unpalatable, even impractical. But if we do, is it because our sacramental theology reflects a richer, more expansive conception of the divine economy and the place of the Church in it, or is it (as I suspect) that we have a far poorer grasp of the connection between our sacramental life and the life of the Church, and of the wondrous prospect that awaits her as the Bride of Christ?

---

[43] Robert W. Jenson, *Systematic Theology, Vol. 2, The Works of God* (New York: Oxford University Press, 1999), p. 369.

Index